INVESTMENT FOR ALL

INVESTMENT FOR ALL

by

WILLIAM G. NURSAW, F.C.I.S., A.C.I.I., F.S.S., F.I.ARB.

Member Society of Investment Analysts

GEE & CO (PUBLISHERS) LIMITED

151 STRAND, LONDON WC2R 1JJ

FIRST PUBLISHED 1971
© GEE & CO (PUBLISHERS) LIMITED
SBN 85258 058 4

Made and printed in Great Britain by
GEE & CO (PUBLISHERS) LIMITED, LONDON AND ST ALBANS

DEDICATION

To those many friends who have helped this book on its way.

CONTENTS

PART III

EQUITIES

PART IV

INVESTMENT THROUGH LIFE ASSURANCE

PART V

LAND AND BUILDINGS

PART VI

OVERSEAS INVESTMENT

PART VII

GENERAL INVESTMENT CONSIDERATIONS

PART VIII

VARYING RULES FOR DIFFERING CIRCUMSTANCES AND FUNDS

PART IX

INVESTMENT MANAGEMENT

FOREWORD

I have endeavoured to cover within the pages of this book practically all fields of investment and there should be something for everybody. The chapters on saving through life assurance, personal house purchase and true yields after taxation will, I hope, have a wide appeal.

In presenting the various investment alternatives I have demonstrated how essential it is that investment must be tailored to circumstances, taxation position, time horizon and how taking all these into consideration an investor is more likely to be successful than in accepting the general advice which is disseminated on a wide scale and which is likely to be inappropriate to his own circumstances.

The book is directed at all who are interested in investment including the serious student of investment – it starts in some sixth forms – and those taking the examinations of our professional institutes, accountants, actuaries, chartered secretaries and administrators, solicitors; also those following the career of investment in banking, law, insurance, pension fund management, stockbroking, investment trusts and unit trusts. I have gone out of my way to present the subject in the simplest terms, no plastering with mystique, no gilding with professional jargon.

Investment in Stock Exchange investments is demonstrably an art and not a science however impressed the layman may be with the erudite stuff that proliferates in investment circles.

Indeed the message in this book to the layman is that there is no precise or certain way of selecting a successful share, and that correctly timing the purchase and tailoring it correctly is fundamental. What is more I have stressed time and time again that before the family man buys a single stock or share in any form, he should in priority purchase the family home by a mortgage backed by life assurance, have adequate life assurance to safeguard his dependants in the event of his death and have £500 or so tucked away against a rainy day in a building society or like safe place. Then, and only then, if he is hooked on equities, should he get diversification through investment trusts or unit trusts, although in the book I have dogmatized that life assurance shares are the supreme equity shares, subject of course to timing the purchase aright. I have stated too that the best way of buying equities is through an equity unit trust scheme linked to life assurance.

Financial journalists will I hope find the book both interesting and helpful. I have tremendous admiration for their work. They have uncovered many a dangerous investment situation. I would not, therefore, wish the fact that I am allergic to their practice of tipping shares, and say so within these pages, to be taken as detracting from the splendid work they do for investors.

I believe there are some matters among the following pages upon which the advanced practitioner might profitably reflect. After thirty-five years in investment looking after funds running into many millions I still find I am still learning.

When writing a book the sequence is first the handwritten script, next the typed script, then the galley-proofs and finally the page proofs. My publishers have excelled themselves in a splendidly speedy time-table, but from the time of writing the first word until yesterday when I finished checking the page proofs much has happened – a reduction in the standard rate of income tax, with surtax to disappear in April 1973 to be replaced by an escalating rate of income tax, capital gains tax has been profoundly changed, the penal rate for short-term capital gains tax abolished and British Government Stocks relieved from capital gains on sales 12 months after purchase. This is to mention only a few of the changes made in the Finance Act 1971. And since I first put pen to paper both Rolls-Royce and the Vehicle & General Insurance Company have gone into liquidation. An equity bear market has changed into a bull market with some of my prophesies fulfilled but because of fulfillment now omitted from the book. A 5 per cent Bank-rate last month for the first time for over seven years has had such an impact upon fixed interest stocks that the gilt-edged market has reached its highest point for four years.

Sympathize with me dear reader when you imagine how all this has effected my first, second and sometimes third set of figures and the text as well.

Still when this book is published, within a few weeks now, few books will start with figures so up to date. At the moment I am stunned with the thought, was all the labour really worth the effort? I can only hope that your verdict will be that it was.

31/10/71   W.G.N.

Part I

Introducing Investment

CHAPTER 1

What is investment?

Investment is a word which has been part of my daily life for over thirty years. It is a word I take for granted. It is a word my business friends and colleagues use all the time. But when I settled down to write this book I asked myself 'What do you mean by investment?' and 'Do your readers know what investment is?'.

My first answer to my own question was that anyone who reads through these pages or even the contents will soon know what investment is. That irritating inner voice niggled me: 'You are dodging the issue, you should start by defining investment'.

I turned to my massive volume of the latest *Oxford English Dictionary* and somewhat to my surprise read as follows:

'(1) The act of putting clothes or vestments on – clothing, vestments.

'(2) An envelope, a coating.

'(3) Investiture.

'(4) The surrounding or hemming in of a town or fort by a hostile force, beleaguerment, blockade.'

But I got there at last:

'(5) Commercial – The investing of money or capital; an amount of money invested in some species of property – a form of property viewed as a vehicle in which money may be invested.'

Two quotations were given:

'(*a*) Before the investment could be made, a change of the market might render it ineligible.' *A. Hamilton.*

'(*b*) I do not put myself in the way of hearing about profitable investment.' *1837.*

A little disappointed I turned to my seven-volume *Lloyds Encyclopaedic Dictionary* given to me by my late grandfather, William Thomas Davis, and published seventy-five years ago. This never disappoints me, well hardly ever. It had the first four definitions in the *Oxford Dictionary* almost word for word and then I read:

'The act of investing or laying out money in the purchase of some species of property usually of a permanent nature as the investment of money in railway shares or in land.'

'Money invested.'

'That in which money is invested. [And gave as an example] A certain portion of the revenues of Bengal has been, for many years, set apart to be employed in the purchase of goods for exportation to England and this is called investment' – *Burke on the Affairs of India.*

At the back of my mind was the query whether an investment had to have an element of change in value in itself. Must it be – a stock or share – a house – a piece of land – or the like? Must it have a capital element which can change in money terms and an income element in the form of interest or rent or the like as a return on the money laid out?

In the story of the Talents – Matthew's Gospel 25 (*New English Bible*):

'the man who had been given one bag of gold went off and dug a hole in the ground and hid his master's money'.

His master admonished him on his return with:

'You lazy rascal – you ought to have put my money on deposit and on my return I would have got it back with interest.'

You will note from the contents of the book that I include cash deposits under investment and the nearest authority I have for this is the definition given above, 'A vehicle in which money may be invested', but the weakness of the definition is the word invested, particularly so if the word is read in conjunction with the other definitions. I am satisfied that investment includes putting money out at interest. So I offer a new definition.

'Investment is the use of money in the purchase of any species of property or in the deposit of money for the purpose of earning interest.'

In other words you are not investing money by keeping it in your pocket, or in your long stocking or in a hole in the garden, or on current account at the bank, neither is a farmer who keeps his currency notes in a milk churn – you are like the man with the one bag of gold, preserving it.

The term property is an all-embracing term and not of course restricted to bricks and mortar. *Stroud's Judicial Dictionary* devotes ten pages to various definitions of property and gives cross-references to twenty-six other definitions which are relevant. Here's one from *Blackstone's Commentaries:*

'Property includes money, goods, things in action, land and every description of property, whether real or personal and whether situated in England or elsewhere; also obligations, easements, and every description of estate interest and profit, present or future, vested or contingent, arising out of or incidental to property as above defined.'

Extent and variety of the various investment groups

Having through our definitions discovered the wide scope of investment it would be interesting to have some figures of the amount involved under the various and manifold headings. Obviously these figures are both approximate and historic. There is also some double counting, so here, rather as a matter of investment titillation than a precise statement of fact are some figures.

The first broad group is cash deposits or their equivalent, the investor receiving on demand or at the end of a stated period his money back in full plus interest in one form or another.

GROUP I

		£ million
(a) Cash deposits		
Bank deposits		32,250
National (Post Office) Savings Banks:		
Ordinary account	1,470	
Investment account	327	
		1,797
Trustee Savings Banks:		
Ordinary account	1,125	
Investment account	1,519	
		2,644
Building societies ..		8,723
Local authorities – deposits		360
(b) National savings certificates		2,500
(c) Government premium bonds		813
(d) Save as you earn (SAYE) ..		32
(e) Government bonds issued by National and Trustee Savings Banks:		
National development bonds	244	
British savings bonds	503	
Defence bonds	6	
		753

N.B. – Other Government stocks on National and Trustee Savings Bank register total £232 million.

GROUP II

I now give details of stocks and shares quoted on the London Stock Exchange as at March 31st, 1971. It will be noted that market values of these investments exceed £120,000 million. Ten years ago the corresponding figure was £51,000 million – an impressive growth. There are, of course, provincial Stock Exchanges but there are many investments which are quoted both in London and on the provincial Stock Exchanges. I have not been able to get at the figures for stocks and shares quoted exclusively on the provincial Stock Exchanges.

Stock Exchange investments at market values, quoted on the London Stock Exchange:

	£ million
British Government and guaranteed stocks	17,160·8
Corporation and county stocks ..	1,575·9
Public boards	238·5
Commonwealth Government stocks ..	518·8
Commonwealth corporation stocks ..	42·6
Foreign Government stocks	1,301·3
Foreign corporation stocks	26·5
	20,864·4

Companies:		
Loan capital	3,649·9	
Convertible loan capital	1,023·5	
Preference and preferred capital ..	862·0	
Ordinary shares (equities)	94,104·3	
		99,639·7
		£120,504·1

These are interesting figures but they certainly do not begin to give the capital investment in Great Britain and in any case the figures for equities include a heavy investment overseas. There will too, be some double counting to the extent that companies, shown under equities, invest in each other. With investment trusts (Chapter 12) it is very much a case of double counting. Moreover, many financial and commercial undertakings are not quoted on the Stock Exchange. The ordinary shares of J. Sainsbury, the well-known grocers, are not quoted on the Stock Exchange as they are privately held, mainly by the family. And there are many similar cases.

Many insurance companies, particularly life offices, are mutual offices owned by their policyholders – they have no shareholders. Investment in a mutual office, the biggest is the Norwich Union, is therefore limited to taking out a life policy, while in the case of a life office which has a share quotation there is the alternative of investing in the shares or taking out a life policy. The market value as at December 31st, 1970, of the quoted ordinary shares of the insurance group totalled £2,076·3 million, whereas (see group III) life assurance funds alone totalled £13,070 million, to which should be added non-life insurance funds of £2,463 million.

Funds which in a less direct degree represent savings are listed under Group III.

Group III

	£ million
Life assurance funds	10,710
Non-life insurance funds	2,463
Industrial life assurance companies and collecting societies	2,360
Friendly societies	843
Industrial and provident societies	957
Trade unions	133
Railway savings bank	42
Authorized unit trusts	1,398
Superannuation and other pension funds	7,404

With all figures there is an element of double counting but not such as to reduce the usefulness of the figures.

Group IV

Land and buildings

I have tried without success to get an estimated value for land and buildings and had I been successful there would certainly have been much double counting. Clearly the market value of the ordinary shares quoted in Table II includes the value of land and buildings owned by the companies whose shares are quoted on the Stock Exchanges. The value of land and buildings is also included in the funds listed in Group III.

GROUP V

Miscellaneous

This will include the following:

Treasury bills .. .. £2,244 million

Treasury bills, indeed all the various groups of investments, are dealt with in the following chapters of this book and the reader should study the contents (pages vii to xi) to note how the book is split in Parts and Chapters so as to get a grasp of the general form and approach of this book.

Two main classes of investment

I would, however, stress at once that there are essentially two main divisions:

FIXED-INTEREST INVESTMENTS
and
EQUITY INVESTMENTS

Fixed-interest investments (see page 12 et seq.) include those where cash or its equivalent is a static factor and where this cash or its equivalent grows merely by the addition of interest at a fixed or varying rate, the investment being on a day-to-day basis or on a fixed-term basis and in the latter case possibly subject to penalties if an early repayment is desired.

Those listed in Group I (page 4) are obviously fixed-interest investments. So are Group II with the exception of ordinary shares (equities), but there is the complication that the market price will vary with supply and demand, also with day-to-day interest rates and the assessment of future interest rates. Current interest rates are readily related to irredeemable stocks. The price of a redeemable stock will reflect also the fact that the stock is repayable at a fixed date and at a fixed price. The effective rate of interest (termed redemption yield) will take this and current interest rates into consideration.

Obviously another fixed-interest group is mortgages, which for convenience are included with land and buildings under Part V. Treasury bills, also cash deposited with some of the funds shown in Group III, mentioned earlier, clearly come under the heading of fixed-interest investment.

Subject to the investor carefully choosing his media and not being tempted by advertisements offering exceptionally high rates of interest, his investments are safe and free from any risk other than inflation. Over recent years inflation has indeed proved a big risk and investors with risk-free fixed-interest investments have found that at the end of a ten-year period even with added interest the investment will buy less goods than the cash would have purchased originally.

Equity investment immediately calls to mind ordinary shares, indeed they are now more often referred to as equities. Equities in their various forms include unit trusts (page 97) and investment trusts (page 85). Equity investment carries with it no certainty that the investor will be able to cash his investment for what he originally paid for it and what is more he could choose what turns out to be a dud share. Land and buildings are obviously not fixed-interest investments and a well chosen piece of land or a building just as in the case of a well chosen ordinary share has all the advantages of an equity investment – indeed is an equity investment. Both should grow in value because of inflation and also with the economic growth in the country.

Investment in life assurance (see Part IV) can be either of a fixed-interest or equity nature. An assurance policy which does not share in the profits of the life funds upon which it is secured is clearly a fixed-interest investment. Whereas a policy which through added bonuses does share in the profits of the life fund is in effect an equity investment.

Before leaving this introductory chapter the term 'financial director' or 'financial controller' is often used for a senior executive of a large company. He is not an investment manager. He is usually a super accountant who is responsible for seeing that the liquid and other resources of the company are used to the best advantage. Investment in its widest term is raising money in a variety of ways – by bank overdrafts, by loan capital, by mortgages, by debentures or by preference or equity share issues etc., in order to promote the success of a company. It is also ploughing back profits for the same purpose.

However, in this book I have restricted myself to the type of investment which is available to individuals, companies and other funds when their money is in the hands of third parties. Quite enough too, I have discovered by the painful process of what is included within the bindings of this book.

Finally there is no magic in the order of this book. The reader can quite satisfactorily start with Parts III, IV and V and then return to Part II. Quite frankly I got less pleasure from writing Part II on Fixed-Interest Investments. It is a very essential section of investment but it is certainly unglamorous compared with Part III on Investment in Ordinary Shares or indeed Part V on Land and Property or Part IV on Life Assurance Schemes. However, I feel it is right and proper to put Fixed-Interest Investments next, as Part II – it is, of course, the oldest form of investment.

Part II

Fixed-Interest Investments

CHAPTER 2

Cash deposits and the like

These can be divided into two main classes: those withdrawable on little or no notice and those fixed for a term of months or years and thus not immediately available except perhaps upon payment of a penalty.

The variety of deposits in both cases is legion. They include banks, the joint stock and merchant banks, building societies, savings banks, hire-purchase companies, local government authorities.

The deposit rate varies with current money rates, and current money rates have a close connection with Bank-rate and a closer still connection with the current rate on Government Treasury bills (Chapter 3).

Bank-rates

Here are the Bank-rates since June 30th, 1932. They tell their own story of the ups and downs of interest rates:

	Per cent			Per cent
June 30th, 1932	2		October 5th, 1961 ..	$6\frac{1}{2}$
August 24th, 1939	4		November 2nd, 1961 ..	6
September 28th, 1939 ..	3		March 8th, 1962	$5\frac{1}{2}$
October 26th, 1939 ..	2		March 22nd, 1962 ..	5
November 8th, 1951 ..	$2\frac{1}{2}$		April 26th, 1962	$4\frac{1}{2}$
March 11th, 1952	4		January 3rd, 1963 ..	4
September 17th, 1953 ..	$3\frac{1}{2}$		February 27th, 1964 ..	5
May 13th, 1954	3		November 23rd, 1964 ..	7
January 27th, 1955 ..	$3\frac{1}{2}$		June 3rd, 1965	6
February 24th, 1955 ..	$4\frac{1}{2}$		July 14th, 1966	7
February 16th, 1956 ..	$5\frac{1}{2}$		January 26th, 1967 ..	$6\frac{1}{2}$
February 7th, 1957 ..	5		March 16th, 1967	6
September 19th, 1957 ..	7		May 4th, 1967	$5\frac{1}{2}$
March 20th, 1958	6		October 19th, 1967 ..	6
May 22nd, 1958	$5\frac{1}{2}$		November 9th, 1967 ..	$6\frac{1}{2}$
June 19th, 1958	5		November 18th, 1967 ..	8
August 14th, 1958	$4\frac{1}{2}$		March 21st, 1968	$7\frac{1}{2}$
November 20th, 1958 ..	4		September 19th, 1968 ..	7
January 21st, 1960	5		February 27th, 1969 ..	8
June 23rd, 1960	6		March 5th, 1970	$7\frac{1}{2}$
October 27th, 1960 ..	$5\frac{1}{2}$		April 15th, 1970	7
December 8th, 1960 ..	5		April 1st, 1971	6
July 26th, 1961	7		September 2nd, 1971 ..	5

The difference between the interest rate on short-term deposits and the long-term deposits will depend on market conditions and supply of money and demand for money. Sometimes the long-term rate is higher than the short-term rate – sometimes vice versa – or the conditions can be such that they approximate to each other. It requires skill and judgement to take advantage of a long-term rate because it means taking the view that money will get abundant and interest rates fall. On the other hand one can be badly caught if one buys a stock which is redeemable in the distant future or is irredeemable and interest rates rise because as interest rates rise the market value of the stock will fall, and the longer the date to maturity the greater the fall.

Bank deposits

Probably deposits with the joint stock banks are top of the league for temporary deposits. Until the recent rivalry all banks quoted 2 per cent below Bank-rate. The merchant banks are competitive but generally they go after the bigger deposits. The banks quote for money withdrawable on seven days' notice, but deposits can be withdrawn on shorter notice on a small penalty.

Hire-purchase company deposits

The hire-purchase companies generally quote higher deposit rates than the banks. Sometimes you will see an advertisement whereby a finance house offers interest rates well above Bank-rate. Treat these with caution. History is strewn with companies which have taken money on deposit and gone broke, depositors losing most of their deposits – sometimes the lot.

Local government authority deposits

Local authorities will often give a better rate than banks but they generally prefer larger sums and to fix the term for a month or more. The money is required for short-term financing but I fear that often the short-term borrowing arises from a reluctance to fund their borrowings in long-term loans because treasurers and chairmen of finance committees hope that eventually borrowing terms will improve and interest rates fall. Over the last decade or so this has proved a false hope and some authorities have been told by the Official Auditors to get on with funding their short-term borrowings. Shades of the past, I know some authorities which were reluctant to fund their borrowings on a 5 per cent rate – they having been not unnaturally mesmerized by the low interest rates of the Dalton and post-Dalton era, 1946–47.

Building society deposits
Building society rates are influenced more by long-term rates than short-term rates. It is essential for building societies to get in the money because it is the money provided by depositors on share, deposit or savings accounts, collectively referred to as deposits, which is lent on mortgage, to buy houses. Building societies are particularly vulnerable to the supply of money. If their deposit rates become uncompetitive then the intake falls and the amount available for lending drops. Building societies are governed by the Building Society Acts and must keep 7½ per cent of their funds liquid. In normal times there is little to choose between deposits on share accounts and on deposit accounts, except that the share account rate is usually ¼ per cent higher than deposit rate. Deposits can be withdrawn immediately whereas according to the rule book share account deposits need one month's notice. One of the attractions of all classes of building society deposits is that the interest is not subject to income tax, as building societies pay tax at a composite rate. But for those not subject to income tax there is no way of reclaiming the tax suffered by the building society. This seems a little unfair. Building society interest is liable to surtax and for this purpose the going-rate is grossed up at the standard rate of income tax and surtax is payable at the appropriate rate on the grossed-up figure. To demonstrate, a 5 per cent building society interest rate is equivalent to £8·10 gross and surtax is payable on that figure. Regular savings through building society deposits have been linked with life assurance to the end that the saver gets life assurance relief on his savings. This is an attractive method of safety first saving.
· Deposits are used by investors pending a permanent investment or to take advantage of a special investment situation which may crop up. In the days when I administered many trust investment portfolios for an institutional investor I had a building society deposit account for each trust so that we could readily take up rights issues without having to incur the expense of having to realize a small proportion of an investment. As the deposits shrunk I fed them by keeping back some cash when an investment change took place. Some new investments, particularly debentures

and unsecured loan stocks (see page 33), are payable by instalments over a period. Whilst awaiting the instalment dates it is sensible to put the cash on deposit.

National savings certificates

National savings certificates are in the nature of deposited moneys because they can be encashed at any time at nominal value plus interest. As with building society deposits the certificate holders get compound interest. In the case of most building societies the interest is credited half-yearly and, at the next half-year, interest is calculated on the deposit plus interest and so on. This method is worth another 0·0625 per cent per annum with interest at 5 per cent.

The basic rate earned in the first year on national savings certificates is usually lower than building society rates, but there are carrots offered in the form of extra credits, sometimes after three years and always at the end of the last year of the term.

The current issue of certificates, the Decimal issue, has a nominal value of £1 per unit and the units increase as follows:

	£		£
End of first year ..	1·03	End of third year ..	1·15
„ second year ..	1·075	„ fourth year ..	1·25

The yield if held to the end of the period is £5·70 per cent which is free of all taxes, but see comparative yield table, page 184. The yield in the earlier years is unattractive. Interest on national savings certificates is not subject to income tax or surtax but the amount permitted to any one holder is rationed – for the current Decimal issue the permitted amount is 1,000 certificates for each holder. There have, of course, been previous issues – some on more attractive terms than others, they having been geared to interest rates current at the time. As a general rule savings certificates which are not cashed at the end of their normal term continue to attract interest but it is usually at a fixed rate so the longer they are held the lower the effective rates of interest.

National (Post Office) and Trustee Savings Banks

The latest figures I have available show that £1,469·6 million were deposited with the National (Post Office) Savings Bank on ordinary account, and £326·6 million on investment account. The figures for the Trustee Savings Bank are £1,125·1 million ordinary account and £1,519·3 million on investment account. The Post Office Savings Bank has been going for over one hundred years and it is amazing that the rate of interest has stayed at 2½ per cent for so long despite the fact that over the period Bank-rates have been as low as 2 per cent and as high as 8 per cent. However, the Chancellor has taken powers to increase the rate of interest to 3½ per cent from December 31st, 1971, but for accounts in existence on December 31st, 1971, the increased rate will apply from January 1st, 1971. In truth facilities offered by the Post Office Savings Bank have improved tremendously over the years.

Although the Post Office does not offer a service equivalent to that offered by the joint stock banks, it offers a pretty full service and, unlike the joint stock banks, pays interest on current account. As from January 1st, 1972, the first £21 (previously £15) of Savings Bank interest is not subject to income tax but surtax payers have to pay surtax on the £21 grossed up at the standard rate. Surtax payers have discovered this at times much to their surprise.

The facilities offered by the Giro have added greatly to the attractiveness of the Post Office Savings Bank. Further, in recent years it has become possible to have an investment account with the Post Office Savings Bank provided the ordinary account has a credit of £50. The rate of interest on the investment account is close to current interest rates and at the time of writing it is 7½ per cent. One useful facility with the Post Office is the ability to withdraw £20 on demand from any Post Office in the United Kingdom provided the depositor can produce his Post Office Savings Bank book.

British Government securities can be purchased and sold through the Post Office Savings Bank at commission rates which work out considerably cheaper than those charged by the Stock Exchange. Dividends on Government stocks purchased can be credited to the owner's Post Office Savings account and they are paid without deduction of income tax. The latest figure for these stocks on the Post Office register is £232 million.

Trustee Savings Banks
Trustee Savings Banks have a fascinating history, going back to 1810. They are pioneers in the encouragement of thrift. The management of the Trustee Savings Banks is usually vested in trustees who are local public-spirited men and women serving the interests of the bank without reward. There are some one thousand

four hundred branches all over the country, some ten million active accounts with, as we have seen, total balances of some £2,644 million, with over half on special investment account.

The rate of interest offered and the facilities are rather similar to those of the Post Office Savings Bank. Whereas the Post Office Savings Bank management is centralized with branches all over the country the Trustee Savings Banks enjoy considerable local autonomy which results in their facilities being a little more elastic. To give one extreme example, some Trustee Savings Banks issued, certainly until recently, travel vouchers to depositors at a discount of 5 per cent on the normal rail fare. As in the case of the Post Office Savings Bank a depositor who has £50 on an ordinary deposit account can open a special investment deposit account.

Save as you earn scheme – SAYE
In the Finance Act 1969 a Government 'Save as you earn' scheme was set up to start on October 12th, 1969. Under the scheme the saver has to agree to save a fixed amount regularly of not less than £1 with a maximum of £10 monthly (£20, September 1971), or alternatively the equivalent weekly sums of 25p or 250p respectively. The amount can be deducted at source by the saver's employers or the saver can make his own arrangements for payment. The whole object of the scheme is to ensure that the saver saves regularly for five years because at the end of the five years he gets a bonus including accrued interest, of 20 per cent, which is equivalent to another year's savings and further, if he allows the money to remain for another two years, the bonus goes up to 40 per cent. All interest and bonuses are free of income tax and surtax. The equivalent yield over the five-year period after allowing for the fact that no income tax is payable is 11·79 per cent per annum and for seven years over $12\frac{1}{4}$ per cent. Higher still for a surtax payer. The free of tax yields are respectively 7·22 per cent and 7·56 per cent.

If the maximum is not taken up in the first place further savings schemes can be taken out up to the maximum amount of £120 per annum.

The rate of interest is only $2\frac{1}{2}$ per cent free of tax if the money is taken out before the five years are completed and no bonus arises. Interest is only payable if the particular saving has been going for a year or longer.

There are provisions where a saver gets behind in his payments. He is given a maximum of six months extension to catch up and repayment is delayed accordingly.

Here are the figures for £10 a month. Total paid in five years, £600. Bonus, including interest, £120. Total repayable, £720. After seven years the total repayable is £840.

The building societies have been allowed by the Government to come into the SAYE scheme. But one individual cannot save under any one or more schemes more than the maximum of £120 per annum.

So far as Britain is concerned this is a savings breakthrough, a pioneering venture which will no doubt be adjusted to meet the requirements of the years to come.

National (Post Office) and Trustee Savings Banks issues

In recent years the Government has borrowed from the public at large through the Post Office and Trustee Savings Banks, by means of: (*a*) defence bonds; (*b*) national development bonds; (*c*) British savings bonds.

Defence bonds were on sale until May 14th, 1964. They were issued for various terms of years and at various rates of interest but most, if not all, had the carrot of a tax-free extra at maturity. The last issue was made on May 14th, 1964, at 4½ per cent interest with an extra £2½ per cent on maturity free of tax at the end of the seven-year period.

The amount outstanding is £5·7 million.

National development bonds superseded defence bonds and were on sale for the period May 15th, 1964, to March 30th, 1968. There were three issues, two with interest at 5 per cent per annum and redeemable at the end of five years at 2 per cent extra, free of tax, and one with interest at 5½ per cent also redeemable in five years at a premium of 2 per cent.

The amount outstanding is £244 million.

British savings bonds succeeded national development bonds. The first issue was on April 1st, 1968. The rate of interest was 6 per cent per annum. The period was five and a half years and the tax-free premium at the end remained at 2 per cent. The issue ended on April 26th, 1969, and was replaced on April 28th, 1969, with 7 per cent British savings bonds, the period again being five and a half years and the premium at the end again 2 per cent. The amount at issue is £503 million approximately.

Defence bonds and national development bonds were rationed as to the total amount an individual could hold but the figures are now merely historic. With British savings bonds which are still being issued the present limit is £10,000 for each individual, but the Government could increase this at any time. They can be bought in multiples of £5.

Premium savings bonds, usually called premium bonds, is the only British lottery so far. The maximum holding is £1,250. The full purchase price is repayable on application. The bonds carry no interest but interest at $4\frac{1}{2}$ per cent is credited on the total amount of the bonds outstanding and paid out in the form of prizes. A draw is held every month for prizes which vary in number and amount according to the monthly amount raised. The highest monthly prize is £50,000 but there is a weekly prize also of £25,000. A bond becomes eligible for a draw after being held for three months and remains eligible until it is repaid. Prizes are exempt from income tax, surtax and capital gains tax.

The amount at issue is £813 million approximately.

CHAPTER 3

Treasury bills

Treasury bills are issued by the Treasury under 40 Victoria C.2 for money borrowed by the Government from the banking system and these bills form part of the country's floating debt.

They are offered for tender each week on a Friday, except when Friday is a public holiday when they are tendered for on the previous day. No tender may be for less than £50,000 of bills. The bills are issued in denominations of £5,000, £10,000, £25,000, £50,000 and £100,000.

The bills, which have an issue period of ninety-one days, are issued at a discount which is determined by the current short-term interest rate. The amount offered depends upon the Government and the amount of cash in the various coffers of the departments, because the departments use Treasury bills for their spare cash.

The discount market tenders for the bills each week but its members first meet to decide on a tender price.

Once allotted the Treasury bills are available to any individual or corporation through their bankers, and others who obtain them from the discount houses. As there is a weekly offering of Treasury bills the market has in theory a pool of Treasury bills with from one day to ninety-one days' unexpired. The bills are in bearer form, thus they can be readily transferred from one person or corporation to another.

The running rate of interest at the present time is about $4\frac{3}{4}$ per cent, which is very little different from the rate for day-to-day money, such as local government deposits. But in the case of the latter income tax is deducted in paying the interest, whereas with Treasury bills the interest, which is represented by the discount the holder gets, comes to him gross and it is his responsibility to disclose the interest to the Inland Revenue when he makes his tax return. At the minimum he has the use of the gross interest and at the maximum he or his principals may not be liable to tax. Treasury bills outstanding on December 31st, 1970, totalled £2,244 million. The average weekly issue is £180 million.

CHAPTER 4

Fixed-interest stocks
As I have already stated, unlike equities, no glamour attaches to fixed-interest investments, including fixed-interest stocks. Indeed I have invited readers to turn first to equities before reading about fixed-interest stocks.

There are, however, considerable skills attaching to operations in fixed-interest stocks and as a result institutional investors reap satisfactory harvests for their funds in this field with the help of specialist stockbrokers. The skills of gilt-edged specialists are growing all the time and the computer has been a great help in the development of these skills. The object is to find which stocks are out of line and to set up a switch.

Fixed-interest stocks have a nominal value, usually £100, the par value. On this interest is paid at the stipulated rate. The stock is sometimes issued at par, sometimes under par, and sometimes over par. The market value is quoted per £100 of stock and the value varies with supply and demand and the current ruling general interest rates. Some stocks have a redemption or maturity date. Others are irredeemable.

Generally
The description could be fixed rate of interest stocks because, as the name implies, the investor is entitled only to a fixed rate of interest; unlike equities where the rate of income will depend upon the dividend which is declared annually and can go down as well as up. He has, therefore, only to concern himself with the security aspect of his investment. Obviously when he buys an ordinary share he is speculating as to the future prospects of the company. When he buys a fixed-interest stock he must be sure that there is no danger of his not getting his interest or his capital when the stock matures or before by selling in the market.

There is a large variety of fixed-interest stocks and despite what has been said against British Government securities, the premier fixed-interest investment is a British Government security. Unlike many of the nations of the world, the British Government has never defaulted either on interest or on capital account.

There are two divisions of fixed-interest stocks. Those which

21

are irredeemable and those which are redeemable at a certain date and at a certain price. Stocks are usually redeemable at par (100 per cent), but they are sometimes redeemable at other percentages. Irredeemable stocks can never be redeemed or are redeemable only at the option of the borrower, that is when it suits him. An example of this is $3\frac{1}{2}$ per cent War Loan which is redeemable at the option of the British Government on December 1st, 1952, or thereafter. Oddly enough, in 1947, there was talk of its being redeemed in 1952. The rates of interest then were of the order of $2\frac{1}{2}$ per cent and the price of $3\frac{1}{2}$ per cent War Loan around 110 per cent but no Government is likely to redeem War Loan at par when the current borrowing rate is nearer 9 per cent and £100 of stock has fallen to about 40 per cent. The price of a fixed-interest stock will, indeed, fluctuate with interest rates. The irredeemable stock or the long-dated stock, which is a stock which has a long time to run before it matures, is very vulnerable to current interest rates. Part of the skill of investing in fixed-interest stocks is to choose a spread of maturity dates so that the fund is not at risk in having a lot of money repaid at a time when interest rates are low.

A fixed-interest stock gives the investor no protection against inflation. He gets a fixed rate of interest and if the true value of money depreciates he gets less and less and less each year in true value terms. On the other hand the market value of fixed-interest stocks does not show the same fluctuation as equities. To give an example, the *Financial Times Industrial Share Index* (see page 61) dropped by 22 per cent in the first six months of 1969, whereas the fall in the *Financial Times Fixed-Interest Index* was 12 per cent only. Of course, it is the irredeemable and the long-dated stock which are more vulnerable to market changes. A short-dated stock is fairly immune from drastic changes in value because its maturity date is near at hand.

The flat yield, sometimes called current or running yield, on an irredeemable stock is straightforward. It is just the interest rate and the market value of £100 of stock worked out as a percentage. The yield on $3\frac{1}{2}$ per cent War Loan at 50 is obviously 7 per cent. A redeemable stock, like the irredeemable stock, has a flat yield calculated similarly and also a redemption yield which takes into account that at the end of the period when the stock has matured the investor is entitled to the difference between what he paid for the stock and the price at which it is redeemed. In calculating both the flat yield and the redemption yield interest which has accrued up to the date of purchase has to be taken into account. In the case of stocks which have gone ex-dividend negative accrued interest has to be taken into account. He can, of course, pay more than the redemption price. In that case the redemption yield is less than the running yield. It is the redemption yield which truly evaluates the comparative yields of redeemable stocks.

In quoting the yields on redeemable stock it is usually the practice to quote both the gross redemption yield and the net redemption yield. The gross redemption yield is what an investor not subject to tax receives. To get at the true gross redemption yield before taxes of an investor subject to income tax and to surtax and capital gains tax it has to be remembered that the yield consists of two elements, capital subject to capital gains except for British Government Stocks held for more than one year and interest which is subject to income tax and surtax where appropriate. Obviously the capital portion is more favourably taxed than the interest portion and the higher the individual's tax liability the higher the gross return to him.

There is a very large selection of fixed-interest stocks, indeed a very large selection of British Government stocks, and it would be possible to select a portfolio of fixed-interest stocks which would be redeemable over a period of consecutive years. Such a portfolio would certainly minimize the risk of having a large proportion of a fund paid off at a time when re-investment was unattractive due to a low interest rate.

In selecting a fixed-interest stock it is a general rule that the investor not subject to income tax or subject to income tax at a low rate will select a high coupon stock whereas the surtax payer, indeed the investor paying income tax at the standard rate only, would select a low coupon stock. This is obvious because the flat yield is subject to income tax and surtax whereas the amount of additional capital payable at maturity is only subject to capital gains tax and not even that, with British Government stocks held for more than one year.

Fixed-interest stocks having reached, during the last two years, an all-time low there have been suggestions that the rate of interest should be linked to Bank-rate with some formula tying the redemption price to a cost of living index. One or two company loans have been tied on a formula to the cost of living index. I expected others to follow but this has not yet happened.

Obviously the yields on all fixed-interest stocks are affected by Bank-rate, although there is not any direct relationship. It just means with periods of cheap money it is possible to borrow more cheaply. In periods of dear money the borrower has to pay a higher rate of interest and make his terms generally more favourable if he is to get his money.

British Government stocks

The British Government finances its expenditure out of the issue of Treasury bills and its various stocks. The national debt grows every year but it is backed by considerable assets. Gas, electricity, coal mines, the railways, the hospitals and all the nationalized industries are all financed out of Government borrowing. On the short-term the Government borrows with Treasury bills and on the long-term it makes its issues of stock. The Government brokers, Mullens & Co, advise the Government how best to borrow the money, whether on the short-term or the long-term. It would, of course make sense if the Government borrowed on the long-term when interest rates are low and on the short-term when interest rates are high, hoping in the latter case that it will be able to borrow on better terms later.

The importance of British Government stocks on the London Stock Exchange cannot be over-emphasized. They represent by nominal values nearly 45 per cent of all securities quoted on the London Stock Exchange and 64 per cent of the nominal and 65 per cent of the market value respectively of all fixed-interest stocks. Also nearly $14\frac{1}{4}$ per cent of the market values of all quoted stocks and shares.

The market in British Government stocks is probably one of the finest markets in the world. Huge blocks of stock running into millions of pounds can be bought and sold without any difficulty. Very close prices are made, indeed it has been known for a mere one-sixty-fourth to separate the buying and the selling price of some British Government stocks. You can sell and obtain the proceeds within twenty-four hours of your bargain. They are referred to as cash stocks. You have to pay cash immediately when you buy them and entitled to receive cash immediately when you sell them. Immediately in this case means within twenty-four hours. They are really money stocks in the true sense because the difference between getting money at once and at the end of an account, as in the case of equities, can in some cases be of tremendous and paramount importance. In subsequent paragraphs I have drawn attention to the unfortunate experience of British Government stocks bearing in mind inflation and the dramatic rise in interest rates over the last twenty years. Prior to that bad period their performance was exemplary and one can understand how they became to be termed gilt-edged stocks. Certainly the gilt has lost much of its brightness and I only hope that the performance over the last twenty years is not indicative of the next twenty years and that the time will come when they will settle down to stable interest rates and inflation can to some extent be controlled. If so, one has almost the perfect investment. The British Government, unlike many other Governments and unlike many companies, has never defaulted on an interest payment or on a repayment of capital.

Undoubtedly among fixed-interest stocks, British Government stocks are the prima donnas. A ready liquidity and much closer dealing prices make them superior to all other fixed-interest stocks. Indeed no portfolio of fixed-interest stocks should be without them. The yield differential in favour of debenture stocks is, more often than not, too small and on top of this debenture stocks are subject to capital gains tax, however long they are held, whereas British Government stocks are as we have seen only subject to capital gains tax if they are held less than one year.

Until the passing of the Trustee Investments Act 1961, trustees had to invest the whole of their funds in fixed-interest stocks and this meant that the majority of trust funds were in British Government securities. Since the passing of the Trustee Investments Act 1961 funds subject to statutory powers of investment can invest half their funds in equities. This is, perhaps, an over simplification, but see Chapter 27.

I have prepared a short table with a selection of British Government stocks at varying coupons (another term for rate of interest) and maturity dates (see page 26).

There is no significance now in the varying titles of the stocks – only inconsequential historic significance.

It will be noted that the flat yield varies considerably. The lower the coupon the lower the flat yield but note the fact that the flat yield on similar coupon stocks increases as the term of years to maturity increases. Where two redemption dates are given it means that the Government has the option to suit itself to redeem the stock at par on the first or second date. Four per cent Consols,

SELECTED BRITISH GOVERNMENT STOCKS

Stocks on which the interest is payable free of tax to non-residents of the U.K. are marked *.
Stocks redeemable at option of British Government are marked †.

Name of stock (1)	Coupon	Redemption date (2)	Price (3)	Flat yield per cent (4)	Redemption yield: Gross per cent (5)	Redemption yield: Net after tax at 38·75p on interest (6)
British Transport	3	1967–72	97⅝	3·07	5·52	3·38
*Exchequer	6¼	1972	100 19/32	6·21	5·69	3·49
*Exchequer	6¾	1973	100 13/32	6·65	5·76	3·53
British Transport	3	1968–73	95⅞	3·13	5·51	3·37
*Savings	3	1965–75	88 29/32	3·37	6·09	3·73
*Treasury	6½	1976	99⅜	6·71	7·24	4·43
British Transport	4	1972–77	86½	4·63	6·63	4·06
*Exchequer	5	1976–78	89½	5·67	7·12	4·36
British Electricity	4¼	1974–79	83½	5·16	7·12	4·36
British Electricity	3½	1976–79	78⅝	4·48	6·99	4·28
Treasury	3½	1977–80	76⅝	4·58	7·10	4·35
North of Scotland Hydro	3½	1977–80	73½xd	4·74	7·54	4·62
*Treasury	8½	1980–82	100½xd	8·44	8·38	5·13
*Funding	5½	1982–84	80⅝xd	6·81	7·95	4·87
British Transport	3	1978–88	54½	5·51	7·92	4·85
Treasury	9	1994	97⅝	9·33	9·37	5·74
British Gas	3	1990–95	47½	6·39	8·03	4·92
*Treasury	8¾	1997	97½	9·26	9·31	5·70
*Treasury	6¾	1995–98	77¼	8·87	9·16	5·61
Funding	3½	1999–04	45¼xd	7·72	8·43	5·16
*Treasury	5½	2008–12	63⅞	8·85	9·00	5·51
†Consols	4	1957	42⅞xd	9·26	—	—
*†War	3½	1952	38⅜	9·20	—	—
Consols	2½	—	27⅛xd	9·21	—	—
†Treasury	2½	1975	27¾	9·22	—	—

$3\frac{1}{2}$ per cent War Loan, and $2\frac{1}{2}$ per cent Consols can be redeemed at any time on the Government's option. Two and a half per cent Treasury can be redeemed by the Government in 1975 or thereafter. None of these stocks are likely to be redeemed in the foreseeable future.

The stocks marked with an * are payable free of tax to non-U.K. residents as also are the following stocks which are not listed:

4 per cent Victory bonds
$5\frac{1}{4}$ per cent Funding stock, 1978–90
$6\frac{1}{2}$ per cent Funding stock, 1985–87
$5\frac{3}{4}$ per cent Funding stock, 1987–91
6 per cent Funding stock, 1993.

Neither are they liable to British estate duty, unlike other Stock Exchange investments in the hands of non-residents.

The British Government table and the tables on pages 36 and 37 for debentures and unsecured loan stocks include a net redemption yield column, but in the case of British Government stocks after income tax only.

The point is that, exceptionally, British Government stocks are not subject to capital gains tax if sold a year after purchase.

The yields are historic and before the 5 per cent Bank-rate but they are comparable. They will be different when you read this chapter.

The following graphs which give the relative performance of British Government stocks and equities since 1925, show up the poor performance of British Government stock since 1954 and how, over the last two or three years, it has been absolutely appalling. Timothy Forsyte in the *Forsyte Saga*, was absolutely right when he said 'hold on, hold on, Consols are going up' because in 1946 they almost reached par. Some high and lows since are as follows:

$2\frac{1}{2}$ per cent Consols	1946	1949	1950	1955	1960	1965
High	99·5	82	75	67	50	$41\frac{3}{8}$
Low	91	65	68	55	43·5	$36\frac{7}{8}$

	1966	1967	1968	1969	1970	1971 to date
High	$39\frac{3}{16}$	$39\frac{15}{16}$	$35\frac{5}{8}$	$31\frac{1}{4}$	30	$47\frac{5}{8}$
Low	$34\frac{1}{16}$	$34\frac{3}{8}$	$30\frac{1}{2}$	$25\frac{3}{4}$	$25\frac{1}{8}$	$40\frac{1}{4}$

Note again the appalling performance of British Government stocks, as shown by $2\frac{1}{2}$ per cent Consols, over the years and in particular in the recent years. This is, of course, only part of the

INVESTORS CHRONICLE
GILT-EDGED AND INDUSTRIAL SHARE INDEX CHART
1925 – 1965

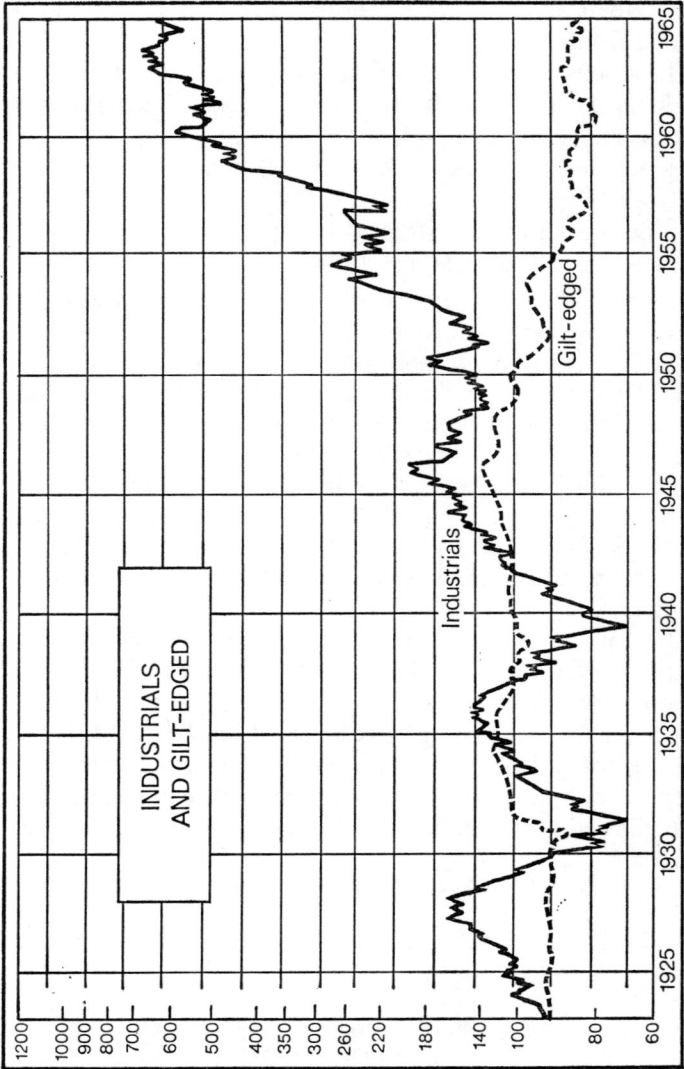

INDUSTRIALS
AND GILT-EDGED

TABLE I

By courtesy of the *Investors Chronicle*

GILT-EDGED AND INDUSTRIAL SHARE INDEX CHART

1965 – 1970 (until discontinued)

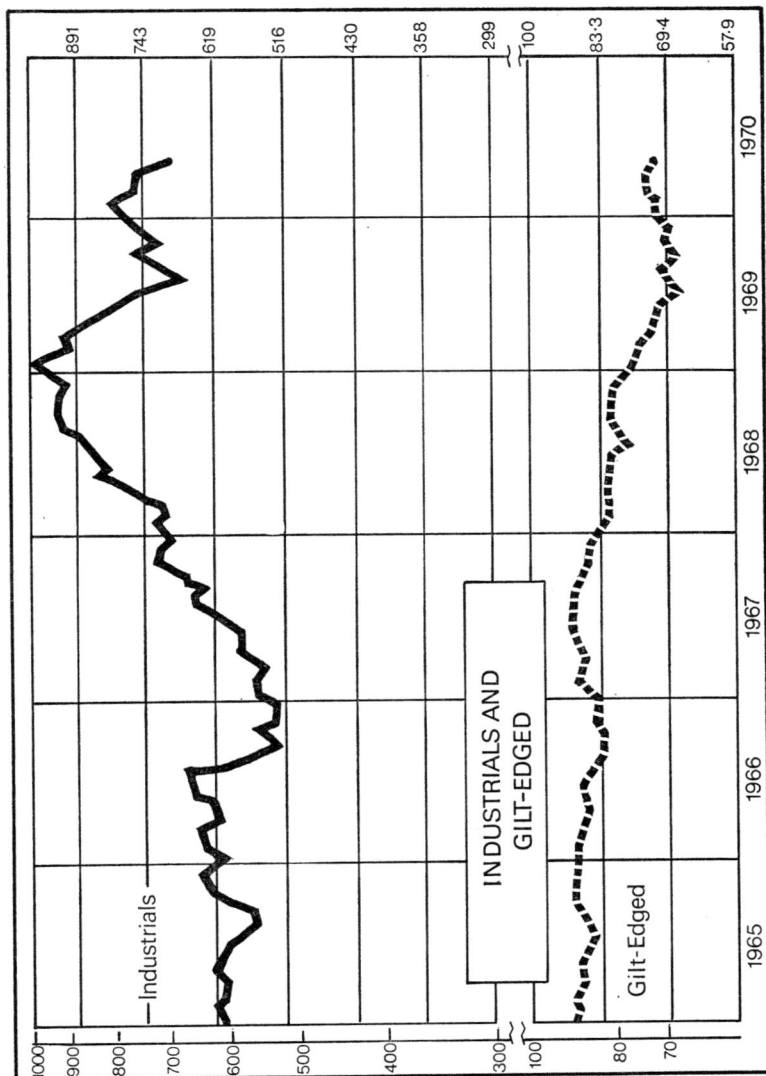

TABLE II

By courtesy of the *Investors Chronicle*

story. In addition to depreciation in money terms there has been a substantial depreciation in money's worth due to inflation. The investor who put £100 into 2½ per cent Treasury which was issued by the late Doctor Dalton, the Socialist Chancellor in 1946–47, at 100 would today have a stock which he could only sell for about £27. The true value of money has halved over the period, thus his £100 is only worth £13·50. However, the poor performance of British Government stocks is shared with all fixed-interest stocks.

Since the Finance Act 1969, British Government stocks are as already mentioned, no longer subject to long-term capital gains tax but they were subject to short-term capital gains tax. This bonus in favour of British Government stocks did little to stop the fall in British Government stocks in 1969, but one wonders how much worse the fall would have been had they not been exempted.

The total quoted British Government and guaranteed stocks is nominal, £22,595 million, market value £17,161 million.

Corporation and county stocks

Stock Exchange figures give these as nominal £1,816 million market value, £1,576 million. Amounts outstanding have more than doubled in the last four years. The British Government is, of course, not the only borrower, the county councils, the county boroughs, the local boroughs, and the like all have to raise money to finance capital expenditure. Indeed, with larger and larger boroughs and with greater powers, borrowing under this heading is likely to increase even more rapidly. Later in this chapter I will deal with the differentials between the borrowing rates of the various types of fixed-interest stocks, but obviously if you lend money to a corporation or buy a corporation or county stock you would obviously expect to get a slightly higher return on your money than if you bought British Government stocks. The difference, however, varies and there are times when corporation stocks are cheap and times when they are dear by comparison with British Government stocks. The borrowing status of corporations will differ and some will be able to borrow on slightly better terms than others. You will not, however, lose your money or stand any risk of losing your money if you invest in a corporation stock.

Corporations, temporary deposits, and mortgages

As mentioned in the chapter on deposits, the local authorities and corporations raise a lot of money in this way. The money is required to finance temporary activities or to finance on the short-term, while an authority is negotiating a loan on a long-term. As indicated it is not unusual for a corporation to borrow temporarily and for its temporary borrowings to become rather permanent because the authority is waiting, sometimes in vain, for a fall in interest rates. At the time of going to Press here are some examples of interest rates:

	Per cent		Per cent
Seven-day call money	$5\frac{7}{8}$		$5\frac{1}{4}$
One month fixed	6	*and after the*	$5\frac{3}{8}$
Three months fixed	$6\frac{3}{16}$	*reduction in*	$5\frac{3}{8}$
Fixed for up to 365 days	7	*Bank-rate to 5%*	6
Two-year mortgages	$7\frac{5}{8}$		$6\frac{3}{4}$

The last item indicates the fact that the corporations will raise money on mortgages, indeed, for varying number of terms longer than two years and in that case they offer the ruling rate of the day. With such a mortgage you are locked in. They are not investments which you can in the usual way sell although they can be repaid on paying a penalty. These deposits and mortgages are arranged direct with the corporation or through a stockbroker.

Public boards – Harbour and dock boards, port authorities,
water boards, etc.
They in turn give a slightly higher return than corporation stocks. The latest figures are nominal value £343 million; market value £238 million.

During 1970–71 these stocks suffered a status reverse when the Mersey Docks and Harbour Board defaulted on its interest payment. This highlighted the fact that these stocks must stand on their own merits and have not necessarily got a benign Government behind them ready to bail them out of trouble.

Colonial and Commonwealth Government Provincial and
corporation stocks
This heading obviously covers the Commonwealth countries of Canada, Australia, New Zealand and sadly, currently defaulting, Rhodesia; also developing countries in the Commonwealth. Obviously some will be able to borrow on better terms than others. The amount outstanding has not varied much over the years. Countries like Canada and Australia now tend to go elsewhere

for their money than Britain. Latest figures: nominal value £732 million; market value £561 million.

Foreign Government, provincial and corporation stocks
These are stocks issued in London in contra-distinction to stocks issued abroad.

These have a nominal value of £2,186 million with a market value of £1,328 million. You will note the depreciation of over 39 per cent. This, however, gives no indication of what has been lost in this type of stock. Many countries and towns which have defaulted are now excluded from the lists. National bankruptcies, repudiation by new régimes, the effect of two World Wars, have resulted in appalling losses by investors under this heading. Enormous sums were also lent to China and these debts have been repudiated by the Communist régime.

Industrial loan capital
This is a very large and growing item, and the nominal amount of quoted loan stock outstanding has increased by 52 per cent in four years. Loan capital includes debenture stocks, unsecured loan stocks and convertible stocks. A short selection of each of these groups giving current prices and yields is set out respectively in tables on pages 36, 37 and 38.

Debentures and loan stocks have always been favoured by the institutional investor but until the passing of the Trustee Investments Act 1961 they were not authorized investments for trustees limited to statutory powers of investment. These stocks can now be bought in the narrower range fund (see page 190).

Industrial companies finance their growth in a number of different ways. They plough back profits, they borrow temporarily on bank overdraft, they issue debenture stocks, loan stocks, sometimes with special rights of conversion into ordinary shares, preference shares or further shares to the shareholders by rights issue. Loan stock is a particularly favoured method employed by industrial companies to raise capital.

The advent of corporation tax has improved the borrowing position of debenture and loan stocks because the interest is a charge before arriving at the amount of corporation tax, unlike preference share interest which is a charge after arriving at corporation tax. This has interesting consequences. It means that in future it is unlikely except in exceptional circumstances for a company to raise money by the issue of preference shares. For example a 10 per cent yield on a debenture costs the company 10 per cent less corporation tax of currently 40 per cent, which means a net rate of 6 per cent, whereas a preference stock which in any case would have to bear a higher rate of interest because on winding up or a liquidation of a company it ranks after a loan stock, would cost the company the full 10 per cent. On the other hand preference share capital is franked for corporation tax. Franked means that it has borne corporation tax. Thus, a company which pays corporation tax and which has invested in a preference share does not pay the tax again on the preference share interest. Thus 10 per cent is equivalent to 17 per cent, subject to corporation tax, which makes it a greatly superior interest-bearing security to a debenture or loan stock, the interest on which is liable to corporation tax in the investor's hands if, of course, the investor is a company.

The incidence of taxation is an important aspect of finance and of investment and elsewhere (see page 177) I deal with this aspect. But it will be observable at once that whereas a 10 per cent interest rate on a debenture or loan stock is, on the face of it, exorbitant compared with the past it is only equivalent to 6 per cent and it may be that the willingness of the borrower to pay 10 per cent at the present time is due to the fact that after corporation tax the rate is not penal. Another factor with investment is the cost of purchasing an investment. This is dealt with elsewhere (see page 195). Expenses consist of stamp duty at 1 per cent with none for British Government stocks, most British corporation stocks and Commonwealth stocks, and stockbroker's commission, which is a varying rate. There is usually an active market in debenture stocks and loan stocks when they are in partly-paid form and are not subject to stamp duty, but after the stock has got into firm hands there is not much of a market even in the very big issues. Thus on a sale you do not get a close price like you would with a British Government stock.

Debenture and loan stock issued through the Stock Exchange are as indicated, usually issued first in partly-paid form. In other words the debenture or loan stock is issued and paid up by instalments. This is the time to buy a stock because as we have seen it is not subject to stamp duty.

The investor when considering a purchase of, say, loan or debenture stock will have regard to the nature of the company and the security in the case of a debenture. A debenture or loan stock issued by a company like I.C.I. or Shell is obviously as sound as a British Government security but a company which is developing a new process which may or may not be successful is a risky investment and before taking even a debenture which is secured on the assets of the company one must be satisfied that the company is likely to succeed. For example, a factory built specially to develop a certain process may be of no value as an asset if it has to be liquidated and sold for a different type of manufacturing process. I well remember a valuer putting a very low value on a factory costing many thousands of pounds, built in the country to produce radio sets. His comment was that if this building had to be sold for any purpose other than for making radio sets it would probably only fetch a knock down price in view of its situation and the expensive plant would be of practically no value.

A debenture as the name implies is usually supported by a charge on the company's assets. This can be a specific charge or what is termed a floating charge. In the case of a specific charge it is equivalent to what a purchaser of a house gives when he buys a house under mortgage. Debenture stocks subject to specific charge usually include a floating charge on all the floating assets such as stock, cash, plant which can be changed from one place to another and so on and are changing in value all the time. Even a debenture with a first charge on all the assets of the company, freeholds, leaseholds, plant, etc., can be of doubtful value as an investment if the company cannot make enough profits to cover its debenture interest.

Some debentures have only a floating charge as security, and this usually means that there is a previous debenture with a first charge or that the company has given its bank a first charge on all its assets. Whilst the company is paying the interest on its debenture and carrying out the terms of the trust deed governing the debenture no problem arises. If, however, the company defaults in paying its interest or in carrying out one of the chief provisions of the trust deed then the trustees can appoint a receiver when the floating charge is said to crystallize. However, the trustees of the debenture stockholders would, where the bank has a first charge in priority, immediately act to protect their interests.

In considering the security of a debenture, whether it is for a specific or floating charge, the issue should be covered by assets by a minimum of twice and as regards income the cover should be at least two or three times and more in the case of companies which are in cyclical business; a business which is subject to variation in the demand resulting from, say, restriction in hire-purchase arrangements. In deciding whether or not to take an interest in a particular stock, investors should look at the historical performance of the company, including its profit record for the last five or ten years. All this apart from considering whether the terms fully reflect current market conditions.

An unsecured loan stock as the name implies is not backed by any security. It does, however, have a trust deed and one of the provisions of the trust deed is that if the company fails to pay the interest on the loan stock or defaults on one of the provisions of the trust deed the trustees can appoint a receiver to take what steps may be necessary to protect the investor. In such cases it is most likely that there is a first mortgage or a borrower in front of the unsecured loan stock and the most that the trustees and the receiver of the unsecured loan stock holders can do is to consult with them and do whatever is necessary to ensure that the unsecured loan stock holder is protected as far as it is possible.

The nominal amount of quoted stock in issue excluding convertible stock is £4,860 million, with a market value of £3,650 million. Note the depreciation of about 25 per cent, a measure of the rise in interest rates and consequent fall in stock values.

Some debenture trust deeds provide for the issue to be repaid by means of a sinking fund. The trust deed may include provision for the sinking fund to be utilized in market purchases by the trustee in which case the trustees would go into the market and bid for stock. They would obviously do this when the stock was standing at a discount, that is a price below the price at which it will eventually be repaid. The trust deed may also provide for stock to be drawn in which case there will be a ballot to ascertain which units of stock will be repaid. This ballot will be supervised by a solicitor or notary. The company if it has the option will usually adopt this method when the market value of the stock is above the price at which it is eventually redeemable. Some issues provide for repayment by drawings only. In which case the stockholder is a lucky man when he is repaid at par at a time when the stock is quoted on the market at a heavy discount.

Convertible loan stocks
There are times when a company finds it most difficult to borrow

money. There is a long queue for loans and the company wants its money quickly so it decides to issue a convertible loan stock. The attraction of this is that under the terms of the issue the loan stock holder can convert into ordinary shares at fixed prices and on fixed dates. This option is worth some money and because of this it is usually possible to float a convertible loan stock at a lower rate of interest. You might well comment 'if an investor wants ordinary shares why doesn't he buy them and not buy the convertible loan stock?' The point is that he can buy the ordinary shares eventually through the convertible stock, but in the meantime he has a much higher return on his money. Obviously when

LIST OF TYPICAL DEBENTURE AND LOAN STOCKS

STOCK	PRICE	Yields per cent after buying expenses and accrued interest		
		Flat	Redemption	
			Gross	Net after tax 30p per cent on capital and 38·75p per cent on interest
DEBENTURES	£	£	£	£
ALLIED BREWERIES 7¼ per cent Debenture, 1988–93	78½	9·33	9·72 (1993)	6·19 (1993)
ASSOCIATED PORTLAND CEMENT 9 per cent Debenture 1992–97	96	9·54	9·59 (1997)	5·95 (1997)
BASS CHARRINGTON 3¼ per cent Debenture 1987–92	43¼	7·55	9·57 (1992)	6·70 (1992)
COURTAULDS 7 per cent Debenture 1982–87	78¼	9·03	9·84 (1987)	6·34 (1987)
UNITED DRAPERY STORES 10¼ per cent Debenture 1989–94	101½	9·81	9·85 (1994)	6·25 (1994)

a convertible stock is issued the ordinary shares can be bought at a lower price than the option terms in the trust deed. If the options never become of any value then the investor is left with a fixed-interest stock for which he has probably paid too much. On the other hand, if the loan stock is floated at a time when equity share prices are well down, and no investor knows when the bottom is going to be reached, it is a comforting thought that at least he can buy shares at a fixed price even though it is higher than the current

LIST OF TYPICAL LOAN STOCKS

STOCK	PRICE	Yields per cent after buying expenses and accrued interest		
		Flat	Redemption	
			Gross	Net after tax 30p per cent on capital and 38·75p per cent on interest
LOANS	£	£	£	£
DISTILLERS 5½ per cent Consolidated un-secured loan redeemable at 101 at any time by company	52¾	10·57	—	—
COURAGE 6¾ per cent Unsecured loan 2004–09	64xd	9·79	9·93 (2009)	6·37 (2009)
GUARDIAN ROYAL EXCHANGE 7 per cent 'B' Unsecured loan 1986–91	72½	9·57	10·14 (1991)	6·58 (1991)
NATIONAL WESTMINSTER BANK 9 per cent Unsecured loan 1993	93	9·56	9·64 (1993)	6·05 (1993)
IMPERIAL TOBACCO 10½ per cent Unsecured loan 1990–95	103	10·25	10·20 (1990)	6·30 (1990)

LIST OF TYPICAL ISSUES – CONVERTIBLE LOAN STOCK

Stock	Conversion rights and Redemption terms	Price	Yields per cent		Equivalent buying price of ordinary	Ordinary stock	
			Flat	Redemption Gross		Price	Gross yield per cent
BEECHAM GROUP 5 per cent Unsecured loan 1984–94	For £100 stock; September 21st, 1972–81 – 40 ordinary 25p shares. Redeemable September 30th, 1984–94 at 100	142	£ 3·49	£ 1·43 (1994)	353¼p	314½pxd	1·7
BROOKE BOND 7 per cent Unsecured loan 2003–08	For £100 stock: January 31st, 1971–75 – 138·88 'B' ordinary 25p shares; redeemable June 30th, 2003–08 at 100. Interest May 6th, November 6th.	105½	6·61	6·55 (2008)	75½	68	3·7
GENERAL ELECTRIC CO 7¼ per cent Unsecured loan 1987–92	For £100 stock: September 15th, 1971–76. – 88·88 ordinary 25p stock units. Redeemable March 31st, 1987–92 at 100.	119½	6·07	5·40 (1987)	133¾	122	2·9
GUEST KEEN & NETTLEFOLDS 6 per cent Unsecured loan 1988–93	For £100 stock: May 31st, 1972–75 – 29·63 ordinary £1. Redeemable June 28th, 1988–93 at 100.	116	5·10	4·50 (1988)	389½	365	3·4
THORN ELECTRICAL 5 per cent Unsecured loan 1990–94	For £100 stock; October 31st, 1972–82 – 14 ordinary and 14 'A' ordinary 25p shares. Redeemable July 31st, 1990–94 at 100.	119xd	4·12	3·47 (1994)	423	357½	1·47

price; and the convertible option price, taking the long-term view and the past history of the share price into consideration, could be a satisfactory one.

When a Bear market in equities starts no one knows how long it will continue. It certainly could continue for two years and has been known to last longer. It, therefore, may be a comforting thought that in the meantime the investor is getting a satisfactory return of money, not as high as if he had invested in a loan stock or debenture direct but a satisfactory return, plus the fact that one day he may be able to convert his convertible loan stock into shares at a price much below the then current market price.

Convertible loan stocks have the further advantage that the price of the stock will vary with the price of the equity and if the equity starts going up before the first conversion date the convertible stock will go up, so the investor has in a way an indirect investment in an equity but with a higher return on his money.

The rate of interest which is payable on a convertible loan stock will, of course, depend on the security which the company can offer in the way of profit records, etc. The investment in an investment trust convertible would only carry a low rate of interest of, say, 4 per cent, whereas a first-class industrial company would probably have to offer as high as 6 or 7 per cent if interest rates were on a 10 per cent level.

The nominal amount of quoted stock is £1,057 million and the market value £1,023 million. Surely there is an investment lesson in the superior performance of convertibles compared with normal fixed-interest stocks, but remember the investor has received less income from the former.

Preference and preferred capital

The present amount quoted on the London Stock Exchange is nominal £1,326 million, and market value £862 million. Note the nearly 35 per cent depreciation. Rising interest rates have hit preference shares even harder than loan stocks. The amount outstanding has shown a strong tendency to go down each year. The explanation of this is the taxation position under corporation tax to which I have referred on page 32. Because of the unfavourable taxation position of preference shares many companies have offered their preference shareholders unsecured loan stock in lieu, with a comparatively higher rate of interest and with a redemption date. Most preference shares are irredeemable but occasionally preference shares are issued which are redeemable at the option, usually of the company, at a fixed price.

In a winding-up or liquidation, a preference share comes before ordinary share capital but after debentures and unsecured loan stock, whether convertible or non-convertible. Some companies issue their preference shares in a cumulative form which means that if the dividend is not paid in one year it accumulates as arrears and the company cannot pay an ordinary dividend until they have paid off all the arrears of their preference dividend. Otherwise a preference dividend if omitted in a particular year would not be made up in a future year.

The market in preference shares has for some time been a little unusual. The yield ought to be more than an unsecured loan stock which ranks in front of it but there have been many occasions when preference shares have been on a lower yield basis. The lower yield has reflected the demand of investors to secure a high yielding investment which is franked for corporation tax (see page 33), also because potentially all preference shares may be repaid by the substitution of loan stock with a higher income return because of the unfavourable taxation aspect to the company which has issued the preference shares.

Preference shares are not suitable for individuals or funds including pension funds and charities who do not pay tax. These would do better with unsecured loan stock.

In considering an investment in a preference share, the investor must have regard to the record of the company and the amount of times the preference dividend is covered. One test is whether you would be prepared to invest in the ordinary shares of the company and if the answer is in the affirmative then obviously you can feel safe to invest in the preference share which is in front of it for dividend. Some preference shares have a fantastic cover for their dividend. I know one where the cover is nearly a thousand times. There is a method for assessing cover assuming 10 per cent of a company's available profits are required for its debenture interest and 6 per cent for its preference dividend and 60 per cent for its dividend, the priority percentages would be shown as follows:

Debenture interest ..	0–10	Preference interest..	10–16
Ordinary dividend ..	16–76	Carry forward ..	76–100

Yield differentials

Earlier in this chapter I have referred to the differentials in yields for the various groups of fixed-interest stocks, and I now set them out as follows:

		Per cent
British Government stocks	.. .. ..	x
Home corporations	.. ..	x+25p
First-class Dominion and Colonial stocks	..	x+37½p
Public boards	.. ..	x+50p
Good debentures	.. ..	x+75p

I refrained from giving you a figure for preference shares. It should really be x+85p, but under existing circumstances, the dividend being franked for corporation tax, the yield is likely to approximate to or be lower than that of a first-class debenture.

Switching

Switching operations are considerable between the various British Government stocks. Switching is effective when the yield on one British Government stock is out of line with another British Government stock. There is a yield differential expressed by a yield curve between all dated British Government stocks from the shortest dated stock to the longest dated and irredeemable stock. Any one of these stocks can be over or under valued at any point of time and this represents a switching opportunity. Straightforward switching can, of course, be made between stocks of a similar date and the relative cheapness of each stock is expressed by its redemption yield scientifically calculated. Stocks of different dates have a basic pattern, as displayed in the yield curve and when these get out of pattern switching opportunities occur. Switching also takes place with corporation stocks but to nothing like the same extent.

Before the advent of capital gains tax there was enormous business done in switching. The volume has reduced considerably since. Releasing British Government stocks from capital gains tax, where the stock has been held for over a year, has not helped much because most switches are opened and closed within a year. However, although switching has been greatly reduced for taxed funds, pension funds and other gross funds are indulging in much more switching.

Part III

Equities

CHAPTER 5

The case for equity investment

There is a superlative case for investing in equities, but one
reason only need be given, 'inflation'. What has happened over
the centuries in the erosion of the value of money is terrifying.
There are, of course, short periods of deflation or of stable prices
but over the years money buys less and less. During the First
World War four ounces a penny was what the children paid for
sweets – now the equivalent is one shilling (5p). In 1939 anthracite
was 5p a hundredweight, today it is £1·15 a hundredweight.

However, let me reduce the facts to figures with the assumption
of £100 in 1963. In 1914 it would be worth £485 but in 1970 only
£72·60.

THE DECLINE OF THE £ IN YOUR POCKET

Taking 1963 as the base year, the figures show the comparative purchasing
power of £100 over the years 1914 to 1970 inclusive

1914	485	1926	282	1938	310·6	1957	113·6
1915	394	1927	289	1946	183·5	1958	110·6
1916	332	1928	292	1947	171·8	1959	109·9
1917	275	1929	296	1948	159·5	1960	108·8
1918	239	1930	307	1949	155·8	1961	105·7
1919	225	1931	329	1950	151·5	1962	101·8
1920	195	1932	337	1951	138·9	1963	100·0
1921	215	1933	346	1952	131·1	1964	96·8
1922	265	1934	344	1953	128·9	1965	92·6
1923	279	1935	339	1954	126·6	1966	89·1
1924	277	1936	330	1955	122·4	1967	87·0
1925	275	1937	314	1956	117·2	1968	83·4
						*1969	78·0
						*1970	72·6

* Estimated by W.G.N.

With acknowledgements to *The Daily Telegraph*

Inflation will go on and on, in my view, until we in this country
see nearly as many figures on our price tags as in Italy with a
current exchange rate of 1,510 lira to the £ and the time will come
when we shall, like the French, convert old pounds into new
pounds – their conversion was one hundred old francs to one
new franc.

An equity share, being an aliquot part of the ownership of a
company, will rise in value with true values. Ten thousand shares

out of a total of one million shares is the ownership of one-hundredth part of the company. In the same way the profits of a company, measured in money terms, will increase with inflation.

Supposing a company had no real growth but its profits merely kept pace with inflation and supposing, compared with five years ago, £100 buys only £70 of goods and services, the company's profits which were, say, £70,000 five years ago would now be £100,000 with scope for a dividend increase.

So much for inflation but the nations of the world have not only had inflation but there has been a redistribution of wealth and a general increase in the standard of living, also a great population explosion. There are far more customers. In 1939, only a few people had motor-cars. Now we talk of the two sometimes three-car family.

So the next point is the real growth in industrial profits and these belong to the equity shareholder.

True there is a battle going on all the time between Government and industry, as to how much the Government gets of industry's profits and what is left for the shareholders who incidentally are taxed again, on the profits which are paid to them as dividends. True there is a battle going on all the time between the trade unions and the employers, which inevitably ends with higher wages. But in a capitalist society there has to be something left for the shareholder otherwise no one, especially the hard-headed institutional investor, would put any money into business, that is into equity shares.

Governments should never forget that investors have alternatives if equity investment became unattractive.

So buying equities is not only keeping pace with inflation, it is also participating in real growth in profits. For confirmation turn to the graphs on pages 28 and 29 showing the comparative performance of the British Government and the equity share indices from 1923 to 1970 produced by *Investors Chronicle* on their own indices. This graph has been discontinued.

Take warning however, all those who feel that equity investment is one vast bonanza. Industry has to take risks; to market projects at considerable expense which may or may not catch on; to quote for contracts in competition, some of which afterwards show no profit, even losses for a variety of reasons quite beyond the control of the company, such as strikes at other plants, freak weather, etc. Big companies may set out to undercut the smaller companies

which, if left to flourish, would take away business from them.
To the big company with many fields of activity it makes sense to
incur losses to eliminate a dangerous competitor. When he is
down they might even pick him up by buying him out.

So in buying equities the investor is buying risk capital. He
might buy a high flyer or one which is soon to take the long drop.

That is not the only danger to the investor; he might be inspired
by Press comment to buy a flourishing growth company which
has been going from strength to strength in what seems an endless
growth industry. But what no one knows is that that particular
company's profits are about to even out. Sometimes the historic
growth pattern has only to even off for one year to produce disastrous consequences for the shareholders who have put all their
spare cash in the company when its shares were standing at the
top. Lesney Products is a case in point.

Here are the pre-tax profits for the last eleven years – culminat-
ing in a loss on the twelfth year:

		£
1960	.. ..	304,000
1961	.. ..	332,000
1962	.. ..	385,000
1963	.. ..	558,000
1964	.. ..	797,000
1965	.. ..	853,000
1966	.. ..	1,359,000
1967	.. ..	2,262,000
1968	.. ..	3,779,000
1969	.. ..	5,577,000
1970	.. ..	2,960,082
1971	.. ..	1,103,915 (Loss)

Now examine the highs and lows of the share price for the last
six and a half years.

	1965	1966	1967	1968	1969	1970	1971 to date
High	35	43	180	553	$473\frac{1}{4}$	$177\frac{1}{2}$	$61\frac{7}{8}$
Low	27	34	40	176	130	$31\frac{1}{4}$	27

If an investor had bought at the top, as he well might, he would
have within nine months lost over three-quarters of his money if
he had to sell. Further, unless the company can, in the near future
get back to growth on the scale of the past he is going to see them
standing for many years at a price well under what he paid for
them.

Not everyone would have heard of the abject fall in the price of

Lesney Products shares but practically everyone has heard about Rolls-Royce. In 1968–69 they secured massive contracts to build the RB211 engine and all investors, including top institutional investors, thought this was a breakthrough. The shares reached 250p. In 1969 the shares fell mainly with the market. The profits were: 1968 £15·92 million, 1969 £6·41 million, and in July 1970 in announcing the 1969 profits it was stated that profits would fall again in 1970 and there was little sign that that trend would change until 1972 or 1973. The company went into liquidation almost without warning on February 5th, 1971.

So even if equities are the supreme investment they are, nevertheless, clearly risk investments and even the best are subject to the risk of timing a purchase badly and first-class companies can quite unexpectedly go into liquidation. Elsewhere in this book (pages 83–102) I point out what can be done to meet these dangers – diversification, unit trusts, investment trusts, etc.

Perhaps the best way of considering or measuring the performance of equities is by examining an equity index.

As you will read elsewhere in these pages, the main equity indices are the *Financial Times Industrial Share Index*, the *Financial Times/Actuaries 500 Share Index* and the *Financial Times/Actuaries All Share Index* of 621 shares (formerly 600). The latter two have only been going since April 10th, 1962, but the *Financial Times Industrial Share Index* started on July 1st, 1935, and this covers quite a period which in my view is adequate because the numbers of equities available for investment fifty years ago were very limited.

One of the problems of the *Financial Times Index* is that, like the *Dow Jones Index of Wall Street Common Stocks*, it only covers thirty shares. It is, however, surprising how closely the *Financial Times 30 Share Index* has in past years approximated in performance to the *621 Share Index*, although due to the poor performance of some of the thirty shares this did not apply in 1971.

Here are the highs and lows of the indices since its inception, together with current indices:

	Current	High	Low
Financial Times Industrial Share			
Index	420·8	521·9 (19.9.68)	49·4 (28.6.40)
Financial Times/Actuaries All Share			
Index	184·13	187·32 (8.9.71)	83·72 (25.6.62)

and here are the highs and lows for 1969–71 (to date):

Financial Times Industrial Share Index ..	520·1	305·3
	(15.1.69)	(2.3.71)
Financial Times/Actuaries All Share Index..	114·27	187·32
	(27.6.70)	(8.9.71)

On October 27th, 1967, when the *Financial Times Industrial Share Index* reached 400 for the first time in the Index's thirty-two years of its history the *Financial Times* published the graph of the Index since its inception. I reproduce it with acknowledgements on page 49, together with another graph for the same Index bringing in the halcyon of the 500 Index period, page 50.

The difference between the highs and lows in the same years is, I am sure readers will agree, pretty staggering. A perusal of the annual highs and lows of the Index will show that the highs are sometimes not attained again for many years. Nevertheless, the movement of the Index is markedly upwards, although 1969–70 and the first half of 1971 has been a period of recession.

Still the graph and the highs and lows in particular stress not only timing but time horizon which is also dealt with within these pages.

Equities are, if the past is any indication, certs for the long-term investor, for charities, pension funds, insurance companies, and for investment trusts, because however bad the timing the years will eventually justify the purchase of a first-class share. Not so for the individual investor who may not live long enough and who might have fared much better if he had bought a fixed-interest investment and had a higher income yield.

The individual can be very unlucky in his investment lifetime. Take the wonderful United States. At the time of the Wall Street crash in October 1929 the *Dow Jones Index* was 381 – it fell to about 40. It did not get back to 381 until 1953.

In Britain the equity investor had a grim time over the period 1910–45 – an individual investor's lifetime.

History it is said repeats itself and certainly this is my experience. But there have been fundamental changes since the Wall Street crash in the attitudes of Governments. Another Wall Street crash would produce international communism because a Wall Street crash means world depression. New economic skills seem to rule out a repetition of world depression and at most it is periods of recession of trade with which we shall be concerned in the future. But even these can stagger the stock-markets. The

FINANCIAL TIMES INDUSTRIAL SHARE INDEX

1935 to 1967

32 years to get to 400

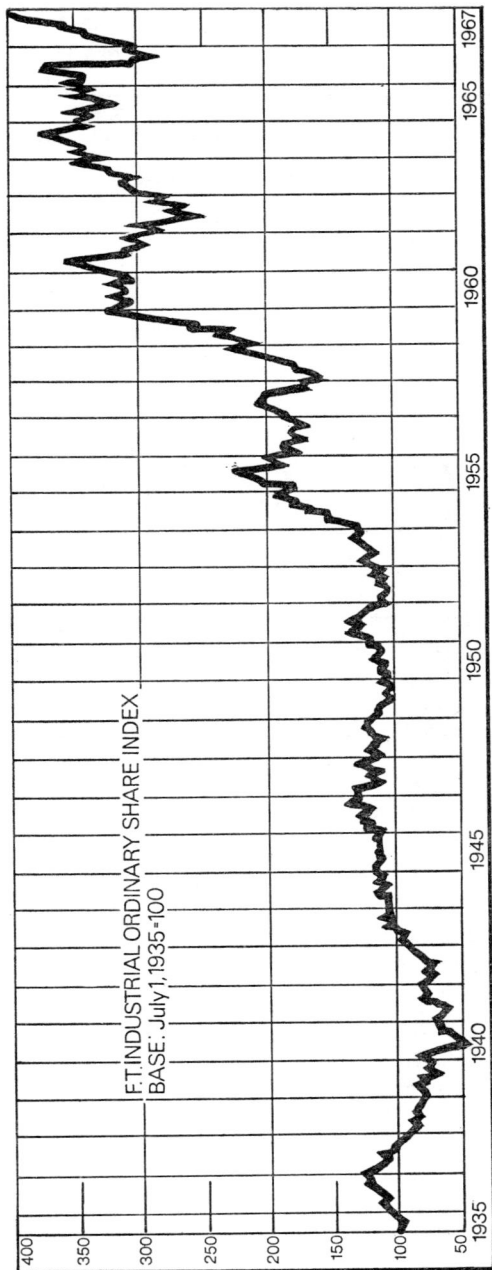

F.T. INDUSTRIAL ORDINARY SHARE INDEX
BASE: July 1, 1935 = 100

FINANCIAL TIMES INDUSTRIAL SHARE INDEX
1959 to 1971 (to date)

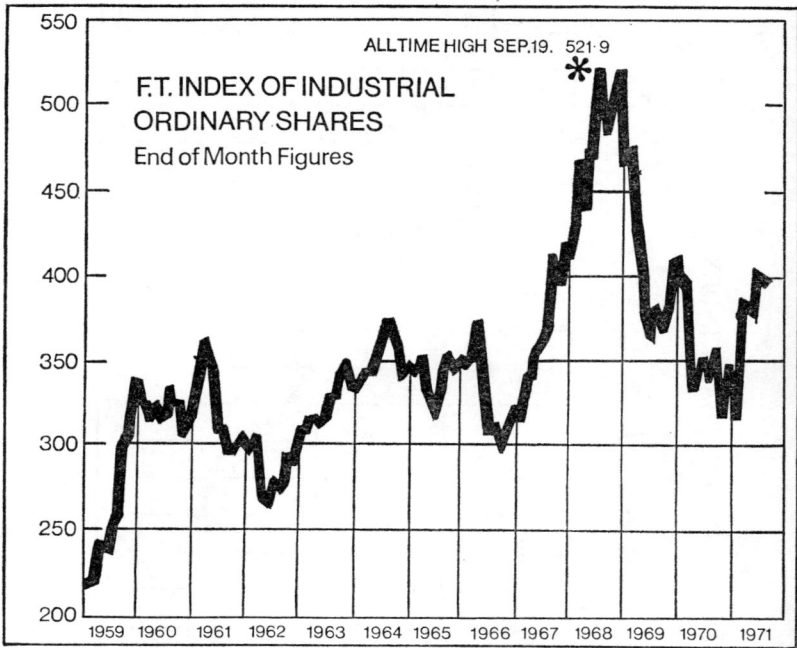

ALL TIME HIGH SEP.19. 521·9

F.T. INDEX OF INDUSTRIAL
ORDINARY SHARES
End of Month Figures

Financial Times Industrial Share Index was 520·1 on January
15th, 1969, and six months later it had fallen to 357·4. In January
1969 the unit trust movement sold its record, up to then, value of
units. My experience teaches me that the majority of individual
investors support a bull market in equities at its top.

In a sentence the case for equities is indisputable but there are
great dangers especially for the untutored investor in timing a
purchase or in selecting a share, dangers from which even the
institutional investment manager is not immune.

In the following chapter I hope to tell how these dangers can be
eliminated or greatly reduced.

CHAPTER 6

Aids for investment, etc.

There is no shortage of aids for investment. By aids I do not mean books on investment. Most of these are introductory anyway. This book itself will enable the reader to grasp much of the scope of investment. It sets the scene, the high peaks, the rough gorges, the nature of the woods, the fertile valleys, the heavy clay land, the sodden areas and it gives much advice out of my many years of experience in practising the art of investment. But, dear reader, I am still a learner like yourself, but perhaps with a lengthy start.

This book is addressed primarily to the student, the individual investor, and all those associated with investment who still feel they have something to learn. I believe many little bits of information will appeal to the professional – and even the professional likes at times to check his experience and opinions with other professionals.

By aids, I am referring to the tools which enable the investment manager or the interested layman to do the job of investing successfully. By aids also I include access to information which will help the mature student to proceed further in his search for information and knowledge of investment.

Newspapers and journals
Most daily and Sunday newspapers devote one or more pages to City news. You should skim through these pages picking out for serious reading matters which may be of importance. It is somewhat invidious to name some newspapers and not others but of the Sunday papers either *The Sunday Times*, *The Observer*, or *The Sunday Telegraph* will suffice. Of the dailies, *The Times*, *The Daily Telegraph*, and *The Guardian* are addressed to the more serious reader, but the *Daily Mail* and *Daily Express* give substantial investment news. *The Times* has its business news supplement, the *Daily Mail* has its weekly *Money Mail*, *The Daily Telegraph* and *The Guardian* their Saturday family finance and insurance pages and for all three these are in addition to their normal financial pages.

Then there is *The Scotsman*, *The Glasgow Herald*, *The Birmingham Post*, the *Yorkshire Post*, the *Liverpool Daily Post*, the *Western*

51

Mail and other provincial newspapers. Some newspapers, the *Daily Mirror* for example, could, I feel, devote more space to financial news. Many a financial journalist is starved for space.

The *Evening Standard* and the *Evening News*, London's two evening papers, carry excellent City columns, but this cannot be said for most provincial evening papers.

Then there is that wonderful investment paper the *Financial Times*, but much more of this later.

The professional investor, the financial journalist, and the stockbroker and stock-jobber cannot afford to ignore any newspaper. There are such things as exclusive news to one newspaper and they must get hold of it as quickly as possible. Every City editor's office will have an up-to-date file of all newspapers and the City staff will skim through the pages as a daily exercise. If it does not produce fresh news it is productive of ideas or even of imitations.

Then there are also the weeklies – *Investors Chronicle*, incorporating the *Stock Exchange Gazette*, *The Investors' Guardian*, *The Investors' Review*, *The Investment World*, and *The City Press*, and of these *Investors Chronicle* is ranked number one but there is good stuff in the others. There is too *The Economist*, with City pages but devoted mainly to economic matters, not that the reader will not find plenty of economic articles in the daily and Sunday newspapers or in the investment weeklies.

Moodies Service and the Exchange Telegraph Cards
These are a must for every investment manager or consultant. Both give vital information concerning almost every stock issued and every company and its subsidiaries. These services give too much information to list fully here. The business of the company and its subsidiaries is given in some detail, a list of the directors, details of share capital and loan capital and the figures for the company including profits for the last ten years. Dividends will be set out for a similar period, also the highs and lows of the shares over the same period. It will show a consolidated balance sheet in brief detail and extracts from the chairman's statement at the last annual general meeting and any information which has come out since.

Moodies Investment Handbooks
These are in two parts. Part I covers industrial trustee companies,

namely, companies which qualify for investment by trustees under the Trustee Investments Act 1961, Part II includes banks, hire-purchase, insurance, investment trusts, mining finance, property and smaller industrial and overseas companies. The two books together comprise the shares of nearly one thousand companies. For each company there is a chart of share price performance and other very valuable information, not of course on the same scale as the *Moodies Cards* or the *Exchange Telegraph Cards*, but nevertheless very useful information. The books are published quarterly and the service costs £17·50 per annum. There is a short edition for the small investor priced at £2·40.

Charts
There are some operators who base all their judgements on charts. Charts are particularly well developed in the United States and Australia. In these countries full particulars of the turnover of every share is published and this information is probably essential to efficient charting. They claim that they can, with the help of their charts, establish a buying or selling signal. I believe that charts can be useful but the chartists have a language all of their own and quite a mystique has developed around prediction by charts. One has to remember too that if a lot of chartists all come to the same conclusion and advise their clients to buy or sell their shares their predictions can well come right merely by their advice being followed. I certainly carefully watch the graphs of the indices.

Bond value tables
In order to calculate the redemption yields on fixed-interest stocks it is desirable to have yield tables covering stocks with coupons ranging from 2½ per cent to 12 per cent. The fact is that the redemption yields which are quoted by the newspapers and by the stockbrokers are on the rare occasion incorrect, and the skilled investment manager has an instinct when the redemption yield looks to be wrong, and it is then that he has recourse to his bond value tables.

Stockbrokers
However experienced the investment manager, he will do well not to under-rate the assistance he can get from stockbrokers, but he is hardly likely to make this mistake. The manager of a large

fund has great advantages because stockbrokers will compete with each other for the business of his fund and that means competition to provide the best service. More about stockbrokers later.

The Stock Exchange

The Stock Exchange is the essential market for buying and selling shares. There the buyers and the sellers are brought together, in their absence, of course, through the stockbrokers they employ. The business is married on the floor of the Stock Exchange, the orders are given to the stockbrokers' dealers and they in turn go to the appropriate jobber who deals in the particular share. The jobber is the man who in the end makes the market. Obviously, a share like I.C.I. can be dealt in readily with very close prices between a buying and a selling order, but a small investment trust or a share not often dealt in would have a wider difference between buying and selling prices and the jobber might have to take the shares on his books and keep them there for a while or even sell short and acquire the shares later.

It is not appropriate here to go into details of how the Stock Exchange works but the fact remains that an investor needs a stockbroker when he buys and sells shares. The stockbrokers' market is in the Stock Exchange and this market is provided by the jobbers who could be at risk if they are not able to balance their sales orders with purchases in any particular stock. The stockbroker incurs no financial risk, he is paid by commission. The jobber takes all the financial risk and his remuneration consists of the turn (the difference in his favour) between the orders he gets to take or provide shares. By overloading his sales or his purchases he could make a lot of money but equally he could lose a lot of money. Certainly the jobbers on the London Stock Exchange do a good job and it is rare for one to come a financial cropper.

The majority of stockbrokers also do a good job. Some have research departments run by trained analysts which are so efficiently conducted that the big institutional investor does not find it necessary to have a research department in his own office. He relies on the research work of his entourage of stockbrokers, just applying his own unique investment experience learned over the years to the massive information which comes to him from stockbrokers and other sources, sorted out first by one of his own junior analysts.

I am glad here to pay a tribute to the research department of the larger stockbrokers and to their work generally. I have seen big strides made by stockbrokers, particularly in the last twenty years. Few, however, can give much time to the small investor but he is well catered for by the unit trust movement, the life assurance offices, and the many types of deposits, see page 12, particularly so now that so many saving schemes are linked to assurance with income tax advantages. The research departments of stockbrokers are manned by young and devoted analysts, some of whom are women. I am pleased that the ladies are invading this hitherto male preserve because I have a high opinion of women when it comes to investment. Women, and my view is based on considerable experience as a trustee manager of a large institution, are better with their own money than men.

A number of stockbrokers are using computers to help them with investment analyses. Messrs Phillips & Drew, for one, rank 160 shares weekly by computer. All known information concerning a company is fed into the computer together with various estimates as to future profit growth, etc. In this way they arrive at a price which they compare with the market price of the share and then rank it by percentages, so much cheap, or dear, or fully valued. One has to remember all the time that the result is not infallible because investment is not a science and the unexpected may happen to any company and to the market as a whole. But I find the exercise useful and I am always keen to know how Phillips & Drew rank a particular share. If they confirm my own feelings, fine, but if we are poles apart I regret to admit I am disinclined to accept their conclusions. Hoare & Co, Govett also rank shares for cheapness and dearness but on an historic basis – still this is a useful exercise because most investment managers are ranking shares in this way 'out of their heads' – that human computer which, when in high-class order and backed by years of reading and experience, is not to be under-rated. Don't be put off entirely by the analyst who wants chapter and verse for your judgement – you may have fed a lot of forgotten material into that head of yours and when it gives you a buy or sell signal don't debase it by words such as hunch. Fed with the right information the human computer can supply some cannily correct judgements.

Literature
Stockbrokers' reports on companies and shares will heap up on

the desks of all investment managers. One or two reports would suffice for the student for careful study because they are all very similar in scope. The investment manager and his staff develop a technique for skimming through the plethora of reading material quickly. The sensible stockbroker will start with his conclusions and recommendations and go into details with figures, etc., afterwards. It is a great burden dealing with a dozen stockbrokers. It is so easy to be snowed under by their glossies and circulars but a quick glance through the lot has its rewards. You may find one worthy stockbroker telling you to buy a particular share while another, equally worthy, tells you to sell. Incidentally if stockbrokers have a fault, indeed all investment advisors too, it is that they do not give enough sale recommendations. The experienced investor will approach all recommendations with a very open mind and will not be rushed into a decision which does not match the signal that head of his gives.

Company accounts

I have had in my time a stack of these two feet high on my desk. I have got behind, but for a fund with holdings of some four hundred equities and two hundred and fifty debentures they come fast, at certain times of the year. I might only have been a fortnight behind – one has to acquire a skill for turning over pages quickly and an eagle eye for spotting the unusual. My first test was whether the dividend had been increased, the comparative profit figures, and whether the carry forward in the profit and loss account had gone up. Still, half the time I already knew broadly what had happened through reading the financial papers. But I do recommend a careful perusal of a company's report and accounts by the investment student, it gives much useful information, much of it in compliance with statute. You can also get a good idea of what pay the executive directors receive and whether the directors have a substantial stake in the company. The latter can work favourably but not always for dividend increases. They might prefer to keep more money in the company – to keep the cash-flow running high.

Figures, figures, figures

I wonder that Walt Disney did not do a ballet of figures for the tired businessman. They are inexhaustible – company figures – stocks and share prices – highs and lows – statistics of this and that – Gold Reserve – trade figures – balance of payment figures – unemployment figures – retail sales for individual industries – turnover figures – projection of this and that. Many by the time you get them hot off the Press are already out of date, referring to a period of three or six months ago or even more. There is always a dreadful feeling that you may miss some important ones.

It is desirable to skim through as much reading as possible but here again the research department of the brokers will come to your aid. They all issue market and economic reviews and summaries of trends as indicated by figures.

One firm of stockbrokers provides an excellent monthly market review covering the economic situation by a prominent economist. The various partners in charge do a piece on British Government stocks, debentures and other fixed-interest stock, equities generally, and investment trusts, insurance shares and property companies particularly. They have found it desirable, to my silent amusement, to give on the first page of the report a very short summary under the above seven or eight headings. First-class communication is an art!

Economic reviews and prognostications

I have to confess to a healthy distrust of all economists. What is an economist? Are not we all? Is it someone who has read a P.P.E. at Oxford or taken an Economics Degree at London? In both cases including a good deal of stuff best forgotten from the practical standpoint. The economist I recognize is someone who has an economics degree but has then devoted his life to studying the economic facts of life, both nationally and internationally. Then I like to know his politics, from Blue Tory through the many shades to communist leanings; for his views will be coloured. I can often guess his politics by what he writes.

Then I have the final reservation, the figures which are the economist's stock-in-trade are almost always out of date. They are based on the estimate of others, in some cases, as we have seen, wildly out of date, and sometimes on estimates in which there is every intention to deceive.

May I take a little misguided pride in what I wrote in a paper on investments in trust for one of the conferences of the Chartered Institute of Secretaries when commenting on the adverse effect out-of-date figures have on economic prophesies? 'The trouble often is that the cyclone which the statistics predict will soon hit us, has already blown itself out in the form of a modest storm and in reality we are about to experience a period of good trading weather but owing to the delay in supplying figures there is not even an identifying patch of blue sky as big as a pocket hand-kerchief on the distant economic horizon.'

Investment analysis

This book is not the place to go into this except very briefly. In the United States, where it is much more advanced and where its exponents are the doyens of Wall Street, it is called security analysis.

The aim is to get together as much data as possible for the various industrial groups and to estimate future trends. Similarly for individual companies to get as much information as possible from their reports and accounts over a period of, say, ten years, to read chairmen's speeches and assess the chairman's worth and the reliability of his statements, taking into account whether he is a cheerful optimist or an incorrigible pessimist. And with the help of as much data as possible to forecast the future growth and prosperity of the company, whether it is earning enough on its assets – whether it is using its working capital efficiently.

Investment analysis is a study in depth – the deeper the better for the analyst. He is an enthusiastic seeker after investment truth. Unfortunately he may begin to feel that investment is a science. In my view it is definitely not and never will be. There are far too many imponderables – political changes – taxation changes – fashion changes – management changes – wages escalation – com-petition – emergencies, etc. But the exercise teaches a lot and I admire these men and women, only a few of the latter so far, who go to all lengths including visiting the company, inspecting the factory, chatting up the chairman, all to the end that their final analysis of the future of the company may be near enough correct.

Financial Times

Now for the *Financial Times*. The *Financial Times* – called the 'Pink un' by the late Harold Wincott, that splendid financial journalist and very dear man, is a truly great financial paper. When I went to the City there were two financial dailies, the *Financial News*, printed on creamy yellow paper, and the pink *Financial Times*. The latter has for many years incorporated the *Financial News* which by an odd quirk owns the *Financial Times*.

Those who had to read both heaved a sigh of relief when there was only one daily financial paper to read.

Well I hope all my financial journalist friends who write for the newspapers or weekly journals will forgive me but if I had to choose one source for all my financial reading my choice would fall undoubtedly on the *Financial Times*. Much that the others publish is splendid and cannot be ignored but what the *Financial Times* provides in investment and economic information would serve any investment manager if he were left with only one source of information.

Let me list what the *Financial Times* provides:

(A) **The Financial Times Share Information Service.** This appears on the penultimate pages of the *Financial Times*. It is in effect the closing prices of certain fixed-interest stocks and equity shares. The price is the mid-market price. Fixed-interest stocks are divided into British funds and other headings. The British funds are further divided into shorts, namely, stocks with up to five years of life, stocks of five to fifteen years, stocks over fifteen years, and undated stocks. Other headings include corporation stocks, Commonwealth and African stocks, Foreign bonds and rails, London; U.S. dollar and Deutschmark issues; and American.

The bulk of the information relates to equities which are grouped as follows: banks and hire-purchase; beers, wines and spirits; building industry, timber and roads; chemicals, plastics, etc.; cinemas, theatres and TV; Drapery and stores; electrical and radio; engineering and metal. The next heading is food, groceries, etc., followed by hotels and caterers; industrials (miscellaneous); insurance, which includes composite insurance companies, life assurance companies and insurance brokers. The next is machine tools, motor and aircraft trades, divided into motors and cycles, commercial vehicles, aircraft, components; garages and distributors; followed by newspapers, publishers; then paper, printing, advertising; property; shipbuilders; repairers; shipping; shoes and leather; South Africans; Steels; textiles – general, textiles – wool; tobaccos; trusts; finance and land divided into investment trusts, finance, land, etc., followed by utilities (this is a small miscellaneous collection), then oils; rubbers – Malaysian, rubbers – miscellaneous; sisal; teas divided into India and Pakistan, and Ceylon; followed by mines – Central rand, Eastern Rand, Far West Rand, O.F.S., Finance, Diamond, Platinum, Central African, Australians; followed by tin – Eastern tin – Nigerian tin –

tin miscellaneous; then copper and finally miscellaneous mines. Incidentally there are 2,550 equities quoted in the *Financial Times*.

In the case of the fixed-interest stocks the running yield and the gross redemption yield are both shown and this applies to all the fixed-interest stocks quoted and the high and low for the current year. The price movement on the day is also given in all cases.

For equities either the dividend or the percentage dividend is shown and the number of times covered, the gross yield on the dividend and the price earnings ratio. The price earnings ratio is the number of times the price exceeds the earnings per share. It is impracticable to give the price earnings ratio for every type of share and for a variety of reasons. Indeed when the changes in taxation become effective and a lower rate of corporation tax applies to distributed profits, the price earnings ratio, if it is to survive, will have to be redefined.

There are some share prices which every newspaper would have to quote as a news item, but for the smaller companies if they want a quotation for their shares to appear on the back pages of the *Financial Times* they have to pay a fee of £250 per annum.

Of course, all share and stock quotations are given daily in the *Stock Exchange Official List*, but whereas the *Financial Times* now costs 6p a day and provides a variety of news as well, as we shall see later, the *Stock Exchange Official List* is just a list of quotations, but they are official in law and fix the price at death for probate. The stocks and shares are not so helpfully distributed as they are in the back pages of the *Financial Times* but you can be sure that every company which has an official quotation will either be quoted in the *Stock Exchange Daily Official List* or the supplementary list which appears once a month. It will be appropriate here to give the division of the daily list, the monthly list follows it: British funds, etc.; corporation and county stocks – Great Britain and Northern Ireland; public boards, etc. – Great Britain and Northern Ireland; Commonwealth, Government and provincial securities; Commonwealth corporation stocks; Foreign stocks, bonds, etc.; (coupons payable in London); foreign stocks, bonds, etc. (coupons payable abroad); corporation stocks – foreign, United Kingdom and other Commonwealth railways, American railroads, foreign railways, banks and discount companies, breweries and distillers, canals and docks, commercial, industrial, etc., electric lighting and power, financial trusts, land, etc., gas, insurance, investment trusts, unit trusts, iron, coal and

steel, mines – Australian mines – miscellaneous mines – Rhodes-
ian and East African mines – South African mines – West African
mines – diamond, oil, property, rubber, shipping, tea and coffee,
telegraphs and telephones, tramways and omnibus, water works.
The daily list is now giving for equities a code showing where a
particular share appears in the *Financial Times/Actuaries All Share
Index*. For example, I.C.I. is quoted under commercial and
industrials and has against it 68, which implies chemicals and
plastics.

Stock and share price indices. The *Financial Times* provides
daily indices for: (1) British Government securities; (2) fixed-
interest stocks; (3) industrial ordinary shares; (4) gold mines,
the starting dates being respectively 1926, 1928, 1935 and September 12th, 1955. These are the *Financial Times'* own indices.
In addition and of more recent vintage are the *Financial Times/
Actuaries Indices* which are worked out by the *Financial Times*
together with the Institute of Actuaries for: (*a*) twenty-year
Government stocks; (*b*) twenty-year redeemable debentures and
loans; (*c*) Investment Trust preference shares and (*d*) commercial
and industrial preference shares, and the *Financial Times/Actuaries
Index* of 500 equity shares and its *All Share Index* which consists
of 621 shares. These date from April 10th, 1962. In contrast the
thirty-five-year-old *Financial Times Industrial Share Index* comprises only thirty shares.

The 500- and 621-share indices are divided into the following
groups: Capital goods, group 185; Consumer goods (durable),
group 56; Consumer goods (non-durable), group 176;
other groups – chemicals, 19; office equipment, 10; shipping, 10;
oil, 2; unclassified, 42. There is now a 498-share index which
excludes oil. The 621 *All Share Index* is the 500-share Index plus
the 121 shares of the financial group. The various groups are
further divided into sub-groups, full details of which appear
under 'Investment indices', page 238.

By perusing the index you can ascertain what is happening
daily to every group and sub-group as well as what is happening
to the index as a whole. The indices provide, in addition: (*a*) the
index change on the day; (*b*) the estimated earnings yield; (*c*) the
estimated price earnings ratio; (*d*) the dividend yield; (*e*) the indices
for the previous four days and a year ago; (*f*) the high and low
of the year; and (*g*) the all-time high and low giving dates in each
case.

There is a share index for the commodity group which is divided into rubbers (10), teas (10), copper (4), mining finance (11), tins (8), and similar information is given for each of these groups.

For fixed-interest stocks the yield of 2½ per cent Consols is shown for the day, the previous six days, and for one year ago.

As we have seen, *Financial Times/Actuaries* indices are provided for: (*a*) twenty-year Government stocks (6); (*b*) twenty-year redeemable debentures and loans (15); (*c*) investment trust preference shares (15); (*d*) commercial and industrial preference shares (20). These give the yield on each index, the index for the previous six days, for a year ago, also the high and low of the year and the high and low since the inception with dates.

Unfortunately the magnificent *Financial Times/Actuaries* indices were not started until April 10th, 1962, while the base date for some of the sub-indices does not start until December 29th, 1967. Indeed the index is one which is being varied and added to fit circumstances and three indices: (*a*) wines and spirits, (*b*) toys and games, and (*c*) office equipment were not included until January 16th, 1970.

Indices are also provided by *Investors Chronicle*, the *Daily Mail*, *The Times*, *The Exchange Telegraph* and *Moodies Services*, *The Economist* and others. *Investors Chronicle* indices for equities and gilt-edged stocks are forty-seven years old but have unfortunately recently been discontinued. A graph for the whole period appears on pages 28 and 29.

(B) Graphs of the *Financial Times* indices and of the group and sub-group indices appear from time to time. Also graphs of industrial activity and other matters.

(C) Stock Exchange Report. There is a daily Stock Exchange report which comments on the activity of the day, under the headings of gilt-edged, fixed-interest stocks, equities, and mining stocks. A list of the principal rises in price and falls in price is given, together with a list of the most active stocks. Another column gives the new highs and lows for the year. Also from time to time the *Financial Times* gives a list of those groups which have beaten the index as a whole and those which have lost out to the index as a whole, dividing the two into what they call leaders and laggards.

(D) General investment news is obviously given and for investment managers the most important section of this is under the heading *Company News and Comment*. This lists the more important company results which have come out on the day.

These pages are divided into issue news, mining news, bids and deals. On these pages too will be the current quotations for recent issues split into equities, fixed-interest stocks, and rights issues. The well-known commentator, Lex, and there must have been many dozens of them over the years, will comment on the back page – he was on the front page for many years – on what he regards as the most interesting figures or results.

(E) Dealing prices. Next to the *Financial Times* share information service is a list of Stock Exchange dealings. It is a list of dealings in the shares named which took place the previous day. The division follows the Stock Exchange Official List, details of the division appear on page 60. At the end of the dealings page there is what they call a special list, and these are bargains marked under rule 163 (1) (*e*) in securities for which quotation has not been granted and which are not recorded in the Official List.

(F) A list of current option rates is also given. I have explained options on page 78.

(G) Details of dividend announcements.

(H) Company meeting reports.

(I) Wall Street including some common stock prices, the *Dow Jones* and the *Standard and Poor* indices and other international indices, but see Chapter 21 on 'Overseas investments'.

(J) A money market report.

(K) Quotations from some provincial, commonwealth and Continental Stock Exchanges.

(L) Base metal and commodity price changes.

(M) Learned articles by economists on the state of the economy and their views as to the future.

(N) When it comes to general news the paper is split up into letters to the editor, food and raw materials, American news, export news, European news, other overseas news, a technical page, the executive world where management and technology are dealt with, labour news, political news, appointments (most people in the City read through the appointments column to note what changes have taken place in the management of the major companies), property market, international company news, Parliament.

Then there is the daily leading article and the 'Men and Matters' column, in which any financier or industrialist likes to see his name. All this and not forgetting the page on the arts which some feel is absolutely first-class. Then there is Trevor Bailey on soccer or cricket, which I confess I sometimes read first of all.

In a sentence it is a wonderful paper.

CHAPTER 7

The course of equity share prices

It is an over-simplification to state that equity share prices depend upon supply and demand. Too many shares for sale and too few buyers, share prices go down. Too many buyers and too few shares, prices go up.

But one must probe deeper than that and I must state at once that after thirty-five years of day-to-day investment management I am baffled by the highs and lows of individual shares. One is aware of the factors that affect the share prices of individual shares, the hard facts as set out in the company's annual accounts and the chairman's statement: the company's half-yearly and sometimes quarterly figures of profits – news as distinct from opinions. Then there is the assessment of these figures and the comments on the company's activities from time to time. Assessment takes the form of stockbrokers' circulars and financial journalists' comments. Lex, for example, of the *Financial Times*, and remember that this covers more than one reigning Lex – in fact a team – and over half a century the column has been written by dozens of different individuals. Like all assessments they have sometimes been wrong, particularly when there is an absence of definite information, assumptions are made and from these predictions.

As I have stressed elsewhere stockbrokers and financial writers are, on the whole, trying to do an honest job of work but they are often concerning themselves with prophecies. The price of a share will largely depend on the nature of the company's future prospects or otherwise and these prospects are vulnerable to the slings and arrows of outrageous fortune – to many things quite outside the control of the company. To politics. To taxation. To fashions. To new inventions. To factors quite unforeseeable.

An investment manager will have some knowledge of the performance of some companies over many years and obviously he gets a fair notion if he has had a share on his portfolios for a number of years. Also he reads the financial papers and skims through the dozens of stockbrokers' circulars that fall on his desk. The scope of the aids to assist him in forming an investment judgement are legion – see previous chapter. He gathers a clear notion of the current opinion on a particular share. Sometimes he has the refreshing experience of reading that one stockbroker, for reasons stated, regards a share as a firm buy whilst another, for equally good reasons, firmly recommends a sale.

On page 225 I have referred to the tipping of shares by financial journalists and the effect of these tips on the market and how jobbers mark up a share as soon as it is tipped and continue to mark up a share as more and more buying orders come in. The jobber as we have already seen is in effect the market for shares. Apart from cases where the stockbroker marries a large sales order from one institution with a large buying order from another institution, and these are not infrequent, the jobber is the market for shares. He is vulnerable, not the stockbroker, who buys and sells shares on commission. The jobber who finishes the day with a substantial balance of shares of an individual company – he has agreed to buy them or alternatively he has agreed to sell them – is wide open to dangers of news, whether concerning the company or generally which breaks during business hours or worse still after hours when he has closed his books. If he does not balance his buying and selling orders at the end of the day he is at risk. But he is in business and each day he is not going to find himself in this happy balanced position.

For every share on his books his protection is to raise or lower the price of his bid, sometimes substantially. When faced with an unbalanced position he takes protective action. He has interpreted for his own protection the news which directly concerns a company and also news which may affect it indirectly. Indeed, I have often been surprised at a share price movement and on inquiry have found it is the result of a piece of news I have missed or felt was of no particular significance to the share in question.

In my view this marking up or down on news remotely affecting a company is often overdone, but I remind myself it is the jobber safeguarding himself. I will mention two heavy markings up and down which I considered at the time were excessive. They related to the insurance brokers group – many other examples could be given. In the first place there were clear indications that the insurance companies – certainly some of them – wanted to get tough with the brokers on commission rates. Down came the share prices of quoted insurance broker shares and they stayed down for a long time, even though it became clear that whatever happened insurance brokers would continue to prosper. A year or so later came Lord Cromer's report on Lloyd's, with forecasts of future growth in premiums following the raising of underwriting levels. Up went the shares. Indeed I looked for and expected the rise.

Certainly share prices are very sensitive to news. Bad news, or what is interpreted as bad news, causes sharp falls in the share price of the companies which seem to be affected. This often provides good opportunities of buying shares. The news is invariably seen in a one-sided fashion, as if the company concerned will put its hands behind its back and accept a knock-out on the chin, whereas a little thought would reassure the investor that the company's first-class management will stand firm, ward off the blow, and fight back.

There are certainly fashions in shares and it is dangerous to follow fashions when they have been going some time. Disastrously fashionable shares have in the past been those heavy engineering shares dealing with the development of nuclear energy, and with computers. Obviously these were things of the future but problems face new inventions. Here I am referring to first-class shares which became fashionable because investors and their advisors regarded these as new exciting growth industries, quite overlooking all the problems known and unknown which completely new and large projects involve. Mergers have largely disposed of all the British computer companies. There is left only one large predominantly British company – International Computers (formerly International Computers & Tabulators). This has had a chequered history. Here are the highs and lows:

			1961	1962	1963	1964	1965	1966
High	..	..	556¼	650	402½	295	245	188¾
Low	..	..	295	391¼	270	193¾	135	130

				1967	1968	1969	1970	1971 (to date)
High	..	..	..	283¾	326¼	276¼	316¼	175
Low	..	..	..	161¼	202	165	175	104

Mergers too have been prominent in the nuclear energy field. Here are the high and lows of Babcock & Wilcox, which is at the time of writing still independent – a take-over may bail out some investors but not those who bought at the top of the 1951 boom. Here are the highs and lows:

			1951–61	1962	1963	1964	1965	1966
High	..	..	490	183	231	230	200	193
Low	..	..	126	99	167	150	150	137

				1967	1968	1969	1970	1971
								(to date)
High	..	..	..	185	234	285	236¼	299
Low	..	..	..	137	155	189	180	225

With hindsight one can understand that the high of 1955 was based on very false premises. Notwithstanding, the highs and lows of shares generally both baffle and fascinate me. I recall as a young junior clerk in one of Britain's greatest insurance companies, a leader then and a leader now, that one of my jobs was to take down the daily prices morning and afternoon of the company's shares. I was fascinated by the wide divergences of prices during the months I did this job. These were the days before the Company Law Amendment Act of 1929, and well before investment thought required regular interim figures. Looking around my office, and I was the most junior staff member on the management floor, everything seemed very calm and I detected no special worries among the management, indeed, I saw a lot of confidential documents as messenger and in the post and if anything was apparent it was that our profits and investment income were going up all the time. All this taught me early in life that timing was fundamental to the purchase of shares and that if they went up they also came down – granted that the case for equity investment is indisputable, investors can lose a lot of money by bad timing.

Here are the 1969–70 highs and lows of a number of shares:

				High	Low	Sept. 30th, 1971
Lesney products	..	..	..	473	20	31
Vehicle and General	..	..	352½	in liquidation	
Gala Cosmetics	..	..	..	85	35	70
Granada	..	..	..	407	147	395
Alfred Herbert	..	..	..	253	39 3⁄16	54
Rolls-Royce..	..	..	..	245	in liquidation	
					(March 4th, 1971)	
Burmah Oil	..	..	..	673	237	430
Avon Rubber	..	..	..	369	119	314

These are my 'Chamber of Horrors' – many other companies are lucky to escape representation – these have come to my mind almost without thinking.

Now for the indices – highs and lows over the same period:

	High	Low	Per cent Diff.
Financial Times/Actuaries 621 Share Index	187·32	114·27	39·00
Financial Times Industrial Share Index ..	520·1	315·6	39·32

To quote one outstanding performance the other way during a similar period (1969–71), Cunard, which has since been taken over by Trafalgar House Investments Ltd:

	Low	High	(July 1st, 1971) Now
Cunard	100	272½	186

The vulnerability of companies engaged in engineering, in building construction, in competitive fields, in luxury goods, is obvious and big differences in share prices over the years are understandable. But surely banking is a pretty steady business in each individual year and with not much real competition. How then can you account for the highs and lows of Barclays Bank in some of the years quoted?

			1961	1962	1963	1964	1965	1966
High	..	..	339	375	307	285	335	345
Low	..	..	232	281¼	262	223	264	279

					1967	1968	1969	1970	1971 (to date)
High	..	..	..	..	400	484	450	417½	622
Low	..	..	..	..	279	335	305	265	327½

We have already seen that the equity market itself is subject both to rapidly rising prices and to rapidly falling prices, to bull and bear markets, but although all shares are subject to the influence of bull and bear markets as measured by the share indices, many shares comprised in the indices fared very differently from the indices.

The *Financial Times/Actuaries All Share Index* of 621 shares was 172·00 on January 1st, 1969, and 147·34 on December 31st, 1969, a fall of 14·34 per cent. Eighteen sub-groups fell more than the index and the following sub-groups fell by over 20 per cent in the year:

Aircraft and components — 43·27 per cent
Newspapers and publishers —26·03 per cent
Rubber manufacturing —25·32 per cent
Machine tools —32·67 per cent

Oil —24·63 per cent
Insurance brokers —23·19 per cent
Building materials —22·54 per cent
Investment trusts —21·32 per cent (partly due to the fall in Wall
  Street because investment trusts have big U.S. holdings)
Electricals (excluding radio and TV) —21·25 per cent
On the other hand twenty-one sub-groups did better than the index:
Hire-purchase, +36·00 per cent
Shipping, +27·18 per cent
Discount houses, +9·69 per cent
Property, +2·15 per cent
Electronics, radio and TV, +0·72 per cent
Rubber, —0·70 per cent
Insurance (life), —2·50 per cent
Entertaining and catering, —3·10 per cent
Stores, —5·49 per cent
Insurance (composite), —7·43 per cent
Household goods, —7·79 per cent
Building construction, —7·96 per cent
Breweries, —8·85 per cent
Motors and distributors, —10·57 per cent
Tobacco, —11·15 per cent
Chemicals, —12·0 per cent
Food retailing, —17·10 per cent
Tin, —12·19 per cent
Food manufacturing, —12·59 per cent
Shipbuilders, —13·51 per cent
Here are two other indices over the same period; Gold mines,
—41·49 per cent; Copper +86·96 per cent.
These changes in 1969, and the figures for any year will serve
equally well, destroy any notion that share prices rise and fall on
any precise pattern or on any general economic background,
although investment analysts, as will be seen from the references
to them on page 58, attempt to forecast the share price trends of
individual shares with, on the whole, only moderate success. And
although chartists claim (and others dispute it) through their
charts to get buy, hold, and sell signals for individual shares, the
extent of the movement of share prices remains somewhat of a
mystery. But the movement is such that many opportunities are
provided for the shrewd investor to buy shares, when absurdly
cheap, his profits being subject to capital gains tax.

CHAPTER 8

How to select equities
This will be a hypothetical question for many of my readers. As to the small investor, I have elsewhere in the book strongly counselled him not to buy equities in any form unless he owns a house, or is buying one by a mortgage protected by life assurance, has adequate additional life assurance for his dependants and an adequate sum available for a 'rainy day' on deposit with the National (Post Office) or a Trustee Savings Bank or a building society or any other deposit form described in this book under 'Cash deposits', page 12. And then I have told him if he wants to buy equities to get his equity investment through investment trusts or unit trusts, or life assurance linked to equities. These each have a chapter to themselves in this book.

Notwithstanding, every individual who reads the financial pages of newspapers will be under pressure to buy equities. The virtues of equities will be brought home to him by comment, by investment recommendations, or shall we call them tips, or by the many different advertisements which compete for his money in Eldorado terms of varying blazing brilliance. He will be under pressure to buy from those friends and acquaintances who will boast of their success in buying particular shares. Incidentally, no boast need be heeded until the share has been sold and profits, after capital gains tax, become a reality, because an unrealized gain can disappear. Take the fellow who bought that first-class share Lesney Products for 190 in early 1968 and saw them rise to 475 in early 1969 with the future still looking rosy. He did not sell and they fell to 36. The company, after reporting falling profits, made a loss in 1971.

Nevertheless, and as the reference to Lesney Products splendidly illustrates – see page 68 – they eventually fell to a low of 20p. Big money can (especially with hindsight) be made on a single share. And the temptation to have a go can be very strong. Equally, as our example demonstrates, big losses can also be made on a single share. For peace of mind I do not recommend either the regrets of the man who has failed to take a good profit or the man who is aware every time he picks up a newspaper that his one share shows him a big loss which it looks as if he never will recoup – unless he has a successful go with another share!

However, a not inconsiderable number of my readers could, now or in the future, get involved in the business of buying equities on behalf of their company or pension fund. Others might even acquire a small fortune, either by their own efforts or by the efforts of a rich relation. Some even may find their way into the investment management field; in a bank, in an insurance company, a merchant bank, a pension fund, an investment trust, a unit trust, or a stockbrokers' office, or in many of the company or Government departments which become involved in investment. And I can assure my readers that there are some very good openings in the investment field.

Those anticipating work of this kind might well ask how I select equities and even those who are already involved, indeed some of the old hands in investment, might be interested to read this chapter.

I am not going to pretend that there are special skills which can be learnt from this book. This chapter will not help you if you have no flair for investment and are not able to make prompt decisions or have not a good memory, then for you it can never be of more than academic interest.

I do not feel that there is any scientific way to select equities. I admire the 'backroom boys' who are striving for methods of selecting investments. I have known some of them, dedicated analysts, who always seem to have a reason for taking no action until the market trend is more or less observable to all. Perhaps it is a case, to quote a sage, of 'too much thought inhibiting action'! On the other hand, I have known successful investors who seem to be able to manage with only a modicum of scientific aid who are able to make quick and correct decisions apparently more by flair and instinct. Maybe these are helped by a good memory and a natural shrewdness. The human computer, the brain, is a great storehouse of forgotten information and many a right judgement may well be the result of forgotten information stored there.

Choosing equities seems to present no great difficulty to someone who has been choosing them for years. He will have his own panel of equity shares to choose from based on years of experience and knowledge.

He will have his own opinion as to when shares are dear or cheap and he will not be far wrong. The shares in his panel he will know very well. These will amount to less than 500 shares, perhaps nearer 200 and he will make no attempt to acquire knowledge in depth on the 3,400 or more equity shares quoted on the London Stock Exchange.

In choosing whether to buy a particular equity at a particular time it is helpful to have the following information:

NAME OF SHARE	PRICE	DIVIDEND YIELD Per cent	DIVIDEND AND EARNINGS YIELD FOR LAST TWO YEARS	HIGH AND LOW FOR THE YEAR	PRICE EARNINGS RATIO

If the list submitted to me contained only shares which were on my panel, the only consideration necessary would be whether they were suitable to the particular portfolio and, if so, whether the price was right. If, however, the list included shares with which I was unfamiliar or upon which I had some reservations, I would consult, in the first place, the Moodies sheet or the Exchange Telegraph card and would look at the following information concerning the company:

(a) the nature of the business carried on by the company;
(b) the list of its subsidiaries and the business they transact – great dangers can lurk in subsidiary companies;
(c) the names of the directors;
(d) the amount of capital and capital structure of the company;
(e) the yield on capital employed;
(f) the trend of earnings over the last ten years;
(g) the dividend record over the last ten years;
(h) details of any scrip or rights issue;
(i) the current prospects as perhaps revealed in the chairman's statement and in quarterly and half-yearly statements;
(j) the opinions sometimes of investment managers and of stockbrokers.

In a sentence, has the company had real growth in the past and if so is it likely to continue?

In considering whether a share is appropriate for any individual or fund other factors to bear in mind are:

(a) The company should be of reasonable size – to qualify under the Trustee Investments Act, for example, a company must have a paid-up capital of £1 million. I realize there is great scope for growth in small companies but it is easier to

pick a dud than a good one and my conservatism in investment causes me to stick to the tried companies.

(b) The company's business must, so far as possible, be a stable
one and the industry an expanding one.

(c) The management must be good; this can be judged on past
results and market opinion.

(d) As to the company's record, the earnings must show a
steady growth trend. I find that companies with long and
exceptionally favourable records of earnings usually prove
to be the best investments.

(e) With corporation tax the dividend cover can be less than
before its advent. I would plump for a cover of 1·5 times.
There are some blue chip exceptions to this rule – Marks
& Spencer has been as low as 1·2; investment trusts are in a
special category – but for some equities the cover should be
twice, e.g., motors, to mention only one group.

(f) As to the dividend yield, it must be 'right' for the share.
This in the main is a matter of judgement. Some feel the
true yield on an equity can be calculated only in retrospect.
Others, helped by investment analysis, endeavour to project
the yield for the next five years in an effort to assess what
future dividend increases are likely to be made. All judgements must have reference to future dividend prospects
because the share price often assumes too much.

(g) The price of a share as compared with its net asset value is
important. A share with a poor dividend record but which
is priced lower than its net asset value could be a take-over
prospect and especially so if the company has a high proportion of cash assets. There is no doubt that shares are
normally valued on an earnings and dividend basis. Some
unexciting shares do become under-valued on an assets basis,
but do not assume that they necessarily have take-over
prospects.

(h) Rights issues often provide good opportunities for acquiring
shares, except when a boom is in full blast, the mere mention
of a rights issue, unless it is a very modest one, depresses
the price of a share. The shares are further depressed by
shareholders selling where they are unable to take up their
rights in whole or in part. Another favourable factor is that
rights are not subject to stamp duty, and the stockbroker's

commission is obviously less when rights are nil paid or partly paid.

(*i*) Popular support can over price a good share. Beware, therefore, of fashionable shares.

(*j*) Alternatively, as often happens, a share becomes unpopular temporarily, the company's difficulties being exaggerated. This gives opportunities for acquiring the shares cheaply. Good management usually successfully overcomes present difficulties.

(*k*) Avoid a share that has not a free market.

(*l*) Avoid too the shares of countries which are unfavourable to the investor.

(*m*) The shares of any company which has had one very bad setback should be treated with great caution when it appears to have recovered. History often repeats itself with companies.

(*n*) Share prices ebb and flow according to general market conditions, and there is scope for intelligent buying.

(*o*) There being so many imponderables – politics – taxation – unexpected competition, etc., there is no precise method of telling when a share is cheap. In the end the decision is a matter of judgement and two experts can differ in their conclusions.

Panel of shares

There is much to be said for an investment manager having his own particular panel of shares. Two to three hundred equities carefully chosen are sufficient for even the largest portfolio, provided of course they cover the whole financial and industrial field. Increasing the number of shares under consideration to an unmanageable number is not necessarily diversifying a fund. The panel must not, of course, be immutable, the components will have to stand up from time to time to vigorous tests, and if any fail the test the shares will have to be dropped from the panel and replaced by others which, in the meantime have become worthy of panel status.

Timing

This is an essential aspect of buying shares and with it goes the ability to act promptly. There is no doubt whatsoever that first-class investments can be bought or sold at the wrong time. There are times when investors temporarily neglect individual first-class shares or alternatively over-chase them. There is always greater interest at dividend times or in anticipation of the accounts. The highs and lows of some very sound shares can, as we have seen, rarely be justified. The competent investment manager endeavours to buy shares when they are cheap and not when everyone is buying them. And remember this in every market, whether it be a blazing bull market or a plummeting bear market, some shares are worth buying because they are cheap. No advice can be given on this matter of timing other than to keep closely in touch with the market. A number of systems have been devised based on indices and charts but, although these are useful, they are by no means in themselves sufficient. I believe a person close to the market frequently has an 'instinct' as to whether a share is dear or cheap or is it his own head computer working efficiently?

Going liquid
Sometimes there is talk of 'going liquid'. This implies realizing part or all of a portfolio and getting back into the constituent equities at appreciably lower levels. This is a very difficult operation, because it involves not only foretelling the future but also overcoming a 7 to 10 per cent handicap. The 10 per cent covers stamp duty, two lots of commission and the jobber's turn. Even then the incidence of capital gains tax may ruin any effort to go liquid.

To give an example, supposing the *Financial Times/Actuaries All Share Index* has reached 170 but still looks like going down. A 10 per cent fall brings the *Index* down to 153 and at that point the portfolio could in theory by repurchased without loss or profit. Obviously, a fall of 15 per cent, taking the *Index* to 144·5 is a minimum to make the trouble and worry of going liquid worthwhile and that is a total fall of $25\frac{1}{2}$ points. But the chances of making a decision to sell at 153 when the *Index* is falling rapidly is rather doubtful. Action would probably get deferred until the market had fallen to 140 which would give a re-entry *Index* of 119, a total fall of 51 points. All right in theory, all right with hindsight but not easy in practice. It is not easy to get out of a share and to get back on attractive terms. Capital gains tax has added to the difficulties of successfully 'going liquid', because it means a bigger margin is necessary.

Do's and don'ts

Here are some thoughts culled from my experiences. The most important:

(*a*) keep in daily touch with the market;

(*b*) make all decisions calmly, do not rush into action;

(*c*) having made a decision act quickly;

(*d*) always be prepared to cut a loss;

(*e*) do not fidget with your investments; buy good shares and try to forget them;

(*f*) instead of selling off the whole of a first-class holding which looks dear skim off some cream, say 25 or 50 per cent of the holding;

(*g*) and use the proceeds of (*f*) in further diversifying the portfolio.

My view is that little benefit is derived from so-called inside information. I am quite sure that some tips are 'planted'. Even the opinions of a company's director or its chairman are often coloured by his own rose-coloured spectacles – and all chairmen like their company's shares to be rated high on the Stock Exchange. They are much more likely to talk them up than down.

CHAPTER 9

Option dealing
These are options to buy or sell shares at fixed prices over a period, normally three months.

With options you can either *give for the call* or *take for the call* or *take for the put* or *give for the put*. The give for the call option gives you the right to buy shares within a period of three months. Likewise the give for the put option gives the right to sell within the same period.

Once, usually on the Thursday in each Stock Exchange account, which incidentally varies from a normal period of two weeks to three weeks when public holidays are involved, you can exercise your option. It is called Declaration Day. The option cannot be exercised at any other time.

The cost of a 'give' option is generally about 5 to 10 per cent of the price of the shares you wish to deal in. The leading option rates are quoted daily in the *Financial Times*. The 5 to 10 per cent consists of a fixed amount plus commission on the number of shares involved. It will be seen that with both call and put options there is another party, it is he who either takes for the call or takes for the put. He is the one who receives the cash in the option transactions and will have, in the case of the call option to sell his shares to you, or in the case of a put option to buy your shares, both at a stipulated price called the striking price.

In a sentence, the giver in an option limits the risk to the cost of his option. The taker has a practically unlimited risk with only the option cash he receives to protect the transaction.

I have always regarded option dealing as a speculation and have not used it myself and have rarely used it with funds, except in special situations.

Before writing the above I had a long talk with someone who is familiar with this kind of exercise. Obviously it is a very sophisticated field including having two-way options which is, of course, at double the cost. The expert soon lost me in a maze of alternatives including operating in the shares as well during the account. There are also various protective actions which the taker can utilize. But on the face of it, it does make a lot of sense if you feel the market has gone high enough to accept option money to have the shares called off you at the current price when you are about to sell them anyway. Then instead of selling in the market immediately you allow someone the option to buy them at the current price within the next three months and you pocket the option money as well as the proceeds, that is if the shares are called off you. If, of course, the share price falls the giver for the call of the option will not call them off you. You could then have missed your sale opportunity. A fall of practically 10 per cent would be covered by your option money. If, however, the proceeds of the sale, when the option is taken up, have to be reinvested then you should, in order not to be left behind in some violent swing of the market, reinvest the proceeds more or less on the day the money comes in.

The give for the put option works in a rather similar fashion. In this case likewise you feel the market has gone high enough and you give money for the right to sell your shares at the current price within the next three months. If you are right and the share price falls you are out of the shares at the higher price. If, however, the price continues to rise you will retain your shares and have paid an insurance premium against selling at too low a price.

CHAPTER 10

Mergers
It will be noted from the fall in the number of equities quoted
on the London Stock Exchange over the last four years that this
is due to successful mergers and take-over bids.

In theory mergers make a lot of sense – too much sense perhaps.
They are hailed by the Government, the Press and the take-over
barons of the City as ministering angels, leading to increased
productivity, rescuing the dull and inefficiently managed company
– the attainment of what was assumed went with big battalions;
greater efficiency and reduced costs, tuned to such grandiloquent
words as streamlining, rationalization, computerization, etc.

Sometimes I feel the term 'merger' has lost its true meaning,
which surely is the merging of two firms of like or complementary
activity. Many mergers knock for six this conception and make
nonsense of the *Financial Times/Actuaries Share Index* groupings.
What has Imperial Tobacco in common with the Ross Group –
tobacco with food? Or Consolidated Gold Fields with Greenwood
(St Ives), gravel with cement; or Grand Metropolitan Hotels with
Express Dairies; London Rubber with Lovibonds – rubber goods
with wines and spirits? British American Tobacco with Yardleys
and Lenthéric – tobacco with toiletries and perfumes? Burmah
Oil with Rawlplug or Phonographic with Butlins, which they
nearly succeeded in getting?

The fact is that merger support money is stacked on the side-
lines and few companies, whether major or minor, are not in
danger of a successful take-over bid. Take-overs are indeed a
dreaded disease. The fear of them cause boards who would prefer
to stay independent to look around for likely bedfellows rather
than have one forced upon them.

Insurance mergers, especially have in theory a *raison d'être*.
They seem to make a lot of sense when one considers only the
multiplicity of branch offices but many have real doubts, whether
they have been good for the insured or for the staff and there is
certainly plenty of evidence of problems, difficulties and doubts.

There might be many good reasons to have five banks (regret-
tably now four) and five insurance companies, but ask management,
staff and the customers whether there is any noticeable improve-

ment in service, unfortunately there is plenty of evidence that service and efficiency are the poorer.

True lazy board members have been jerked into activity and shareholders baled out of shares which have fallen in value, but there is so much poppycock talked about the Stock Exchange truly evaluating a share price in those dogmatic words 'the share price is the crystallization of all the known factors'. However, when one company buys another it is buying that company, lock, stock and barrel and as a going concern. The current price thus bears no relation to this and most take-overs are got on the cheap. Reflect how some bids have been uplifted three or four times in the course of a take-over battle and the shareholders have received a price more in keeping with true value and the directors who resisted it have got the sack.

The directors themselves are indeed on the horns of a dilemma. They have to choose between agreement and satisfactory terms for themselves, or defiance with complete elimination. Even successful resistance could antagonize many shareholders if the bid failed and the shares plummeted.

In the stratagems of take-over warfare the merchant banks are prominent. Some have been known to ring up the large institutional holders and offer prices well above the market price. Some have even rung up modest shareholders when the percentage acceptances have got near to success. One sent last minute telegrams to all shareholders who had not accepted their client's bid. One elderly shareholder thinking the telegram brought bad news nearly died of shock.

There have been instances of bullying circulars which boiled down, mean, if you don't hurry up you will be a minority shareholder and you know what that means. Even the Companies Acts, although giving some protection to minorities, make a take-over absolute if 90 per cent of the company's shares are secured.

Shareholders are at times forced to accept cash or part-cash involving capital gains tax problems or to take tiny amounts of unsecured loan stocks or preference shares, as well as some equity shares, instead of clear-cut equity stake for equity stake. I feel that an investor should get equity for equity and not have foisted on him unwanted holdings of unsecured loan stock – or be paid cash and forced to pay capital gains on a share they had no intention of selling.

The skills of in-fighting are developing all the time and the

Stock Exchange take-over panel, deserving and hard-working as it is, seemed always many jumps behind. And is it unfair to state that management and staff seem the last to be considered in a take-over?

It is easier to set out the defects of the situation and its attendant evils than to prescribe remedies. The list of bad cases is too long to cite and clearly the take-over code needs strengthening and to be given stronger teeth.

CHAPTER 11

Diversification
Having stressed the vulnerability of share prices the need for diversification becomes obvious to the end that an investor does not commit his funds, whether they be large or small, to a single or a few shares.

Object is to beat the Index
It is easy with hindsight to choose a share which handsomely beats the performance of the equity market as measured by a share index, but with foresight and only a blank piece of paper in front of you it is very difficult and the odds are very much against you. Indeed you might end up picking a dud. The remedy is to choose a number of shares limiting your participation in each share to a reasonable amount. For a fund of £5,000 twenty shares, for a fund of £50,000 thirty shares, and for £5 million fifty to one hundred shares. But selecting the shares you require as far as possible by choosing shares from the whole spectrum of British industry. Alternatively buy diversified investment trusts or unit trusts. I have listed the component groups of shares of the *Financial Times/Actuaries Index* (see page 238). If an investor could buy units of this *Index* he would certainly have bought diversification in depth – the antithesis of too many eggs in one basket.

However, it must not be overlooked that the shares of many companies, whether included in the *Index* or not, have an element of diversification in them. Imperial Tobacco for example has large food interests; C. T. Bowring, grouped as an insurance broker, owns Bowmakers, the hire-purchase company and nearly 46 per cent of its profits come from that source. It also has a fair stake in shipping. There are also the conglomerates – an American term. We used to call them the 'rag bag' companies. These company groups contain many companies operating in entirely different fields. The most successful in England is Thos Tilling. Before the nationalization of transport it was one of the biggest passenger bus companies. It used its compensation money to buy up many smaller companies. It has since from time to time raised money to continue this policy. Its interests extend from insurance – Cornhill Insurance Co, 11 per cent; to glass, 18 per cent; from

D   IFA

motors, 11 per cent; to building materials, 20 per cent; from engineering, 8 per cent, textiles, 9 per cent; to builders' merchants and electrical wholesaling, 17 per cent; and miscellaneous, 6 per cent.

Tillings have been reasonably successful, dividends have increased two and one-quarter times in ten years but, personally, I do not like conglomerates, particularly the United States pattern. There the idea is much more developed and includes the lumping together of very big and diverse companies, and they have come under much criticism. In my view, unless each company in the group is given wide individual responsibility, group management is more likely to be a disadvantage than an asset. Obviously from the financial angle the conglomerate has real advantages but, apart from marketing, what has food and tobacco in common with insurance and gravel, textiles with glassware? The danger is that group management will interfere with individual company management. It has to be admitted that it often takes a lifetime to acquire the skills of a particular industry and the overlord of a group company has got to be a pretty amazing individual if he can more successfully manage and direct a completely diverse group of companies than if the companies had complete freedom to manage their own affairs. There are obvious advantages but I feel they are outweighed by disadvantages. A number of conglomerates have fared rather badly. In England, as mentioned, Thos Tillings is perhaps the one exception of any size, where the shares have performed rather like the market as a whole. Others have rocketed in price only to fall abysmally. Probably what success Tillings have had is due to the cautious manner in which they have approached the problem. Apart from the Cornhill the group contains relatively small companies and in its formative years it had the great advantage of being led by the late Lionel Fraser, a dedicated man of business and finance.

However, all this is by way of introducing the reader to the three groups of investment – investment trusts, unit trusts, and insurance, where one investment only secures the purchaser a considerable amount of diversification. With the general and composite insurance companies there are some added worries arising from underwriting fire, motor and marine insurance generally but as I propose to deal with the three groups separately we shall come to these worries later.

Diversification is illustrated in Chapter 12 on investment trusts.

Investment trusts

An investment trust is a much more sophisticated animal than a unit trust. As we will see in the following chapter, a unit trust is in essence a portfolio of investments held in trust for the unit holders; with managers selecting and from time to time making somewhat limited changes in the list of shares; with a trustee who keeps an overall eye on things; and with regulations made by the Board of Trade to be complied with. What sophistication there is comes from the variety of unit trusts which are available providing varying portfolios both by selection and group of industrial, commercial and financial shares and catering for varying investment objectives.

By contrast an investment trust is a joint stock company whose purpose is investment and which is, like all other joint stock companies, established under and regulated by the Companies Acts. Hence it is a single unit run by directors.

Perhaps you would like a definition and there is one which I like and which I have quoted before, it appeared some years back in the *Stock Exchange Gazette:*

'An investment trust is a limited company which uses the capital subscribed by its shareholders to purchase shares in other companies. The object is to hold these shares as fixed assets with a view to obtaining a gradually increasing income. But just as an industrial company may, from time to time, dispose of plant and machinery that is not fully productive, so may an investment trust sell one investment and buy another, which seems to offer better prospects. Many industrial companies issue preference capital and debenture stock, thereby borrowing money at a fixed rate of interest. This fixed-interest capital is used to buy assets which will eventually produce an income greater than the interest on the money which has been borrowed (the gearing factor). Likewise, an investment trust will borrow funds in the same way and for the same purpose. At first the return may be less than the interest on the borrowed money, but once the fixed-interest dividends have been covered any further increase is profit for the ordinary shareholders alone.

'Like any other joint stock company its share capital is held by shareholders and, if it has a quotation on the Stock Exchange, its shares can be bought and sold in the normal way on a supply and demand basis, the share price varying accordingly.

'Like any other joint stock company it can raise money within the terms of its borrowing powers. The borrowing can take the form of bank loans, or issues of loan stock or debentures. Some investment trusts have also raised money by the issue of preference shares which, as we have seen earlier, take precedence in a winding up or liquidation of a company over the ordinary share capital.'

Since the advent of corporation tax, preference shares are no longer a satisfactory method for a company to raise capital. The dividends, like ordinary share (equity) dividends, have to be paid out of profits after the payment of corporation tax – unlike debenture and loan interest which can be charged against profits before arriving at the amount payable for corporation tax.

Loan stock, debentures, and preference shares are all fixed-interest investments. The amount that the company pays out is fixed. The rate of interest the company pays when raising money varies with the market rate of interest at the time the company makes the issue. I have known loan stock issues being made with interest as low as 3 per cent per annum. Recently a first-class investment trust would have to offer as much as 9 per cent. The current dividend yield on the *Financial Times/Actuaries Investment Trust Group Index* is 2·83 per cent and I have known the top trusts to yield in bull markets a mere 1½ per cent. There is thus not much joy in raising money at 9 per cent, even if it can be charged against profits before tax. Indeed in recent high-interest rate years investment trusts have turned to convertibles to raise money, offering yields of around 4 per cent with conversion rights into their ordinary shares.

Gearing

The great point, however, of raising money by fixed-interest borrowing is that, once the investments purchased with the proceeds yield more than the cost of interest on the amount borrowed, the surplus is available for the company's ordinary shareholders. This is called gearing. Just imagine the extent of the gearing of an issue made at 4 per cent in 1950, the proceeds then being invested in equities. It could be quite fantastic. British equities then on average yielded 1½ per cent more than British Government securities, say, 5 per cent, and dividends have since increased at the rate of 7·3 per cent per annum according to some figures supplied to me so that the current yield of the money invested at 5 per cent would be 22 per cent. Investments in U.S. common stocks have done even better plus bonuses from the devaluations of the £, and most investment trusts hold U.S. common stock, some up to 50 per cent of their funds.

Gearing is not, of course, restricted to investment trusts. Most companies raise loan capital and the additional income this provides is available to the shareholders. The disadvantage is when the company is unable to earn on its activities an average rate equal to what it pays on its fixed-interest borrowing.

An investment trust which has a high proportion of fixed-interest capital is described as being highly geared while one that has a low proportion of fixed-interest capital is stated to be lowly geared.

In good times the highly geared investment trust will perform very well indeed for its shareholders. In bad times it will feel the pinch of any reduction in the dividends received on its portfolio of investments. It follows that if a recession or depression is on the way the investor in an investment trust with a high gearing should get out of the shares and if he wants to stay in investment trusts buy shares with a low gearing. Whereas if there is a blazing inflation with bull markets on the way it will obviously pay to be in a highly geared trust.

On the whole gearing is a great advantage and particularly so for an investment trust which is backed by a diversified spread of investments over the whole industrial, commercial and financial field at home and abroad backed by good investment management.

This brings me to two further advantages of investing in investment trusts – expert management and investment overseas.

Skilled investment
The managers of investment trusts are among the most skilled investors in this country and like all expert investors their skills are growing all the time. They will follow an active investment policy but not one of all-out change. Changes will be based on special situations and the need to change, not on taking a speculative view.

Basic decisions will be taken as to the amount in a particular industry and the need to cut down at certain times. Decisions too will be made as to the extent to invest overseas; in particular in the United States.

Some reliable calculations of one stockbroker show that £100 invested in investment trusts in 1952 would have done twice as well as putting the money in the *Financial Times Industrial Share*

Index. The figures on November 18th, 1966, were, respectively, £597 and £245.

It always intrigues me that the unit trusts which are top performers – here I exclude unit trusts with Australian, United States and overseas portfolios generally – are the trusts of investment trusts. My readers should note this fact very carefully when considering the respective claims of unit trust and investment trust management.

Investment overseas

Many British investment trusts will have about half their funds in the U.S., which is an obviously favourable factor because the investment rewards of U.S. common stocks have greatly exceeded those of British ordinary shares, which themselves have not done too badly. I hold the view strongly that whilst it is possible to have a pretty good knowledge of investment in the U.S.A., it requires a specialist in U.S. stocks to look after a portfolio of these stocks. All investment managers should be acquainted with overseas stocks but the executive in charge must be a specialist – just as the executive in charge of a British portfolio of shares must be a specialist in that field. It is too much to ask of anyone to be a top performer in both British and overseas investments.

Here is a typical split of an investment trust, orientated to the U.S. stock-market.

							Per cent
Great Britain	..	..	..	..	..	..	52·1
Commonwealth	..	..	..	..	..	..	2·6
U.S.A. ..	..	..	..	..	..	..	44·2
Other countries	..	..	..	..	..	..	1·1
							100·0

and here is another, typical of those trusts which have only a modest proportion of their funds in the United States:

							Per cent
Great Britain	..	..	..	..	..	..	74·6
Commonwealth	..	..	..	..	..	..	9·4
U.S.A. ..	..	..	..	..	..	..	12·5
Other countries	..	..	..	..	..	..	3·5
							100·0

Diversification

Earlier in these pages I have stressed time and again the virtues of diversification which is the antithesis of too many eggs in one basket, the greatest hazard of any fund.

We have seen that investment trusts are further diversified by having a proportion of their portfolio overseas. They are diversified also by industry.

Here is an example of a diversified portfolio – it is not a current one but it is a very good example and this kind of information is not usually given now. It is a Great Britain orientated portfolio:

(*a*) *Geographical spread*	Per cent
Great Britain	76·66
Commonwealth (excluding Canada)	7·25
North America	11·97
Other countries	4·12
	100·00

(*b*) *Classification of investments*	Per cent
Debentures	1·75
Preference	6·55
Equities	91·70
	100·00

(*c*) *Number of Holdings*	890
(*d*) *Book value of investments* £3,561,779
(*e*) *Market value* £9,168,766

(*f*) *Analysis of investments at valuation*	No. of securities	Value £	Per cent
Foreign Governments and corporations	10	1,102	0·01
Banks	22	271,919	2·96
Breweries, distilleries and wine merchants	25	411,093	4·48
Building and civil engineering:			
(i) Contractors and plant	25	180,329	1·97
(ii) Materials and components ..	35	280,155	3·05
Chemicals and plastics	28	371,456	4·05
Engineering:			
(i) Heavy electrical	13	91,338	0·99
(ii) Light electrical, radio and record	39	375,052	4·09
(iii) Shipbuilding, boilermaking and general engineering	50	481,015	5·25

(iv) Specialist engineering	42	280,320	3·06
(v) Machine tools, metal manu-facturers and merchants ..	48	493,622	5·38
(vi) Office equipment	8	219,734	2·40
Finance and hire-purchase	18	166,448	1·81
Food and tobacco	34	292,948	3·20
Hotels, catering and entertainment..	8	74,908	0·82
Industrial holding companies ..	15	279,148	3·04
Insurance	16	652,074	7·11
Investment trusts	40	1,041,148	11·36
Land and pastoral	10	64,721	0·71
Merchanting and warehousing ..	12	81,717	0·90
Mines:			
(i) Gold mines and mining finances companies	12	87,135	0·95
(ii) Other mines	22	102,749	1·12
Motors, aircraft and components ..	32	243,576	2·66
Oil and natural gas producers and distributors	30	351,459	3·83
Packaging	12	75,023	0·82
Paper, printing and publishing ..	34	243,741	2·66
Plantation companies:			
(i) Rubber	17	100,177	1·09
(ii) Other	10	35,542	0·39
Real property	22	242,008	2·64
Shipping	16	148,419	1·62
Steel	18	224,532	2·45
Stores, furniture and shoes ..	51	452,228	4·93
Textiles:			
(i) Cotton and artificial	11	60,591	0·66
(ii) Wool and carpets	15	70,135	0·77
(iii) Other	14	97,327	1·06
Transport	14	91,509	1·00
Utilities	27	219,731	2·39
Miscellaneous	21	212,637	2·32
	890	£9,168,766	100·00

Specially note the diversification over the whole field of commerce and industry.

Earnings cover
Before the advent of corporation tax the investment trusts used to distribute about 80 per cent of their earnings, ploughing the rest back for reinvestment. This was very good housekeeping. It especially benefited the surtax paying shareholder who only paid tax on what he received as his dividends. This ploughing

back of profits was one of the key advantages of investing in investment trusts.

The Finance Act 1965 limited retentions to a maximum of 15 per cent. However, this is rather academic at present because investment trusts were hit heavily by the change to corporation tax on April 6th, 1965, particularly those dynamic investment trusts which had a large proportion of their funds in America, because not having suffered British corporation tax the dividends from American investments had to pay it. All British equity dividends, having been paid out of profits which had suffered corporation tax, did not have to pay it again. To put it another way they were franked for corporation tax.

In order to help the investment trusts through a difficult period they received transitional relief. The object of this was to enable the investment trusts to adjust their portfolios so as to lighten the effects of the change. The immediate reaction might have been to sell American equities with low yields and to buy British Government securities, but the income from British Government securities is subject to corporation tax and there is, of course, no growth element, whereas U.S. equities have shown dynamic growth.

Clearly the investment trust movement has not yet coped fully with its new taxation situation. Since 1965 many investment trusts have shown no growth in their income, in fact the income in some cases has gone down. Many investment trusts have not increased their dividends and some have only maintained theirs at the expense of a reduction in earlier profits carried forward. As a result of corporation tax the dynamic Foreign and Colonial Investment Trust's five-year trend of earnings to December 31st, 1969, with 65 per cent invested overseas, was minus 6·4 per cent with no change in dividend.

Personally, even when the effects of corporation tax have been corrected, I cannot see the investment trusts securing the same exciting growth rates as they achieved before the advent of corporation tax. As I have already mentioned, British Government securities, and all fixed-interest stocks for that matter (with the exception of preference shares), as well as overseas dividends, are subject to corporation tax in the hands of the investment trust after, of course, deducting expenses of management, whereas before April 1965 overseas tax on overseas investments could be set off against British tax. This was rather absurd in my view but it was a bonus nevertheless, now lost to investment trusts.

Another less favourable current factor is that it is more expensive to borrow money although on the credit side interest on the money borrowed can be deducted before arriving at the liability for corporation tax purposes, and this is a substantial help.

At the time I wrote the first draft of this chapter the dividend yield and the earnings yield of the twenty (out of 360 investment trusts quoted on the London Stock Exchange) constituting the *Financial Times/Actuaries Investment Trust Index*, were respectively 3·27 and 3·22, thus the dividend was not quite covered. This underlines my earlier statement that some trusts were dipping into past profits – very slightly it seems – to pay their dividends. Currently there is some improvement, the figures being respectively 2·83 and 3·03 with a price earnings ratio of 32·95. This is high but misleading as I will show in the following paragraph.

Earnings covered amply by earnings on the shares comprised in the portfolio
The real cover behind the dividend paid by an investment trust is the earnings cover for the dividends paid by the companies whose shares comprise the trust's portfolio of investments. The true cover is not far off the cover for the *Financial Times/Actuaries 500 Share Index* – this excludes the financial group of companies – the dividend yield on which is 3·81 and the earnings yield 5·89, which gives a cover of just over 1½ times. Some investors seem to overlook this earnings cushion, their eyes seem to be cast only on the small earnings (received) cover for their own dividends.

Standard and Poor's Index of U.S. common stocks has a dividend yield of about 2·9 per cent and an earnings yield of 5 per cent with a cover of just under one and three-quarters times.

Break-up value of shares exceed market value
Neither does the layman investor fully appreciate, nor do even some so-called experts appear to appreciate fully, the great advantage which goes with buying investment trusts, the fact that the market price of an investment trust share is in the majority of cases less than its equivalent proportion of the market value of the trust's own portfolio of investments.

This, to my mind, is a remarkable phenomenon. The investor has the advantage of free expert management in depth, of gearing, of diversification and of overseas spread but nevertheless he can often buy the shares for less than their intrinsic worth.

Contrast this with unit trusts where you have to buy the underlying investment at cost price including stamp duty and commission plus added management charges which vary from 3 to 7 per cent.

When you buy investment trust shares you get your equivalent share of the portfolio at a discount which is as much as 20 per cent, sometimes more. The average discount can vary from 3 per cent in bull markets to 15 per cent in bear markets. There are, of course, some trusts which have outstanding records or are popular and their share prices are at times quoted in excess of the equivalent market values of their portfolio.

Some trusts in my view are certainly over-priced compared with others. I recognize that some managements are more dynamic but one can get a little mesmerized at times into paying too much to the neglect of a lesser but very much under-priced trust. Provided the management does not engage in speculation, and this is much the exception in this field, a mixed portfolio of equities is bound on the medium- or long-term to be a flourishing one and to perform at least as well as the average unit trust. So why not get as big a discount as possible provided the reports on management are not adverse? I would not avoid a so-called stuffy management if the discount was high and I would avoid a tip-top management if the current yield was about 1½ per cent and the premium over market value high.

Here are some current discounts for three major investment trusts:

Trust	Market price	Break-up value per share	Discount Per cent
A	88p	102·9p	14
B	146	160·3	9
C	115½	143·7	20

Taxation

As already indicated the advent of corporation tax affected investment trusts adversely. This was a once-and-for-all factor and in the course of the years the investment trusts have trimmed their sails to deal with this adverse wind, but they were helped by the transitional relief which was allowed them. Capital gains tax at 30 per cent, as for individuals, is payable on both short- and long-term gains, a penalty shared with other investors. Before, unlike finance companies, investment trusts were not liable to tax on capital gains. That had a restrictive effect on their investment policy because if they turned over their investments too much there was the danger they would be taxed as a dealing and finance company. The turnover each way used to be from 15 to 30 per cent. They are no longer inhibited in this way. I do not expect investment trusts to become very much more active in switching investments but they no longer have the old fears that excessive dealings might result in adverse taxation.

There is a capital gains concession for shareholders. The managers issue certificates to shareholders certifying the total gains per share after capital gains tax, and shareholders on selling their shares are allowed to add these net gains to the cost price of their shares in arriving at the capital gains liability. One or two trusts have already chalked up pretty considerable credits for the shareholders in this way. One, the Foreign and Colonial, has issued certificates to a total of 17·5p per share.

I believe this rather absurd comedy will be ended and investment trusts and unit trusts relieved of capital gains, the shareholder or unit holder paying the tax on the disposal of his holding in the normal way.

The income from British ordinary and preference shares is franked for corporation tax in the hands of investment trusts and other British investors. That is as we have seen because these investments have already borne corporation tax as the dividends have been paid out of income which has suffered corporation tax. Unfortunately, the income from overseas investment is liable to corporation tax, so to make the investments in the United States viable for investment they must produce a greater growth rate than their British equivalents. More so because to buy U.S. common stocks investment dollars have to be bought at a premium which has been as high as 50 and as low as 15 and seems to have settled around 25. Still worse on a sale of a U.S. stock, 25 per cent of the premium has, under existing regulations (this will not last in my opinion), to be surrendered to the Bank of England at the current exchange rate. Many investment trusts raise dollar loans in America. This does not involve paying a dollar premium, neither is there any penalty on selling a dollar investment bought with the proceeds of the loan. However, the going borrowing rate of interest is currently high and the portfolio of investments acquired will have to be turned over pretty actively and expertly if the expenses of the loan are going to be justified. Some of these loans – other investors were similarly involved, the insurance companies for example – were looking pretty sickly in the early part of 1970 with the *Dow Jones Index* down by 25 per cent from the top.

Income tax deducted at source in the payment of the dividends on the trust's underlying investments can be set off against the income tax deducted in paying dividends to the investment trust's own shareholders.

Disadvantages

From what I have written above the reader will have gathered that I favour investment trusts but I must point out that there is one disadvantage. The shares of the smaller investment trusts are not very marketable. Over half the trusts have assets of less than £10 million and in good times it is a case of buyers only as investment trust shareholders are usually in for keeps. On death shares come on to the market. But if you want shares you need to give your order to your broker. Give him some limits and just wait.

In bad times it is often not easy except on a marking down in price to sell the shares of the smaller investment trusts.

Indeed there seem to be greater swings in investment trusts' share prices between bull and bear markets than for the index generally. This was certainly markedly so in the 1969 bull to bear market.

			Fall Per cent
Financial Times/Actuaries 500 Shares	193·73 (31.1.69)	140·08 (29.7.69)	27·69
Financial Times/Actuaries Investment *Trust Index*	215·04 (31.1.69)	139·71 (29.7.69)	32·03

The marked changes in six months again underline the importance of investment timing.

Here are some large trusts where it is possible to buy up to £5,000 shares on a normal day with some historic 1971 figures.

	Assets £'000	*Price*	*Yield*	*Dividend* *ten-year* *growth* *rate* Per cent
Alliance	117,664	199	2·8	+6·6
Foreign and Colonial ..	121,091	146	2·0	+5·3
Industrial and General ..	109,898	115½	3·7	+5·9
Mercantile	102,267	50¼	4·1	+6·0
Globe	105,133	134	2·9	+9·5
British Investment	105,568	158	2·3	+6·1

I have added the ten-year growth rate per cent in dividends. The last five years which include the inception of corporation tax were less satisfactory and were respectively 4·3, nil, 3·4, 2·6, 6·2 and 3·2.

There are a number of stockbrokers who specialize in investment trusts. They include Myers & Co, Hoare & Co, Govett, Norris Oakley Richardson & Glover, Laing & Cruickshank, Phillips & Drew, and L. Messel & Co. These brokers keep and maintain comprehensive statistics and most publish detailed manuals annually plus monthly figures.

Finally, there are a number of dual-purpose trusts with three main parties to the arrangement. The first are those stockholders who lend money to the trust on fixed-interest terms. Next there are the income shareholders who are entitled to all the net income of the trust and who after a fixed term of years get repaid the nominal value of their shares. Thirdly, there are the capital shareholders who are entitled to all the capital profits of the trust but to no income. The names of some of these trusts are Altifund, Dualvest, Fundinvest, Triplevest.

The high taxpayer gives up his income, which would anyhow be highly taxed, to receive all capital profits on which he pays capital gains tax of 30 per cent.

Here is the capital set-up of Triplevest: £2,500,000 7⅜ per cent debenture stock, 1987–91; £12 million in income shares of 50p; £6 million in capital shares of £1 each. The dividends paid out for each 50p share since the company began, was 1967 (part), 1·976p; 1968, 3·454p; 1969, 3·517p; 1970, 3·677p; 1971, 3·966p. The last distribution gives a yield of 7·9 per cent. The estimated payment for 1971–72 for the full year is 7½ to 8 per cent. Not a particularly exciting return after four years. The income shares issued at 50p had a high of 65p whereas the £1 capital shares have been as high as 271p and even with a *Financial Times Industrial Share Index* of 344·3 they were 192½ and the income units 47¼. Not at all satisfactory for the income shareholders whose capital is there presumably to produce profits for the capital shareholders. The income shareholders receive a return of 3 per cent less than they would get on a first-class loan stock and have received little growth in their dividends.

The investment of the funds of a trust like this has an element of life-tenant and reversions about it, see page 202.

CHAPTER 13

Unit trusts

These are perhaps the ideal investment for the investor with limited funds, although, as you will have gathered, my own first preference is investment trusts. Diversification is the essence of unit trusts.

The essence of the unit trust is that investors put up cash which is invested by the unit trust managers in a mixed portfolio of equities. For convenience the investors' share of cash is represented by an equivalent number of units, the price of which is quoted daily in the newspapers and twice daily at the managers' offices. The price is based on the market value of the shares comprising the portfolio, plus broker's commission, stamp duty and the manager's service charge. The maximum charge permitted for a twenty-year unit trust – the fees of all unit trusts authorized by the Board of Trade are restricted – is $13\frac{1}{4}$ per cent of the cost of the unit. This is usually split as to 5 per cent as an initial charge added to the cost of the unit and the rest split over the twenty-year term and deducted by half-yearly instalments. Most unit trusts promote sales of units by advertising in the newspapers what is known as a 'block offer'. The managers offer for sale let us say £5 million in ten million units of 50p each to give an estimated commencing yield of let us say $3\frac{1}{2}$ per cent. The advertisement may or may not say which shares the managers propose to buy or may only give a rough indication, otherwise the particular shares might be marked up higher in anticipation of the coming purchases.

The investor in our example who buys 500 units secures an investment of £250 in a diversified portfolio of shares. Unit trusts vary as to the number of shares in their portfolios. It may be as low as 40 and as high as 400. I know of no trust which diversifies to the extent of following the 621 shares comprised in the *Financial Times/Actuaries All Share Index*. Indeed, diversification is not the exclusive plank of the unit trust movement's appeal. There are some unit trusts for example which restrict themselves to: (*a*) insurance shares, (*b*) commodity shares, (*c*) investment trust shares, (*d*) bank shares, (*e*) Australian shares, (*f*) U.S. common stocks, (*g*) mining company shares, or (*h*) other *ad hoc* portfolios.

The majority of portfolios offered by the unit trust managers,

97

however, comprise a mixed bag of shares selected out of the 3,400 odd shares quoted on the London Stock Exchange. What the small investor gets is what he cannot get on his own, a proportionate part of the shares contained in the unit trust portfolio. Alternatively he can choose a specialist unit trust as mentioned in (a) to (h) above.

In addition to offering portfolios of a variety of groups of similar shares and a variety of different portfolios of industrial shares generally, the movement offers portfolios of low yielding so-called growth shares and also high yielding portfolios for those who must have the maximum current income. Yields differ from 1 to $7\frac{1}{2}$ per cent, according to the type of portfolio selected. Most of the unit trust managers will now offer their portfolios linked to life assurance provided either by the larger life offices or by their own *ad hoc* companies. The linking of unit trusts to life assurance was a big breakthrough for the movement.

There are some sixty-eight unit trust management groups with a total of over two hundred trusts. Of recent years the big insurance companies and the banks have entered the unit trust field after leaving it to its originators for so many years. The entry of the insurance companies is explained by the enormous growth in equity-linked trust contracts and in the growth of the movement generally. These are dealt with under life assurance on page 124. A number of banks have their own unit trusts which they sell over the counter. It is very useful for a bank manager to be able to recommend his bank's own unit trust. The big insurance companies sell their equity-linked contract through their sales organizations.

All this and particularly the invention of the equity-linked contract has resulted in rapid growth over the last few years.

The figures for 1959 to 1970 inclusive appear on facing page.

I can state at once that the unit trust movement in this country has a clean bill of security health. Authorized unit trusts have to comply with the regulations of the Board of Trade, which exercises its powers through regulations it makes under the provisions of the Finance Act 1958, and these regulations are pretty stringent. In addition the securities comprised in the portfolio have to be registered in the name of a top trust corporation, such as a bank or an insurance company. These are thus custodian trustees for the unit trust holders, but behind the scenes they exercise an influence for good.

TABLE II
Summary (1960–71)

Year	Value of funds (year end) £ million	Net investment £ million	Holdings – millions
1960	201·4	13·51	0·66
1961	236·6	7·36	0·67
1962	272·5	33·94	0·82
1963	371·2	59·68	1·05
1964	428·9	77·04	1·31
1965	521·9	59·02	1·42
1966	581·8	105·43	1·64
1967	853·6	83·91	1·71
1968	1,482·4	258·48	2·15
1969	1,411·9	186·18	2·39
1970	1,397·7	97·80	2·40
1971 (8 months)	1,810·6	50·24	2·35

The movement started in a modest way before the Second World War, the Municipal and General Group being the first of any size to enter the field. Unit trusts were just about to get on to their feet when war came, but the growth since the Second World War, as shown by the figures which I quoted earlier, is a remarkable testimony to the efficiency and soundness of the movement.

The main criticism I have of unit trusts is one of psychology. The hard fact is that the investor seems to want only to buy units in bull markets. The movement gets little response from its advertising and sales organizations when a bear market is in operation. Here are the monthly figures of sales for 1969. I have chosen 1969 because the stock-market was particularly volatile.

1969 – £ million

	Net sales £	Funds* £	Financial Times Industrial Index
January	33·3	1,589	519·2
February	32·9	1,488	464·9
March	24·8	1,507	474·6
April	22·2	1,502	449·8
May	9·7	1,416	416·1
June	10·2	1,316	398·5
July	11·1	1,234	362·9
August	10·5	1,290	374·5
September	7·7	1,329	383·1
October	9·4	1,311	367·0
November	8·5	1,384	385·9
December	5·7	1,412	407·4

* End of month market value.

I have added the *Financial Times Industrial Share Index* at the end of each month, also the market value of all authorized unit trusts. The sales figures clearly demonstrate that unit trust sales are greatest when the market is most bullish.

What worries me, therefore, is that advertising and house-to-house selling in the case of life-linked unit trusts definitely tends to put the investor into shares near the top of the market. This does not matter too much where the investor is buying equity-linked units or units on an instalment plan because over a period of years he gets the advantages of averaging his purchase price. It doesn't matter too much either if the investor is a long-term investor as equities on the long-term are bound to be correct, even if the investor pays too much for them at the time he enters the market. Ten years should put that right. But if the unit trust's advertisement stressed past impressive growth and this tempts the small investor to put money into a unit trust at the top of the market this could prove serious because he may soon need the money for other purposes and he may find himself selling the units well below the price he paid for them. A reference back to the fall in the indices would show how serious it would be for someone who bought units in January having to sell them in June.

It is a fundamental principle of the unit trust movement that the managers will buy back the units. The unit trust movement has been in operation long enough now and has gone through sufficiently difficult times to prove that it can weather the storm arising from a rush of unit holders wishing to sell their units. Indeed the most salutary aspect of the unit trust movement is that the unit trust investor does seem to be a long-term investor and not one who wants to rush out of his units in panic when the market falls substantially. One hopes that it will always be so. Most trusts will send the proceeds of a sale within a few days of receiving the unit certificate duly discharged.

When the unit trust movement started, the portfolio was usually a fixed portfolio of equities which could not be changed except under stringent conditions. Today the unit trust managers make changes in the portfolio but in general the changes are not substantial, and the investor is not likely to wake up one morning and find that all the first-class industrial shares in the portfolio have been sold and the proceeds invested in, say, gold shares. There may, at times, be a temptation on the part of the unit trust managers to make big changes in the portfolio but they would undoubtedly meet with opposition from the trustees. From the conservative angle I regard the presence of trustees of the calibre of the large banks and insurance companies as great protection to the investor. This leads me to mention that a unit trust is not a company incorporated under the Companies Act but an association of investors with a management company acting as investment managers and with an independent trustee holding the underlying securities. This is quite different from an investment trust which is a company formed under the Companies Act as we have seen in the previous chapter. As stated earlier the unit trust linked contract has become a best seller.

The reader will no doubt have noted that the unit trust managers have been ingenious in providing many types of portfolios, and many purpose schemes. In addition they have designed trusts for children, with the generosity mainly of grandparents in mind. These were particularly attractive from the taxation angle but a recent Finance Act took away the taxation advantage, only to be reversed in the Finance Act 1971 as from April 6th, 1972, so no doubt this scheme will be resurrected. Certainly the movement is expert in selling and more and more sophisticated schemes will no doubt appear in the future. They have also a fully developed scheme of accumulation settlements by parents for infant children.

Obviously the skills of the managers of the unit trusts will vary. Indeed some have better investment records than others. Also one finds that the unit trusts under one management will vary in their performance. The *Unitholder* now called *Money Management and Unitholder* from time to time publishes the respective performance of the various unit trusts in the form of a league table. This is helpful as history but it does not tell us what is going to happen in the future. Indeed there are times when a specialized group of trusts will perform in a way inferior to the *Financial Times/ Actuaries All Share Index*. Take 1969 for example. Hire-purchase and shipping beat the *Financial Times/Actuaries All Share Index* by 36 per cent and 27·18 per cent respectively, whereas aircraft and components gave the worst performance, down by 43·27 per cent, and gold mines by 41·49 per cent. Oil had a minus percentage of 24·63, even investment trusts a minus percentage of 21·32, against the *Index* fall of 15·2 per cent, due principally to the fact that their holdings of American securities had fallen in value with the 1969 set-back in Wall Street.

Unit trust managers also design portfolios for particular

investors. There are unit trusts for pension funds, charities, trade unions, for individual and personal and family trusts. Indeed the Trustee Investments Act both encourages and recognizes unit trusts. There are unit trusts run by the insurance companies, by the Trustee Savings Bank and by the Charity Commissioners, apart from those which are run directly for profit by the unit trust movement's various management companies.

Income from units is usually distributed half-yearly and an informative statement issued showing the number of units, the rate of dividend, tax deducted and composition of the portfolio. A unit holder can give a mandate for his dividends to be accumulated for the purchase of further units.

Finally here are some of the provisions which the Board of Trade require to appear in the trust deed setting up each unit trust.

(a) the method of calculating the manager's prices for the units on a sale and a purchase respectively, and the yield from the units;

(b) the mode of execution and the issue of unit certificates: no units may be issued until the underlying investments have been vested in the trustee;

(c) every advertisement, circular, or other document containing any statement with respect to the sale price of units, must state the yield from the units: such an advertisement, etc., must be approved by the trustee before issue;

(d) a fund, for defraying the expenses of the administration of the trust, must be established;

(e) accounts relating to the trust (including accounts of the management company in relation to the trust and statements of its remuneration) must be audited.

A trustee can require the retirement of the management company (subject to any provisions as to appeal contained in the deed) if the trustee certifies that it is in the interest of the unit holders.

Unit trusts are treated similarly to investment trusts for capital gains except for those linked to life assurance. The capital gains position for these is dealt with under equity-linked, page 124, in the life assurance chapter.

CHAPTER 14

Insurance companies
There are two ways of investing in an insurance company's
investment skill, as a policyholder or as a shareholder.

Your investment as a policyholder will be a life policy in one of
its various forms or an annuity. An endowment policy, and
particularly a with-profits endowment policy, is almost as much
an investment as the purchase of an insurance share or a Stock
Exchange investment. The ordinary endowment policy is akin to
a fixed-interest investment and the with-profits policy to an equity
investment. The equity-linked endowment is pure equity investment – investment through life assurance, however, has a separate
chapter – see pages 116 to 129.

A general insurance (non-life) policy is hardly an investment
within our definition – see page 3. You and thousands beside
pay an annual premium to cover a risk which might not happen.
You are in effect joining with lots of other people and the total
premiums received are funded and out of this fund the insurance
company will meet any claims and losses which any one or more
of the group of policyholders suffers. There is a flow of premiums
and investment income. Losses and expenses are met out of these.
Reserves for claims not yet assessed and for unexpired risks are
set up and the policyholder is protected. Protected is the word
although there have been a number of small companies which
have gone broke and the débâcle of the rate-cutting, with paper
asset of £45 million, Vehicle and General Insurance Co was a
blow to insurance prestige.

If you wish to be precise you will refer to life offices as assurance
companies because they are concerned with an event which must
happen, death, whereas an insurance company is providing cover
for an eventuality which might not happen and certainly will not
happen to every one of their policyholders.

But when it comes to becoming shareholders in an insurance
company the choice is very much limited. This is because the
majority of life offices and many general insurance companies are
mutual companies. A mutual office is owned by the policyholders
who generally take very little interest in the company's affairs –
unless things go very wrong. With a mutual company it seems to

me that in practice the reigning management has almost absolute powers.

So to become a shareholder in an insurance company you have a limited choice but nevertheless a choice which includes some of the most famous insurance companies in the world.

As we have seen there are two main divisions of insurance – life assurance and general insurance.

Life assurance is in effect non-risk business. Rates are based on mortality tables which conservatively predict the expectancy of life at all ages for both men and women. The rest is applied mathematics and here the actuaries, fellows or associates of the larger English Institute, the Institute of Actuaries, or of the smaller Faculty of Actuaries in Scotland, play their part. In a sentence the life offices are run by actuaries.

The companies which transact fire, motor, aviation and marine insurance and the many varieties of accident insurance, usually called general insurance business, are certainly transacting risk business. They can only estimate their premiums. They cannot even imagine some of the hazards which will involve them in heavy claims. They know the hazards to date but have no idea of what could happen. There had been bad hurricanes before hurricane Betsy. But hurricane Betsy was many, many, many times worse than any previous hurricane. The trail of damage which it inflicted was terrible but had it hit the north-east coast of the United States its effect on the insurance companies and Lloyd's could have been catastrophic.

Lloyd's is the other big insurance market. It is possible to invest money in Lloyd's but only by becoming an underwriting member. Your investment is the compulsory and substantial deposits you have to make. Lloyd's is run on a syndicate basis. A number of underwriting members group themselves together. The number can be as small as 2 or as large as 700. The syndicate has a manager and an underwriter and the members' deposits of investments constitute the security for the risks which the underwriter accepts. Apart from the deposits which the underwriting member puts up the member's personal estate is liable. Hurricane Betsy hit most syndicates badly and in some cases ate up the reserves which the syndicate is bound to set up, ate up the deposits, and if that was not enough in some cases ate up the entire personal estates of the underwriting members. This is a far cry from the thought that you have only to become an underwriting member of Lloyd's to make a fortune. General insurance business is indeed risk business. Incidentally, if a syndicate cannot meet its losses the Corporation of Lloyd's as a whole steps into the breach.

To set the scene here are the premiums for the year 1970:

Insurance Companies

	£ million	
Fire and accident (non-motor)	1,176	
Motor	683	
Marine, aviation and transport	225	
Ordinary life	1,320	
Industrial life (door-to-door business)	298	
		£3,702

Lloyd's – £668 million

By way of explanation, Industrial Life assurance is business where the premiums are collected door-to-door by the company's representative. With the advent of the affluent society more and more people are making use of ordinary life business and paying their premiums by cheque or banker's order. Nevertheless, industrial life business still grows, mainly in the industrial areas, but its rate of growth is appreciably slower than ordinary life business.

From the Stock Exchange investment angle there are two main groups of insurance companies. The life offices or mainly life offices and the composite offices. The latter are principally in the general business field but also have substantial life departments.

For a list of the insurance companies with Stock Exchange quotations see the *Stock Exchange Daily List* of quotations but the *Financial Times* quotes each day under insurance the prices of the majority of companies in its Share Information Service. However, both lists include insurance brokers under insurance companies. These are to some extent involved in risk business directly when they own small insurance companies, and indirectly where they act as managing underwriters for Lloyd's syndicates receiving a commission on profits. But as their description implies the bulk of their profits come or should come from non-risk brokerage commission on business which they secure and place with the insurance companies and Lloyd's. There is a tendency for some insurance brokers to spread their wings to other activities. Bowring for example owns a shipping company and Bowmaker the large hire-purchase company.

In these days of diversification it is becoming increasingly difficult to know what you are really buying when you invest in a company. I have dealt with this aspect elsewhere in this book.

Unlike insurance companies, insurance brokers are not heavily engaged in investment. More often than not their nominal capital is not covered by assets because their business is goodwill business, the right to receive commission on a block of insurance business and a list of satisfied clients. In some cases the business is tied firmly to a particular firm of insurance brokers but in other cases it is very vulnerable to attack by other brokers. Certainly a broker can sell his portfolio of clients to another broker for two or three years' purchase of the relevant commissions so it has a value but only a goodwill value. It can be lost to another broker or a big client can start its own insurance company.

So much for the broker who in truth performs a valuable function but those shares are not an investment within the terms of the chapter.

At this point I list the large life or mainly life offices and the composite insurance companies. I regard these as group investments, and akin to investment trusts but with a big difference in the case of the general and composite insurance companies. Their risk business can be profitable or unprofitable and recently it has been the latter.

Life or mainly life offices	Price (30.9.71)	Yield	1969–71 (to 30.9.71) High	Low
Britannic	256	3·2	288	150
Equity and Law	310	1·8	350	170
Legal and General	362	2·5	372	170
London and Manchester	157	3·0	191¼	92½
Pearl	294	3·4	310	178¾
Provident 'A'	189	3·9	189	105
Prudential	180	3·0	210	107½
Refuge 'B'	180	3·8	215	122½
Sun Life	181	1·7	183	71¼
Composite offices				
Commercial Union	443	3·5	482	251¼
Eagle Star	468	2·5	492	230
General Accident	182	3·1	197	75
Guardian Royal Exchange	279	2·9	288	118¾
Phoenix	264	3·3	290	121¼
Royal	411	3·2	434	165
Sun Alliance	498	3·4	504	233¾

A composite insurance company is one which transacts all classes of insurance business including life. Separate funds have to be kept for life business.

The accounts of the insurance companies have to be produced in a form prescribed by the Assurance Companies Act and these accounts have to be submitted to the Board of Trade in an even more detailed form than to shareholders.

The first thing that becomes apparent is that the yields on the life companies are decidedly lower than for the composite offices.

The respective historic index yields on the *Financial Times/Actuaries* group indices demonstrates this also:

	December 31st, 1969	June 30th, 1970	December 31st, 1970	30.9.71 Current
Life	2·5	3·95	3·3	2·64
Composite ..	4·2	5·33	4·5	3·17
Insurance brokers	4·4	4·95	3·3	2·57

The yields are further evidence of the mystery of the rises and falls of share prices.

These indices at once provide an investment assessment, and in my view a reasonably correct one, of the three main insurance groups.

With the exception of Equity and Law, all the life offices have some interest in non-life business. It is, however, a relatively small interest compared with their life business but in the case of the Prudential and the Legal and General, quite substantial in themselves.

It will be noted too that although the yield on the *Financial Times/Actuaries Life Group Index* is 2·64 some life offices give a higher yield and some a lower yield. The difference represents the current market assessment of the future growth of the particular company, especially dividend growth.

The same applies to a lesser extent to the composite company. With mergers the list has become shorter and shorter and we are getting down to about five or six, which evens things out. Eagle Star receives a high percentage of its profits from life business and this accounts for its lower yield, plus the fact that it is considered to have take-over possibilities.

On the face of it, it may seem odd that, despite the competition from many mutual life offices, the shareholder-owned companies (sometimes called 'proprietary companies') should exist and do so well. It is another case of theory and practice. In theory the mutual office should win every time but in practice the proprietary companies are every bit as competitive as the mutual and some-

times even more so. It is all a matter of 10 per cent. Let me explain.
The whole of the profits of a mutual company belongs to the life
policyholders whereas in the case of the proprietary companies it
is usual for the with-profit life policyholders to get at least 90 per
cent, the rest inuring for the benefit of the shareholders.

Life business is a growing industry. Here for the last ten years
are the funds and new annual premiums and annuity moneys for
the members of the Life Offices Association, Industrial Life Offices
Association, and the Associated Scottish Life Offices: I regard new
premiums and funds as a sound measure of annual growth.

Life Assurance						New premiums £ million	Funds £ million
1970	..	..	..	..	..	436·00	13,584·00
1969	..	..	..	..	..	351·00	12,564·00
1968	..	..	..	..	..	385·00	11,571·00
1967	..	..	..	..	..	337·00	10,580·00
1966	..	..	..	..	..	301·00	9,667·00
1965	..	..	..	..	..	272·50	8,927·00
1964	..	..	..	..	..	318·00	8,166·00
1963	..	..	..	..	..	291·00	7,403·00
1962	..	..	..	..	..	222·00	6,721·00
1961	..	..	..	..	..	197·00	6,163·00
1960	..	..	..	..	..	167·00	5,642·00

The figures are for both ordinary and industrial (door-to-door)
life. The funds are the security for the life policyholders and
substantial security they are indeed.

If the business grows at the rate of 10 per cent per annum the
profits and possibly dividends will grow at the same rate. There
was a setback in dividend growth due to the introduction of
corporation tax in 1965, but this has now been absorbed.

Contrast this certain growth of the life offices with the general
insurance companies which are dealing with risk business. The
premiums are total premiums, not premiums on new business as
in the case of life; these appear on facing page.

Devaluation has helped general insurance companies because
many have big investments overseas. Underwriting losses have
been appalling in recent years, but they have been more than offset
by investment income which, as the following figures show, has
been on the up and up.

General Insurance

							Total premiums £ million	Funds £ million
1970	..	..	..	..	..	..	2,084·0	2,463·0
1969	..	..	..	..	..	..	1,867·0	2,227·0
1968	..	..	..	..	..	..	1,727·0	1,999·5
1967	..	..	..	..	..	..	1,712·7	1,872·1
1966	..	..	..	..	..	..	1,496·7	1,628·5
1965	..	..	..	..	..	..	1,285·3	1,540·0
1964	..	..	..	..	..	..	1,185·8	1,479·8
1963	..	..	..	..	..	..	1,091·3	1,413·1
1962	..	..	..	..	..	..	1,025·9	1,357·2
1961	..	..	..	..	..	..	982·6	1,303·3
1960	..	..	..	..	..	..	924·1	1,182·5

The B.I.A. have no information on total investment figures earlier than 1969 so, as an indication of the rate of growth in investment of the non-life companies, here are the figures for the Royal Insurance Co, the biggest of the composites, covering a period since their last merger:

	£ million			£ million
1961	.. 12·56	1966	..	18·11
1962	.. 13·57	1967	..	19·66
1963	.. 13·97	1968	..	23·41
1964	.. 14·95	1969	..	27·16
1965	.. 16·23	1970	..	30·36

Source; Extel Card

The figures for premiums and funds for general business are provided by the British Insurance Association, Aldermary House, Queen Street, London EC4. The funds are not exclusively due to the transaction of insurance business. Normally an insurance company will set aside 40 per cent of its premiums annually for unexpired risks. It will provide reserves for outstanding claims and it will set up revenue reserves out of past profits. The figures will also include the assets represented by the company's share and loan capital. Fresh capital has been raised from time to time from shareholders in the form of rights issues. Sometimes this capital has been raised merely for investment purposes.

You would have noted earlier in the chapter that in 1970 life funds totalled £13,584 million, and general funds totalled £2,463 million.

Despite the bad underwriting results of the non-life offices and because of increased investment income the cost of dividends of the composite offices went up as follows:

	£ million			£ million
1961	.. 32·00	1966	..	40·09
1962	.. 33·64	1967	..	43·02
1963	.. 34·22	1968	..	45·75
1964	.. 34·79	1969	..	50·19
1965	.. 37·85	1970	..	53·75

It is this investment aspect of insurance companies, coupled with skilled investment management which is so important. Both are in some ways akin to investment trusts. With a shareholder-owned life office up to 10 per cent of its growing profits go to its shareholders. The total non-life profits of shareholder-owned general insurance companies on the other hand accrue to the shareholders. Fine when they are making profits. Then they are investment trusts plus. But when they are making losses they are investment trusts minus.

It is of interest to note how the funds of the life and general offices are invested and for comparison purposes I set out side by side a recent percentage spread under the various headings:

	Life per cent of total	General per cent of total
Mortgages	17·0	5·2
British Government and British Government guaranteed securities	15·8	8·2
Commonwealth Government, provincial and municipal stocks, and Foreign Government stocks	3·4	18·6
Debentures and loan stock, preference and guaranteed stocks and shares	18·5	21·9
Ordinary stocks and shares	27·5	34·4
Real property and ground rents	13·4	7·2
Other investments	4·4	4·5
	100·0	100·0

The spread is on the basis of book values because at the present time insurance companies do not have to disclose market values of their funds. Some companies are now giving a total figure for the market value of their investments in the form of a footnote on their balance sheets. I think this practice will grow.

It will be noted that the general insurance companies have a much greater proportion of their investments overseas than the life offices, the figures being respectively 18·6 and 3·4. This is due to the fact that companies transacting business overseas have to deposit securities in the countries in which they operate and usually the securities of the particular country. Because of this pre-requisite condition before commencing business in a particular country investments are often bought which normally their investment managers would certainly not buy.

The percentage of life funds invested in mortgages is high. But a life office has to match its investments with its liabilities. This means having securities redeemable at various prescribed dates. It has policies maturing each year. Also it needs to rely on a fixed rate of interest. In the case of a composite office a mortgage can cement, or help to nourish, general insurance business.

Owing to much switching of gilt-edged investments I would expect book values of British Government securities not to be greatly less than market values. The book values of other fixed-interest securities will probably be well above their market values, whereas with equities and property, the market values will be well in excess of book values. I have done some intelligent guesstimates for life and general funds.

I make the market values of the life and general funds £2,850 million and £5,800 million respectively, and the split on market values as follows:

	Life per cent of total	General per cent of total
Mortgages	14·0	4·0
British Government and British Government guaranteed securities	13·5	7·0
Commonwealth Government, provincial and municipal stocks, and Foreign Government stocks	2·5	13·0
Debentures and loan stock, preference and guaranteed stocks and shares	13·5	16·0
Ordinary stocks and shares	35·0	46·0
Real property and ground rents	17·0	9·5
Other investments	4·5	4·5
	100·0	100·0

Taxation

Before leaving insurance companies it is essential to understand in broad outline how they are taxed.

The first point to grasp is the fact that general and life offices are taxed on entirely different bases.

The general insurance companies pay corporation tax on the interest from their invested funds and other income plus or minus profits or losses on underwriting their fire, motor, marine, accident and other insurance business, less, of course, the expenses of running the company. Profits and losses on investments are taken into account in assessing profits subject to tax. The general insurance companies' holdings of British equities and preference shares are of special value because they are franked for corporation tax and can be offset against the companies' liability to corporation tax. The income from funds representing overseas insurance is treated as trade income and thus qualifies for double taxation relief. This is a concession, extracted from the Government at the inception of corporation tax, which many commentators overlook. It is of considerable help to the insurance companies.

The taxation of life offices varies within the company itself. Income from funds in respect of fully approved pension schemes under section 208, Income and Corporation Taxes Act 1970, formerly section 379 of the Income Tax Act 1952, are fully relieved from all tax by the section. Ordinary life assurance business is assessed on interest plus profits less losses on investments less an allowance for expenses of management. The annuity fund is taxed on profits.

Both the life and annuity fund are taxed at the concessional rate of corporation tax of $37\frac{1}{2}$ per cent. This is equivalent to the concessional rate of income tax of $37\frac{1}{2}$p in the £. Profits, after deducting losses on the sale or realization of investments, are taxed at not more than 30 per cent. The advent of corporation tax hit the life offices because franked investment income is apportioned between the profits distributed to policyholders and the portion, usually 10 per cent, paid over to the shareholders. With this kind of split obviously there is not likely to be enough franked income to meet the corporation tax liability so the balance suffers corporation tax. This hit the Legal and General hard because so much of their funds were and are invested in property and the percentage of their income which is franked for corporation tax was particularly low. As a result they were unable to increase their dividend at the triennium following the imposition of corporation tax – an unheard of thing and one of these investment unpredictables which makes investment an art and not a science.

From the table on page 111, where I estimate the percentage split, under the various headings, of the market value of the life company funds, it will be seen that even taking property and equities together only 52·0 per cent of their funds are invested in inflation-protected investments, because with life offices there is considerable matching of liabilities with money stocks. With general funds the corresponding percentage is 55·5 per cent. The general companies keep a fairly high percentage liquid to meet losses, although with both life and general business, particularly life, there is some self-financing out of premiums as they come in. General insurance companies have, as we have seen, to keep pretty substantial funds abroad because of their overseas business. Overseas currencies are often blocked and moneys surplus to requirements cannot be remitted to this country.

I am a great believer in insurance shares as investments. The general insurance companies have had a bad experience with their underwriting over the last five years or so, motor business being particularly difficult. Also difficult has been the business transacted in the United States and although reinsurance through excess of loss transactions took away much of the sting of hurricane 'Betsy' the British insurance companies nevertheless suffered heavy losses.

I regard life companies as the supreme safety growth investment. They have now got over the initial impact of corporation tax and I look forward to growth as good as in the past. This was of the order of 8·8 per cent per annum, compared with 3·1 per cent per annum for general offices over the last ten years.

Taking into account the past growth of life companies and assuming that general underwriting will settle down to a break-even basis, I feel that a dividend yield for life companies of $2\frac{1}{2}$ per cent and for composite companies 4 per cent is about right and takes into account expected future growth in dividends.

Finally here are the highs and lows of 1969–71 (to date) of the *Financial Times/Actuaries* group indices:

	High	Low
Financial Times/Actuaries Composite	140·87 (23.9.71)	67·02 (26.5.70)
Financial Times/Actuaries Life	170·47 (20.9.71)	94·25 (27.5.70)

which is enough to write big that timing is an essential part of the art of investment.

Stockbrokers who are specialists in insurance shares include Read Hurst Brown & Co, Phillips & Drew, Greenwell & Co, Savory Milln, all London brokers, and Tilney, Sing, Parr & Rae of Liverpool.

Part IV

Investment through Life Assurance

CHAPTER 15

Annuities

The term investment, as we have seen from our definition, is a pretty wide one and the objects of investment legion. Outside the scope of this book would obviously fall pictures, *objets d'art*, furniture, postage stamps, coins, china, silver – the list is almost inexhaustible and includes anything which can possibly increase in value, if only with accruing interest.

Annuities, however, I feel should earn a place in these pages, also savings through life assurance policies which are dealt with in the subsequent chapter.

An annuity is simply an annual payment. It can be payable by half-yearly or quarterly instalments or even weekly as are annuities granted to servants on retirement.

I am not here concerned with pension annuities or payment for life to a valued member of the state but to annuities which can be bought with a cash sum by an individual from a life assurance office. In simplest terms the purchaser gives the assurance company a sum of £Y and in return the assurance company agrees to pay £X annually during the life of the purchaser.

You may well comment: 'How do they know how long he will live?' They don't, but with the help of mortality tables, which the life offices have been perfecting over the years, they know what is likely to be the average life of both men and women at various ages from the day they are born and for each year onwards. They know too that, on average, women live four to five years longer than men.

Here are a few examples of the expectancy of life of persons of various ages, according to the mortality tables used by the insurance companies:

Age	Males	Females
At birth	68½	68½
10	61	61
20	53½	57½
30	44	48
40	34½	39
50	25½	30
60	17½	21
70	11	13½
80	6	7½
90	3	4

116

It is apparent at once that with individual lives the life assurance companies will gain on those annuitants that live less than the average and lose on those that live longer but over all will make the profit that they expect to make.

It is the uncertainty of the length of an individual life which makes annuities attractive. The purchaser has a sum of money, the income from which is perhaps inadequate to maintain him at the level he wishes and he knows he will have to dip into the capital sooner or later and, what's more, if he lives long enough and maintains his standard of living the day will come when he hasn't enough money to live on.

He hands the cash to an insurance company and they guarantee him a fixed sum for the rest of his life. What he is getting from them is a mixture of interest and return of capital – the proportions are fixed from the onset. The income proportion is liable to income tax and surtax if appropriate, the capital proportion is free of tax in the normal way, as it should be, but prior to the Finance Act 1956 the whole of the annuity was subject to tax.

If the annuitant is not liable to tax, arrangements can be made with the Revenue and the insurance company for the annuity to be paid gross, that is without deduction of tax.

Supposing a married man, aged 66, had £10,000 invested, half in British Government securities and half in equities, which gave him an overall return of 5 per cent =£500 per annum subject to tax. Supposing also he had a pension of £1,500 per annum. The income from his investments would bear tax at the standard rate so his net spendable income from the £10,000 would be £306·25. Obviously the fund could be reinvested to produce a higher return but even £800 would only bring in £490 after tax.

The £10,000 would currently buy him an annuity of £1,440 of which £740, the capital content, would not be subject to income tax. So his spending money would increase to £700 less tax £271·25 net, £428·75 capital content £740, a total of £1,168·75 per annum. The figures are based on half-yearly payments of the annuity. It costs a little more for more frequent payments.

The purchaser thus transfers the responsibility for investing his money to the assurance company. Their arithmetic will see to it that they will make an all-over profit on their annuity business but if the purchaser who buys an annuity at age 60 lives beyond the age of 78 (see mortality tables) the assurance company is likely to make a loss on the transaction.

Here are some rough examples of what £1,000 will buy for a
male or female at the ages stated. The capital content is shown in
brackets:

Purchase price: £1,000.

Age	Male Annuity		Female Annuity	
	£	£	£	£
60	127	(57)	116	(47)
65	141	(71)	127	(58)
66	144	(74)	129	(60)
67	148	(78)	132	(63)
68	152	(82)	135	(66)
69	157	(87)	139	(69)
70	162	(91)	142	(73)
80	237	(162)	199	(127)

I have made no attempt to quote the cheapest rates. Rates vary
between companies and it pays a prospective purchaser to go
shopping.

Rates generally will vary with the interest rates insurance
companies can secure on their investments. At the present time
purchasers get much better rates than people who at the same age
bought an annuity ten or twenty years ago. One company ties
its annuity rates to the current yield on 2½ per cent Consols. Here
to illustrate how annuity rates can change (and they are changing
all the time) are the average yields on 2½ per cent Consols for each
of the last twelve years:

1959 ..	.. 4·84		1965 ..	.. 6·44
1960 ..	.. 5·44		1966 ..	.. 6·82
1961 ..	.. 6·24		1967 ..	.. 6·73
1962 ..	.. 6·01		1968 ..	.. 7·44
1963 ..	.. 5·60		1969 ..	.. 8·94
1964 ..	.. 6·04		1970 ..	.. 8·65
			1971 (to date)	9·37

In 1946–47 that dizzy Labour Chancellor, Hugh Dalton, mani-
pulated interest rates so successfully that the yield on 2½ per cent
Consols had fallen to a whisker under 2½ per cent. He even issued
a 2½ per cent Treasury stock at 100, which has since been as low
as 26. So clearly it makes a lot of difference not only as regards
age but interest rates ruling when an annuity is purchased.

Many object to an annuity because the purchaser parts with his
capital. But if he is wealthy he gets in effect a bonus when he buys
his annuity. Let us assume he has an invested fund of £100,000

and his total income of £5,000 a year is derived from this source. He is 68 and married. His net income after income tax and surtax would be £2,762. If he died his average estate duty rate is 46½ per cent and his net estate after estate duty £53,500.

Supposing he uses half to buy an annuity. £50,000 buys £7,723 with a capital content of £4,100. Thus his spending money is £7,248 compared with £2,762 heretofore.

Moreover he has immediately reduced his average rate for estate duty to 31 per cent. So his net estate becomes £34,500 after duty compared with £53,500. In effect he has bought his annuity for £19,000.

You might well add – but his wife will have less to live on when he dies, because his estate after duty is reduced from £53,500 to £34,500. This problem could be solved by the purchase of a joint annuity on the lives of himself and his wife. Obviously joint annuities will cost more than a single life annuity and on the assumption that the wife is 64, £50,000 buys a joint annuity of £5,793, capital portion £2,460. The joint annuity being more costly his total spendable income drops to £5,510 but he has nevertheless doubled his spendable income. Having regard to the incidence of estate duty it is preferable for the husband to give the wife the money and for her to effect a joint annuity for half the joint amount. The incidence of estate duty has to be borne in mind wherever capital transactions involving more than one person take place, and the transaction is not for full money consideration. It takes four years before a gift qualifies for any relief for estate duty and seven years before it escapes altogether (see page 200). But in a joint annuity provided by the husband and where his wife survives him, the wife's annuity bears estate duty in full on his death on its then value.

There are plenty of refinements in the annuity field. Arrangements can be made for an annuity to run for a guaranteed period of years irrespective of the life of the annuitant. If he dies during the guaranteed period the company pays out for the remainder of the guaranteed period to his executors or administrators. An annuity can be tied to some extent to inflation by having the annuity increase by a fixed proportion every three years. One company's annuity goes up 7½ per cent every three years, but it is not until the ninth year that the payment becomes greater than the conventional annuity.

These refinements will, of course, cost additional money to

secure the same benefits as a conventional annuity at the commencement.

The greatest virtue of an annuity is the regular payment of a fixed sum as against the worry that the person concerned will run out of money one day. The straightforward annuity is, of course, no protection against inflation but it would be sensible on purchasing an annuity and giving a big boost to spendable income to live well within this amount, putting aside something each year for a rainy day or alternatively not committing all one's capital to an annuity, leaving some as a reserve against contingencies.

CHAPTER 16

Life assurance policies
Life assurance generally is more a means of provision than of
investment. The provision is against untimely death and all its
consequences for the widow, the family or for the assured's
business. This type of assurance is usually called 'whole of life'
or if the life assurance is for a prescribed limited period
'term assurance'. Incidentally, in pedantic circles 'assurance' is
the term used for insurance against certainties such as death
and 'insurance' against what can happen but might not – an
accident.

However, I regard the class of life business referred to as endowment assurance as a true form of investment. The expression
endowment goes back into history. It is a putting aside of money
to endow for a certain event – the attainment of a particular age,
the repayment of a mortgage, the retirement from business. The
object of an endowment assurance is to secure a sum of money at
the end of an agreed period. There is an element of life assurance
with an endowment policy in that if the assured dies before the
end of the period selected, usually ten years or more, a fixed sum
or a fixed sum plus bonuses (which I will explain later) is payable.
But the death provision is secondary, the primary motive of the
transaction being savings. Indeed the cost of the death cover is a
very small proportion of the monthly, quarterly, half-yearly or
yearly sum, called a premium, which is payable during the period
of the assurance.

One of the great advantages of life assurance including endowment assurance, is that there is income tax relief on two-fifths of
the total annual premium provided certain conditions are fulfilled.
These conditions are that the term must be for a minimum of ten
years, the amount of the annual relief on the premium is limited
to 7 per cent of the sum assured, and the total of all such eligible
premiums for relief is restricted to one-sixth of the assured's total
income.

The amount of the premium will depend on the period selected
and the age of the assured at the time the policy is effected. The
premiums for women are usually similar to those for men who are

four to five years younger. Obviously the cost of life assurance goes
up with the age of the assured. He must provide satisfactory evidence of health or pass a satisfactory medical examination.

Endowment assurance policies are usually issued in three main
forms, non-profit, with-profits and equity-linked.

Non-profit endowment secures a fixed sum at the end of a
selected period, no more and no less. The sum assured is the
same whether the assured dies after paying one premium or
survives to the end of the selected term.

The non-profit endowment policy is a favourite method for
repaying a house purchase loan when the borrower pays income
tax at the full standard rate and particularly so if he pays surtax –
see Chapter 20 on 'House purchase'. The gross interest on the
loan is an allowable charge against the borrower's income for tax
purposes and in addition he gets life assurance relief on the
premiums.

This is likely to be the cheapest method for such a taxpayer
(who wants life cover for his mortgage) repaying a house purchase
mortgage. It is cheaper than paying a premium to cover the death
risk in respect of the reducing amount of the loan outstanding
where the house purchase loan takes the form of annual instalments of income and capital to repay the loan over the term. It is
the incidence of tax which works the magic.

A with-profits endowment policy or an equity-linked policy
would almost certainly be the cheapest method of all for repaying
a loan, but the premium is substantially higher to provide the same
initial sum assured as a non-profit policy. And normally the lender
requires the initial sum assured to equal the amount borrowed.
But at the end, the with-profits policyholder is likely to pick up a
considerable surplus over and above the sum assured. Thus
though not the cheapest annual cost to repay a loan in view of the
bigger premium, the transaction as a whole is very much better if
the borrower can afford the higher premium and will give a better
return as the following figures demonstrate.

Now as regards the conventional with-profits endowment
policy, as distinct from the equity-linked policy which I will deal
with later in this chapter, it might assist if I gave you two quotations, one for a non-profit the other a with-profits endowment
assurance, for a man aged 35, for a term of twenty-five years
and for a sum assured of £5,000.

Non-profit endowment assurance for twenty-five years

	£		£
Sum assured	5,000	Net premium after relief ..	118·05
Death cover throughout	5,000	Total of net premiums ..	2,951
Sum payable in twenty-		Sum payable at end of	
five years	5,000	period	5,000
Premium	139·7	Yield after all taxes paid ..	3·8
Life rebate	21·65		per cent
			per annum

With-profits endowment assurance for twenty-five years

	£		£
Sum assured	5,000	Net premium after relief ..	181·59
Immediate death cover,			
plus accrued bonuses	5,000	Total of net premiums ..	4,540
Premium	214·9	Estimated sum payable at	
		end of period	12,347
Life rebate	33·31	Yield after all taxes paid ..	7·1
			per cent
			per annum

Note. – The death cover increases every year with bonuses. If death occurred after ten years the amount payable is estimated at £7,261.

On the basis of the same premium for a with-profits policy as for the £5,000 non-profit policy the figures would be as follows:

With-profits policy	£
Sum assured	3,234
Estimated maturity value	7.986
Estimated death value after ten years ..	4,695
Yield after all taxes paid	7·1 per cent
	per annum

The estimated sums including bonuses to maturity are based on the assumption that the current rate of bonuses continues and that all bonuses are retained – that is, not taken as cash.

The life assurance relief is on the assumption of the continuance of the current rate of relief and with income tax at 38·75p in the £. The percentage yields take into account tax relief.

The non-profit policy offers no complications but the with-profits policy immediately provokes questions.

The with-profits policyholder is entitled to share in the profits of the company. His share takes the form of the issue of bonuses which are added to the policy. In fact they are normally called reversionary bonuses. These bonuses can be cashed at any time but obviously the cash amount will be less than the reversionary amount which is the amount payable at the end of the term.

With mutual assurance companies, which are owned by the policyholders, the assured benefits from 100 per cent of the profits available for distribution after making the appropriate reserves. In the case of the companies owned by shareholders he usually shares in about 90 per cent of the profits similarly calculated. Thus the with-profits policyholder shares in the profits spawned not only by the with-profits contracts but by non-profit policies as well. It must not be assumed that all mutual companies give better bonuses than shareholder-owned companies. It is not so. It pays to go shopping when seeking life assurance.

Reverting to the use of insurance for house purchase, it will thus be seen that there are assumptions with regard to with-profits policies and the cagey lender will tend to ignore the bonuses and look to the sum assured only. However, if the borrower can afford the extra premium I very much recommend the with-profits policy.

A non-profit return is a guaranteed return, and mark well it is over a period of twenty-five years when interest rates can vary greatly. Interest rates are high now, 9 per cent subject to tax on gilt-edged stocks but about twenty years ago they were $2\frac{1}{2}$ per cent subject to tax.

Political repercussions, adverse to life assurance companies, and war excluded, I feel there is a good chance of current bonuses being maintained over the period, indeed increased. If I am correct the certainty of a return of 7·1 per cent per annum compound interest after all tax has been paid, as in our example, is very attractive.

(c) Equity-linked endowment assurance

There are many people, however, who would prefer to go for the equity-linked policy where the rewards could be even greater. Apart from the Equitas policy of the London and Edinburgh Insurance Co, a small life office of under £5 million assets, equity-linked assurance has not been going for ten years yet. However, the London and Edinburgh can claim that equity-linked policies (Equitas they are called) taken out with them ten years ago have out-performed any conventional with-profits policy. I need only cite one case, a ten-year Equitas equity-linked policy effected by a man, aged 30, in July 1959 for an annual premium of £100 was worth £1,552 at maturity. The best comparable conventional endowment I can find to match this sum is £1,475 with an 'Ecclesiastical' policy but the Equitas payment would have been substantially higher if it had been paid out in January 1969, when equity shares were much higher.

The Equitas policy certainly beats most conventional with-profits policies over the last ten years but these years have been fat years for equities, giving birth to the expression 'the cult of the equity', and I question whether the next ten years will be as good.

Here is an example for a man, aged 40 next birthday, paying the standard rate of income tax who undertakes to pay £100 per annum for twenty years as a premium.

Annual subscription – £100.

Income tax relief at 38·75p in the £ on two-fifths of the subscription – £15·50.

Net annual outlay – £84·50.

Total net outlay over the twenty-year period is £84·50 multiplied by 20 =£1,690. Ten pounds of the subscription goes for administration expenses including the life assurance cover and the balance of £90 is invested in units together with half-yearly income. Thus on these figures £1,800 is invested at a cost of £1,690.

During the twenty-year period the life of the policyholder, as the unit-linked investor is termed, is insured for £2,000 and at the end of the period there is a guaranteed sum of £2,000.

We have now to consider what the unit trust-linked policyholder is likely to receive at the end of the twenty-year period. If the income accumulates at the rate of 2 per cent net per annum and the capital increases at the rate of 3½ per cent per annum the units would be worth £3,410 at the end of the twenty-year term. It was impossible to invest in an equity-linked contract twenty years ago but had it been possible the units would have accumulated to a much larger sum than £3,410. But what of the future? Equity investment has been very satisfactory over the last twenty years and all we can do is to assume that it will be satisfactory in the ensuing twenty years.

In my view there is not a better way of buying equities than under the equity-linked scheme.

Not all equity-linked policies have guaranteed sums at maturity – you just get the value at maturity of the units purchased with your premiums. Where there is a guaranteed sum it is less than the equivalent non-profit endowment guaranteed sum and slightly less sometimes than the comparable initial sums assured for the with-profits policy. Further, bonuses once declared stick for good whereas with an equity-linked policy the sum payable at maturity will depend on the market values of equities at maturity. During 1969–70 for example, the *Financial Times Industrial Share Index* has been both around 500 and around 350 and the higher is just over 40 per cent more than the lower. Some equity-linked policies provide for the transfer of the underlying securities to the assured at maturity – if he so wishes – so that he can keep the shares until the market recovers.

Equity-linked was pioneered by the Unit Trust Movement, but now many of the famous life assurance companies issue equity-linked policies to those who prefer them to the conventional with-profits policy.

I feel the change in attitude of the life offices may be reflected in a recent paper given to the Institute of Actuaries by Mr G. L. Melville. He claimed that the unit-linked approach was equally appropriate to investment in equities, property and fixed-interest stocks. It was easier to understand and administer, fairer and more logical than the reversionary bonus system, and there was no need to dispense with a guaranteed sum assured on death.

All that might have to be sacrificed in adopting the unit-linked approach was a guaranteed value at maturity, but Mr Melville felt that conventional policyholders lost more than they gained by having this guarantee. He considered that, on balance, the advantages of the unit-linked system outweighed the additional risks. These views are probably minority views.

The equity-linked policy, being a life assurance contract, the fund is taxed similarly to life assurance funds on slightly more favourable terms, see page 112. The growth in the policy is subject to capital gains tax and whether or not the unit holder receives the proceeds in cash or by transfer of shares, capital gains is payable on any excess over purchase price, I am informed, at a special rate of 20 per cent to reflect a number of factors.

Building society-linked policies
A favourite life assurance-linked policy is the one linked to regular building society savings. It is perhaps the finest and cheapest way to save money without risk. Life assurance relief is secured on the amount regularly saved subject to the usual qualifications.

Life assurance is already linked to unit trusts, building society deposits, property bonds. Why not indeed link life assurance to the high yields which go with fixed-interest investment and get the maximum advantage which goes with compound interest?

New type policies

Life assurance companies have, during the last year or two, brightened up their sales organizations. Some have even gone so far as to have sales promotion departments.

Some single and annual premium endowment assurance policies have been given sales promotion names. Single premium endowment policies are now often referred to as bonds and ordinary endowments plus a few refinements have acquired distinct trade names, with various companies – one which, for example, is termed Profitmaker.

Under pressure from the unit trust movement, which habitually gives estimates on attractive assumptions of future growth, the life offices have recently not been so inhibited in quoting future bonuses.

I give two examples of this new look. The first is a ten-year single premium endowment policy now termed **annuity bond.**

In the event of the bondholder being subject to surtax when the bond matures or is surrendered a surtax liability will arise. It is calculated on the proceeds of the bond in excess of the premium. The difference is divided by the number of years the bond has been in force. The resultant figure is added to the bondholder's income to arrive at his surtax rate and this rate is applied to the whole of the excess over premium. Thus it pays a bondholder to take the proceeds of a bond when his income is low.

The minimum acceptable premium is £500 and the maximum as high as £250,000. The bonds are intended for persons over 50 or under 76, when they mature. The single premium in the hands of the life assurance company pays income tax at $37\frac{1}{2}$p, there is no surtax and the company's effective capital gains tax rate is said to be about 10 per cent. The company guarantees that the bond will attract interest at 13 per cent before income tax. I have seen one scheme with 17 per cent guaranteed.

To quote from one scheme a single premium of £1,000 for a man, aged 65, will provide the following amounts:

					£
After 5 years	..	..	..	..	1,450
„ 6 „	..	..	..	..	1,565
„ 7 „	..	..	..	..	1,685
„ 8 „	..	..	..	..	1,810
„ 9 „	..	..	..	..	1,946
„ 10 „	..	..	..	..	2,080

or alternatively a guaranteed annuity of:

		£
After 5 years	.. ..	159·25
,, 6 ,,	.. ..	172·25
,, 7 ,,	.. ..	185·25
,, 8 ,,	.. ..	199·25
,, 9 ,,	.. ..	213·25
,, 10 ,,	.. ..	229·00

If the bondholder can get better terms in the market he takes the sum assured and goes elsewhere for his annuity.

If death occurs before the end of the selected term, the surrender value of the policy will be 95 per cent plus compound interest of 4 per cent net of tax. Thus after about eighteen months the surrender value will start to exceed the premium.

Now for the **Profitmaker** policy, which it is broadly claimed gives yields of up to 14 per cent gross per annum, plus 'a unique cash loan plan'.

The 14 per cent assumes a continuation of a bonus of £4 per cent for a ten-year term, the term suggested for the policy, the company, pointing out that it has recently declared a bonus of £4·25 states that 'bonuses have gone up strongly on every declaration since 1945 and the odds are that the growth will continue'.

This rather fulsome statement was withdrawn after the first advertisement – conservative caution prevailed.

Life cover varies according to age of entry. It is 'at least 180 times' the monthly premium. Differently described, it is fifteen times the annual amount saved. The premium can be any multiple of £1 monthly with a minimum of £4. All monthly payments must be by banker's order, a very sound pre-requisite from all points of view.

Taking a premium of £10 a month, the ten-year Profitmaker has a unique advantage. It carries with it the right to apply for a substantial loan from the Mercantile Credit Co at any time during the period of the plan. This is not determined by the amount of premiums paid because from the payment of the first premium the loan ceiling is the whole of the guaranteed minimum return at the end of ten years.

Furthermore, as bonuses are added to the policy, the ceiling for loans is automatically increased. Loans have to be repaid over four years but bondholders can re-borrow up to the ceiling even if they have not fully paid off an existing loan.

For a man, aged 35, a monthly premium of £10 costs over the ten-year period after tax relief £1,014. The estimated return after ten years is £1,566. Estimated tax-free gain £552, equivalent to a gross yield to a standard rate taxpayer of 13·7 per cent per annum.

Some assurance companies are involved in property bonds. These are dealt with under 'Mortgages and property', see page 143.

This is only a brief chapter on investing in life assurance, it is not a book, so if the reader wants further information or desires to know whether there is a scheme to fit his own special needs, any life office will help him. There are many first-class companies which are household names. It would be invidious for me just to mention the names of a few.

Married Women's Property Act and other trust policies
However, before leaving investing in life assurance there is one important point I should make. It is that they can be attractive from the estate duty angle if the policy is taken out as a trust policy under the Married Women's Property Act or otherwise.

If a man wishes to benefit his wife and family, then a trust policy is clearly indicated and such a policy would not be subject to death duties if the policyholder's personal representative can satisfy the Estate Duty Office that the premiums have been paid out of income and represent normal expenditure which has not adversely affected the normal standard of living of the policyholder. A trust policy should be a must for all temporary assurance where the cover is high and the premium low. To give an example, the payment of £24·75 annually for twenty years for a man of 30 secures cover after one premium has been paid of £1,500 per annum for twenty years, a reducing maximum of £30,000. If he survives the twenty years the policy cover lapses.

Whole of life and term assurance
I do not regard policies which are concerned only with insurance against death as investments. Some have no value at the end of term. As large sums can be involved they should, where possible, be issued under the provisions of the Married Women's Property Act or otherwise as trust policies.

Part V

Land and Buildings

CHAPTER 17

Mortgages

A mortgage is a fixed-interest investment whereas a purchase of property is an equity investment. The amount of the mortgage is fixed in value whereas land and buildings will vary with market conditions and in an inflationary economy the value is likely to go up all the time.

The property owner who secures a mortgage on his property is termed a mortgagor and the lender who provides the money for a mortgage is called the mortgagee.

A mortgage is for an agreed amount. It is sometimes repayable after a fixed number of years either by instalments or in a lump sum at the end of the period. The rate of interest may be fixed for the term of the mortgage or there may be arrangements so that the rate of interest varies with money market conditions. The rate of interest on building society mortgages varies with market conditions but I am aware of a number of loans with a fixed rate of interest for a term of a minimum of five years.

When two individuals or two institutions are involved, one buying the property, one providing some of the money by means of a mortgage, the two concerned have both made investments. One a fixed-interest investment in a mortgage the other an equity investment in land and buildings.

Personally I would always rather be the owner of the land and buildings than the mortgagee. It is, however, the job of a building society to grant mortgages to encourage people to own their own houses. Local authorities, insurance companies, and others also help in this way. It also suits institutions from time to time to lend money on a mortgage, when interest rates are high and these high interest rates can be secured for a lengthy period. Indeed they can be favourite forms of investment in periods of deflation and when the purchasing power of the currency is stable. They are, however, much out of favour at the present time because we have been going through one of the worst periods of inflation in our history. I know for instance of houses which were built for £400 before the Second World War which have recently been sold for £5,000, and I am not talking about a rise in the price of land due to scarcity, these are just small houses on tiny plots.

There will always be a demand for mortgages and when the demand is greater than the supply, as it is at the present time, the lender can make conditions as favourable for himself as possible. If, for example, an insurance company was the lender it might ask a borrower to transfer all his insurance business. Or if the insurance company already had all his insurance business the insurance company would be inclined to grant a mortgage if required in case the firm concerned were to go elsewhere for a mortgage and transfer its business to the lending insurance company. It is probable that insurance companies are the main source for large mortgages. In the case of the life offices it is necessary to have some of the companies' funds in mortgages so that they can tie fixed liabilities to a fixed investment such as a mortgage.

If you were the manager of the mortgage section of an insurance company how would you set about arranging a mortgage? You would know that there were various types of properties from large private houses to country mansions, maisonettes to large blocks of flats, shops and office premises, hotels and theatres, factories of every type of business, some factories producing goods for which there would be a market long into the foreseeable future. Other factories would be producing goods of a speculative type, something which was in fashion at the time and for which the demand could suddenly end. It emerges at once that in granting a mortgage to a company the mortgagee is very much concerned with the continued success of the user of the property. The mortgagee has got to be satisfied that a mortgagor would be able to pay the interest during the period of the mortgage and he, the mortgagee, is not going to be landed with a property which is going to be empty for a long time whilst another user is being sought. The mortgage manager of an insurance company is certainly going to be under great pressure from would-be mortgagors who want to offer indifferent security and he is going to be overpersuaded by the insurance side of the business to be as accommodating as possible. He must, however, be tough because it doesn't make sense to lend on fixed-interest terms to someone who is engaged in a speculative enterprise which might fail leaving the mortgagee with a property which is, perhaps, unsaleable and cannot be developed for a number of years.

So the first and most important aspect of a mortgage proposal is the type of security which is offered. The next is the value of that security. The mortgagee will not accept the valuation placed on it by the proposer. He will not even accept the valuation placed on it by the proposer's surveyors, even though they be one of the finest surveyors in the City. The reason for this is that a valuation can be made on a number of different bases. It can be based on the value as between a willing buyer and a willing seller. This usually means the cost price. Alternatively it can be based on the value which the property would fetch if it were put up for auction without reserve. Reserve is a figure which the seller puts on the property; the lowest price for which he would sell it. If at the auction no bid is received at the reserved price or above it then the property is withdrawn from auction.

If, therefore, the lending company is prepared to consider a mortgage it has to set down certain terms, the rate of interest, the mode of repayment and a condition that the amount of the mortgage will depend upon the value of the property which will be based on the lender's own surveyor's report and valuation. The cost of this survey and valuation will be borne by the mortgagor. The scale fee for a report and valuation on a property worth £50,000 would be £162·75 and the valuation itself would belong to the lender who would instruct the surveyor. There is usually an arrangement by which one-third of the fee is payable forthwith and the balance only if a loan is granted. It behoves, therefore, both the borrower and the lender to be reasonably satisfied before a surveyor is instructed that the proposition will be viable. Although the lender will indicate the amount of the loan he will require, it is not impossible that he will be satisfied with a lower amount when the time comes.

Mortgage valuations sometimes cause bad feeling between the lender and the borrower. For example, if a company has a factory which cost £300,000 to build which is situated in the country and tape recorders are manufactured there, so far in successful competition with its rivals, it is in reality a business risk and the basic value of the property is what it will fetch in the open market if the business folds up. There are plenty of buildings which, if valued on this basis, would have a value which bears no relation whatsoever to their cost. And the manager of a mortgage department has to temper the wind to the shorn lamb and carefully investigate the company's financial position and growth rate and consider what prospects there would be of dealing with the property in the event of the company's business failing. So let us assume that a mortgage is granted, that the security is acceptable, that the covenant of the mortgagor is first class, there is no risk whatsoever of his defaulting and that the rate of interest and the terms of repayment are satisfactory. It is still an unattractive investment to me. The rate of interest would probably not be more than 2 per cent more than what could be secured on an equivalent dated British Government security, where the collection of the interest is the simplest matter possible. It is just credited to the investor's bank account. In the case of a mortgage, arrangements have to be made to collect the interest. If there are quarterly, half-yearly or annual repayments of capital the interest has to be recalculated and adjusted and application for interest made accordingly. It is not unlikely that there will be changes in the security itself. The mortgagor might want to sell off a piece of land or to buy a piece and add to the security. He might want to vary the building and all these matters would involve the lender consulting his surveyors, particularly if the borrower wanted to keep the proceeds of sale. No doubt the deeds of the property would have to be produced by the lender's solicitors to the borrower's solicitors. On the purchase of additional property the borrower might want a further loan. The lender would have to keep all the deeds of the property – sometimes running into dozens and dozens of documents.

The mortgagee would have to satisfy himself that the property was fully insured, indeed in the surveyor's report a suggestion will doubtless be made as to the amount of the insurance. But he has to satisfy himself that the premium is paid each year. One way or another he is very much involved and in my view the additional rate of interest which he secures in no way compensates him for the additional work compared with the purchase of a Stock Exchange fixed-interest stock. All this is referring to the day-to-day, year-to-year, work connected with a mortgage. But what about the initial work of putting the mortgage on the books? That is very substantial. I just can't see why anybody should grant a mortgage unless there are other advantages as well. If any funds with which I am connected want a fixed-interest investment then I would go to the Stock Exchange and select my term.

One final point, the security which may be offered for mortgage may be a freehold or a leasehold property. In the case of leasehold properties I would want a lease of not less than fifty years and for the ground rent to be a reasonable one. The point is if you are landed with a leasehold property then you are faced with having to pay the ground rent.

With mortgages or loans to property companies I would insist upon securing a stake in the equity, that is the property itself. Why should I lend money on fixed-interest terms to enable other people to make huge gains as properties rise in value with inflation?

CHAPTER 18

Freeholds and leaseholds

Now for a few words concerning the purchase of property as distinct from mortgages on property. Property is of course a first-class investment. In fact it is probably the best equity investment in the world, provided restrictions are not imposed which take the gilt off the gingerbread. Just as in the case of granting a mortgage, there is considerable preparatory work before the purchase of a property can be negotiated. There is at the present time also considerable competition for the acquisition of property. The formation of property unit trusts and the desire of pension funds to invest directly in property has driven up prices, and first class property is attracting higher and higher prices, and this reduces the yields which can be secured on properties. However, most properties are let on leases and most leases provide for periodic reviews of the rent, so that often in buying a property you are buying the next rent increase. Just as when granting a mortgage, you cannot safely embark upon the purchase of a property unless you have a survey and valuation. But this survey need not be in the same great detail as in the case of a mortgage where you have a fixed-interest risk and cannot afford to disregard any unfavourable factor.

With the purchase of a property and the acquisition of the equity an all-over decision taking the rough with the smooth is appropriate, but with a mortgage why should you take any risk whatsoever when someone else is going to gather in all the profit? In considering the purchase of a property I am not thinking of a purchase for personal occupation. This is dealt with in Chapter 20 under 'House purchase'. Apart from the property companies with or without official quotations on the London Stock Exchange, the most likely investors in property are the insurance companies and the pension funds, although individual companies will like to acquire property for the purposes of their own manufacturing processes and generally.

Just as an individual would like to guard himself against inflation by owning his own house, so there is a lot to be said for an organization buying its own factories and office accommodation in the form of property, thereby safeguarding its rents from

137

inflation in the future. The true investor in property is the one who buys property occupied by other people. A pension fund for example which is undertaking to pay pensions based on the pensioner's last year's salary before retirement has obviously got an inflation risk and an investment in property would be one of the means of guarding against this risk.

Before considering a property purchase the investment manager should have a look at the actual property, at least from the outside. He would, of course, have read all the specifications and after seeing it from the outside he would have a general feel of the property. He would then have to secure a report and valuation from his surveyor and, unlike in the case of granting a mortgage, his firm or fund will have to pay for the report. There must be no skimping on the valuation. The very cautious might ask for three sets of values: (*a*) between a willing buyer and a willing seller; (*b*) the value the property would fetch at auction without reserve; and (*c*) the value for insurance purposes. He would expect his surveyor to look into any changes in the security which might be caused by road widening or changes in the centres of population or the chances of motorways going through the site. There are so many factors which can affect the value of the property now and in the future and the surveyor and the purchaser must be very cautious and take all likely and unlikely factors into consideration.

An investment manager with plenty of experience in property investment and, having done his sums as to current and prospective yields on the property and having satisfied himself that the price he had negotiated subject to his surveyor's report was reasonable, might not ask his surveyor to report on the precise value of the property. Nevertheless he would probably want some guidance as to the adequacy of the insurance on the property. Incidentally, the surveyor employed by the purchaser must be entirely independent. The vendor's surveyor, however reputable, must not act for both parties.

A valuation will normally include the land and the buildings on it as one item but in some cases it might be as well to have a separate valuation of the land. On a decision to buy the property the purchaser pays a deposit to the seller's agent, usually the estate agent, sometimes the solicitor. He then instructs his own solicitors to draw up the contract and I would stress that until the contract has been signed by both parties there is no binding contract to buy or sell the property. Indeed the vendor could accept a higher offer from elsewhere. This is very unsatisfactory because in a seller's market it is a one way option as many a would-be purchaser of a house for personal occupation has discovered. Once a deposit has been paid there is no reason at all why contracts should not be signed in the course of a week or two. A contract can be subject to a satisfactory survey. However, there are any amount of excuses which can be put forward for delaying the signing of a contract. Searches at the local council offices are necessary on a variety of subjects. One feels that often these are merely delaying tactics while the vendor is looking for some-one who may offer him a higher price. If you have got one of that type of vendor then my advice is don't stay with him but look around for someone who will be as good as their word, and there are plenty of those people about.

On the completion of the purchase the purchaser obtains control over the deeds of the property. These can be voluminous where the title to the property is split up into various parts, and there are sometimes problems in storing the deeds. In setting up the cost of the property in the books there is the purchase price, the surveyor's fees, the solicitor's costs and disbursements, which would include stamp duty on the conveyance of the property. The rate of stamp duty is as follows:

Not exceeding £5,500 – nil.
Exceeding £5,500 up to £7,000 – 25p for every £50 or part of £50.
Exceeding £7,000 – 50p for every £50 or part of £50.

It has also involved a lot of time and the investment manager should ever contrast this time and the cost and the return with what he can get on a first-class equity share, which is a very simple transaction, just two dividends a year and automatic growth in dividends. I would point out that at the current time the average yield on a first-class equity is $3\frac{1}{2}$ per cent, whereas it is possible to buy a batch of diverse properties to give an all-over yield of $6\frac{1}{2}$ per cent, and here I am referring to first-class stuff.

Apart from the time involved in purchasing a property there are problems during the life of the investment. These are: (a) if the property is not let on a full repairing lease problems concerning the repair and redecoration of the property, but even if the property is let on a full repairing lease it is wise to inspect the property occasionally to satisfy yourself that the covenants are being carried out; (b) to check up that the property is fully insured and that the premiums are kept up to date; (c) you might have to deal with an easement such as granting to the Post Office authorities facilities for a telephone post; (d) it will be necessary to diarize the break clauses in the lease and to be ready to negotiate a new rent and, if the past is any indication, at an increased rate; (e) in case of leaseholds to ensure that the ground rent is paid regularly.

This work during the period of the ownership of the property is only an indication of what will be involved. In the case of some properties there will be work of an unexpected nature.

It could be a mistake to buy a property which is held on a long lease with no break clauses for increasing the rent. But even where there is a break clause every seven years a property investment is at a disadvantage as compared with an equity. With an equity the profits would normally keep pace with inflation and the profits would go up annually and the dividends would also go up annually. There, of course, will be times when there is some form of dividend restraint, but this will usually tie up with periods when there is a squeeze and profits are falling or not going up at the usual high rate. However, with a lease you have to wait, say, seven years for a rent review before you catch up with inflation, then immediately you have increased the rent you have to wait another seven years to catch up with the next bout of inflation. In other words you keep up with inflation only in jerks and in arrear and not year by year.

However, property has one built-in asset and that is the land can be used in a more efficient way thus increasing the value of the property. We are seeing manifestations of this all the time. Here is a piece of land on which there is a house. It pays to pull down the house and build a factory in its place or flats. Local government requirements are being eased all the time, whereas at one stage only a two storey dwelling house would be permitted, in its place is erected an eight-storey block of flats. When you consider that the value of a piece of land is the amount of the units that can be erected on it you will observe at once that the flats have increased the value of the land enormously. We have also seen old office buildings pulled down in the City and taller blocks take their place, increasing the rental value of the building on the site enormously and with this increased rental value increasing the value of the site. I might interpolate here that all buildings which are of a permanent character which are erected on a piece of land belong to the freeholder, even though they have been erected by the tenant. Obviously the tenant would not pull down an existing building and replace it with a larger building without coming to terms with the freeholder. What they negotiate in the way of increased ground rent and the term of the lease would depend on supply and demand. Of course a leaseholder can always terminate the lease or sub-let it and find another site.

Property development
I have already stated that the investor who provides the money for property development ought to insist upon having some equity interest in this investment and in advising pension funds I have suggested that the interest should not be less than 33⅓ per cent. Property development is as we have seen an attractive method of increasing capital. Sites with an existing user can be cleared and new buildings erected in their place. A public house can be pulled down and an office block with a public house on the ground floor erected in its place. You have only got to walk round any district which you know fairly well to recognize what can be done in increasing the potential of a site. There are examples of this everywhere. On the face of it it seems extraordinary that someone can buy a large house and pay quite a high price for it, more than anyone would be prepared to pay to live in it, then be able to pull it down and rebuild on the site and make a lot of money, but this is being done all the time. However, this is a specialist activity and individuals who do their own developing are open to risk and to a lot of worry. It is a job best left to the experts.

Some of the larger insurance companies and pension funds are engaged directly in property development. As a result, some of their investment managers are getting expert in development. But they must secure the best advice and protect all contracts and cover every dangerous contingency. There are many pitfalls apart from politics, and the fickleness of local planning officers. Only a lot of experience will protect the investor from making mistakes and undoubtedly investors will have to pay for their experience. It is not enough to employ the best experts if there is no one sufficiently expert to assess the value of the advice. Even experts can make mistakes because they are often very busy and work is left to their less experienced assistants and the signing of partnership letters does not directly show that the letter has been written or even signed by the partner concerned.

You must bear in mind all the time that property investment is expensive if it is only limited to a few investments. To get the full benefit of experienced property staff you must have enough work to keep them busy. If you dispense with such experts and rely upon outside advisors then you must pay for your experience with the mistakes that you make although these mistakes might not be serious. Certainly there are far, far more problems with property investment than there are with buying selected equity shares, although the rewards could be greater.

An investment manager responsible for the investment of large funds can, what with visits to likely properties and generally, spend a major proportion of his time on property investment to the disadvantage of the performance of the rest of the funds under his care – equities and fixed interest stocks. The risks are even greater where property development is involved. This is greatly time-consuming and I rather doubt whether one man without delegation to efficient and able colleagues can cope effectively with investing both properties and stock exchange investments.

CHAPTER 19

Property shares, property unit trusts, and property bonds
There are at least three ways for the individual or for a fund for
that matter, to participate in the property boom without incurring
management responsibilities and without taking the risks involved.
One is to buy the shares of property companies quoted on the
Stock Exchange. Another is to buy the bonds of property unit
trusts. Yet another is to purchase property bonds.

Property shares
The shares of property companies will, to some extent, be affected
by the general rise and fall of share prices. Property shares themselves will be affected by adverse political factors and news
favourable or unfavourable, to properties. There will be times,
like other shares when, due to over-optimism, property shares will
be over-bought and times, due to pessimism, when they will be
over-sold. Timing a purchase is very important. In the last ten
years there have been times when investors have had an absurdly
optimistic attitude to property shares and other times when they
had been equally absurdly pessimistic.

The property share quoted on the Stock Exchange has the
advantages of gearing and property development where the big
money is often made. As you will have read elsewhere in this book,
gearing results from raising money on mortgage or loan and
re-investing the money in equities or assets which, unlike cash,
will grow in value both as a result of inflation and by careful
cultivation of rents and by development schemes. In an inflationary
society cash can only reduce in value compared with the goods it
can buy whereas cash invested in equity shares, property, goods
and even services can grow in value and usually does. The investor
in a property company which is heavily geared – that is, has raised
a high proportion of its money by mortgages or loans – must
eventually benefit greater than the investor in one that is lowly
geared or not geared at all. The effect of gearing is dealt with on
page 86, under 'Investment trusts'. In a sentence, all income on
the property purchased in excess of the interest on a mortgage or
loan belongs to the shareholder. So once the loan interest is covered
all income from dividends or rentals belongs entirely to the
ordinary shareholder.

143

In buying property shares you are buying some of the most knowledgeable and experienced expertise in the whole field of property management but your return is subject to both corporation tax and income tax and pension funds and other non-taxable funds can only recover the income tax. Any capital appreciation in the value of the underlying properties cannot be directly secured by you although much of the appreciation will be due to superb management skills, skills quite in excess of the average investment manager experienced in property.

Property unit trusts

The property unit trust was designed about ten years ago to meet the wishes of the smaller pension fund or charity which wanted to invest in property; to leave the investment to experts, to secure spread. But some of the larger funds will invest direct in freehold and leasehold properties, see Chapter 18.

For pension funds and charities which are not subject to any tax and for those pension funds whose members have the maximum permitted right to commute their pensions and are thus subject to tax on 25 per cent of their income (a separate fund for each), a stake in property can be secured by investing in property unit trusts, of which there are some fourteen trusts. Each is run by a committee of management. Each has the help of well-known consultant surveyors and each is associated with a bank or merchant bank. Over £150 million have been invested in this way. As in the case of a conventional unit trust of equity shares the investor has a proportionate share in a portfolio of investments, in this case in a mixed bag of properties – offices, shops, flats and some commercial and industrial properties. The price of the units is fixed according to the value of the properties and the yield at entry is quoted on application.

Supposing the trust owns a total of £10 million of properties and that it has issued 5,000 units, the average price of the units would be £2,000 and the purchaser of one hundred units would have an investment valued £200,000 with a yield of probably 7 per cent. A number of these unit trusts are well tried in this form of investment, although there is not quite the same liquidity as you get with an equity unit trust nor is the market value so readily adjusted to true values. Property unit trusts are a form of investment I can recommend as part of an investor's invested fund.

Property bonds

An alternative to units in a property unit trust is the property bond. The only difference in principle between these and property unit trusts is in the incidence of taxation. Property bonds are subject to income tax and capital gains tax at the normal rates. They can be subject to surtax.

However, property bonds can be linked to life assurance and where they are so linked the holder has the advantage of the reduced tax rates applicable to life assurance companies. These are a special income tax of 37·5p in the £ and capital gains at not more than 30 per cent. The premium, that is the annual amount contributed for the property bond attracts life assurance relief of two-fifths of the premium at the standard rate of income tax, provided the term is for ten years or more, total eligible life premium does not exceed one-sixth of the assured's taxable income and provided also the premium does not exceed 7 per cent of the sum assured. Any excess in both cases does not attract life assurance relief.

Where the assured is liable to surtax, surtax can be payable on the bond if it is repaid or surrendered within ten years. The method is to take the excess received over premiums paid and divide it by the number of years the bond is in force. The resultant sum is then added to the assured's total assessable income in the year the bond is surrendered to ascertain the rate of surtax applicable. This rate is then applied to the whole of the excess over premiums paid.

Property bonds have disadvantages in certain circumstances and the investor must follow my golden rule not to buy equities in any form, and that includes property bonds, until he has a house or is buying a house by mortgage, has adequate life assurance for his wife and children (if any), and has accumulated a sum of money against a 'rainy day', which is readily accessible in, say, a Trustee Savings Bank, a building society or some other form of investment where the full amount of cash can be secured without delay.

The disadvantages of property bonds are on the whole short-term ones. Whilst things are proceeding normally there is every likelihood that an investor will be able to withdraw his money immediately pound for pound on demand, or within the six months some property bond trusts stipulate. New money coming in will normally be adequate to repay those investors who want to surrender their bonds because of some unforeseen happening or, worse still, because they have fallen for some attractive advertisement stressing wonderful likely growth and have invested money which they should have kept liquid.

Some of the claims of growth for property bonds may well prove extravagant. Some property bond promoters solicit premium and forecast growth and yield before the properties have even been acquired. In such a case the investor is in fact at the outset investing in cash and promises of performance.

There have been periods in my life when a first-class modern office property, within a half mile from the Bank of England, has stayed empty or substantially empty for years, when flats have remained unoccupied for months and months, when factories built for a particular project have first fallen vacant and then become virtually derelict. I can even recall a number of hotels at seaside towns which remained partially built for years. I can recall times when there was a buyers' market only for properties and when the owner of a dwelling house could only sell at a substantial loss. In a sentence, buyers held the whip hand.

In times when there are buyers only of property it is easy to become over optimistic. In that climate it seems entirely correct for the property bond managers to uplift the value of a portfolio of properties annually. But supposing for some reason or other history repeated itself – and do not forget the boost to building and rental values which the Nazi bombing did for property – and we had a buyer's market or even a break-even market and the bond holders decided that they could do better in equities than in property bonds, the manager would be put to great difficulties in raising the necessary money without depressing property values. The claim by managing companies that property bonds are much less vulnerable to ups and downs in value than equities or unit trusts of equities can certainly be justified over the last fifteen years but it could result in a demand for repayment of bonds when equity shares look attractive and any excessive demand for repayment could be embarrassing.

Unlike unit trusts, property bonds are not regulated by the Board of Trade. This is odd because they are in essence unit trusts, the one of Stock Exchange equities and the other of properties. This means there is virtually no control over them. No supervision of advertisements. No rules for the valuation of properties. No insistence on a trust corporation as trustee for the property bondholders. No Board of Trade approval of the trust deed creating property trusts. No control of the fees chargeable. The field is consequently wide open for exploitation. However, in stressing this I am not pointing a finger at any particular trust, merely pointing out the dangers, and these include inter-group transactions and valuers who are not independent.

In my view property bonds must be brought under the wing of the Board of Trade and be subject to similar controls as for unit trusts or special legislation must be invoked to control them.

There is no association of property trusts equivalent to the Association of Unit Trusts and although not every unit trust is a member of the Association of Unit Trusts it does lay down standards of conduct for its members and does all it can to keep the movement pure. At the time of writing a number of property trusts are getting together and exploring the possibility of setting up an association. Such an association would no doubt scrutinize advertisements critically; watch the comments of newspapers and other publications, provide for a fuller disclosure of the nature of the fund's assets; insist upon independent valuations and the avoidance of property deals between the funds and the managers' associates; curb optimistic forecasts of rises in the value of properties, particularly those yet to be acquired; break down the growth estimates between income and capital values; and ensure that the method of calculating the bid and offer prices is disclosed. Also, perhaps, to agree a standard scale of fees, although on the face of it the scales at present charged, which do in fact vary from trust to trust, are not excessive.

I believe that an association will eventually emerge, but this will be a voluntary act. I still feel it is essential for these trusts to be controlled by a Government department, such as the Board of Trade. It is the small investor who is involved and he has to be protected. The institutional investor can look after himself.

Some large insurance companies issue Property Bonds including The Guardian Royal Exchange Group.

CHAPTER 20

Personal house purchase
The investment claims for property cannot be disputed. Any
owner/occupier of a house who has changed his house once or
more during the last twenty years will know at once how property
values have gone up and up. Indeed it is common knowledge that
since the commencement of the Second World War in 1939 a
semi-detached house with garage has appreciated some six to
eight times in value – expressed as a percentage up by 600 to 800
per cent.

The majority of individuals are now convinced of the wisdom
of buying rather than renting a house for occupation, and building
societies and others, including the insurance companies, are very
ready, and on reasonable terms, to assist the individual to become
the owner of his own house. And in these days of inflation it is a
push over – you raise cash by way of a mortgage and you buy an
asset which appreciates in real terms with inflation. There have
been many short periods in history when it has been better to
have cash than a house – when a forced sale would have resulted
in the seller getting substantially less than what he paid for the
house. But the majority of owner/occupiers have been able to sit
through these periods and the upward swing of house prices has
eventually continued.

Over the last twenty years some owner/occupiers have deliberately rung the changes to very good effect. Others who have had
to move more than once for business reasons have, without
conscious effort, found themselves doing equally well. Let us take
four house changes. The first, a house bought (including expenses)
for £1,000 in 1950 with a mortgage of £800, the purchaser putting
up £200 himself, which he had some difficulty in scraping together.
He sold the house five years later for £1,500 after expenses,
and he had paid £100 off his mortgage. He has thus after expenses
created £800 cash including the £200 he put up. He pays £1,750
after expenses for his next house and borrows 80 per cent, namely,
£1,400. He can easily put down £350 out of the £800 surplus he
has created, leaving £450. In five years he sells his house for £3,000
net, repayments of the mortgage amount to £200, so this time he
has a surplus of £1,800 plus the £450, a total of £2,250. He buys

148

his third house for £4,000 and again borrows 80 per cent, namely, £3,200 and puts down £800 leaving £1,450. This house he sells for £6,000 net – a surplus of £2,800. Allowing for loan repayments of £300 and the £1,450 he has in hand, he has a total of £4,550, out of which to put down 20 per cent, namely £1,500 to purchase his dream house which costs him £7,500 with expenses. He borrows 80 per cent – £6,000, so having put up £1,500 he has cash-in-hand of £3,050, his various salary increases and promotion rises take care of the annual repayments of interest and capital. He has created a total surplus of £3,050, and has invested £1,500 towards the cost of his £7,500 house.

This house in which he still lives has already appreciated to £10,000, and when he started he only had £200 to put down towards his £1,000 house. He has become convinced that investment in property works wonders and he asks himself whether he should not become a property investor by buying another house – one perhaps by the seaside and what is wrong, he thinks, with owning a number of houses.

Provided you keep to the modest rules laid down by the building society there is no difficulty in getting a mortgage on a house for your own occupation. But it is not so easy to get two mortgages unless you have a substantial income. As for more, you will certainly have to go elsewhere for finance.

Everybody, if it is at all possible, should buy a house for personal occupation and buy it through a mortgage.

Once you have a house you have more or less stabilized your rent in any inflationary economy while your earnings grow not only with your responsibilities but with inflation. The average wage has grown five times since the Second World War and the owner/occupiers' rent has remained static. Ignoring the effect of the Rent Restrictions Acts, rents have certainly risen at least as steeply as anything else. Whereas at times before the Second World War and during it, owning a house was a liability – almost an unrealizable asset – since the Second World War it has become a man's supreme asset.

As regards a mortgage, I have always advocated buying a house through a mortgage even when the purchaser has the money in hand to buy it. Obviously if he has the surplus money some can be invested in equities. I do not recommend buying a second house for investment. A house as an investment can be quite troublesome – repairs can cost a lot of money – the tenant can be awkward and he is unlikely to take the same care of it as he would if it was his own. Property investment, although generally extremely profitable, may not be for a single tenanted house. To secure the law of averages – i.e., the average tenant – the average repair cost – the average crop of troubles, you need half a dozen houses. Houses with tenants in war-time are the very devil – of course we will not get another war, not even a hotted up conventional one. But during the Second World War, and for some time after it, rents were restricted by law – repair bills rocketed – some areas were evacuated – others were bombed. I know of one property-owner who gave all his working class houses to the tenants. He was paying in repair bills and maintenance costs much more than the rents – and there was at the time no sign of the end of rent restriction.

But let us return to mortgages and ask the question what sort of mortgage. The source could be a building society, a local authority, an insurance company or some private arrangement such as a company staff purchasing scheme.

The most popular, principally because they have the most money to lend, is the building society mortgage. It is the building society's function to gather in money from their depositors and shareholders and to lend it for house purchase.

What about the method of repayment? The most popular if you count numbers is by fixed annual instalments of loan and interest, although the method of repayment will be by monthly instalments which, of course, increases the stipulated rate of interest. Eight per cent per annum by monthly instalments becomes 8·3 per cent per annum. One of the disadvantages of this method is that in the earlier years the interest proportion is high and the repayment of loan proportion low with the capital proportion rising during the term until at the end of the period it will be almost exclusively loan repayment.

The interest on a personal house purchase loan is a deduction in assessing the purchaser's income tax. If he pays enough income tax at the standard rate, the cost is the interest less an adjustment for earned income relief, that is if he has no unearned income against which to offset the loan interest. Adjusting for earned income relief at two-ninths and tax at 38·75p he saves 30·14p in the £ on every £ of interest he pays. If he is a surtax payer he saves surtax on the gross interest as well. However, some borrowers may not be subject to income tax – their allowances being sufficient to wipe out any liability to tax. There is a special facility to meet such cases which was introduced in 1968. It is known as option mortgage scheme. A mortgagor (the house purchaser who takes out a mortgage as distinct from the lender termed the mortgagee) instead of paying the current rate for mortgages, let us call it 8 per cent, and getting tax relief on the interest can by arrangement with the lenders pay at the reduced interest rate of 6 per cent and get no tax relief on the interest. He must however, elect for one method for the whole period of a mortgage but, of course, he may be selling out in five years to move to a house which demonstrates his one-upmanship to the world. So the election is not a too onerous one.

Our typical borrower may, however, be on a salary scale and he knows that whereas now he pays no tax, it will not be many years before he will pay at the full standard rate in which case he will not elect. Neither, of course, would a man paying tax at the full standard rate.

There is one problem which has to be faced by all borrowers. They really need life assurance to cover the loan. I regard this as essential, having in my capacity of a trustee manager seen the sad effect of a widow with young children inheriting a house saddled with a large mortgage. The cover required is not expensive as, in the case of a fixed-instalment plan, the outstanding amount of the loan is decreasing all the time and what is required is a decreasing temporary term assurance.

Whilst on the subject of life assurance I must point out that a loan can be repaid by an endowment assurance policy, either a non-profit endowment for a fixed amount, or a with-profit endowment policy when the sum assured increases year by year with added bonuses. I have appended a table showing how various methods of repayment work in money terms.

A purchaser of a house usually has to put up, certainly with a building society or an insurance company mortgage, 20 per cent of the purchase price. However, 90 per cent will be lent with an insurance guarantee for the extra 10 per cent. The cost of this is quite cheap, namely, a single premium of approximately·5 to·6 per cent of the mortgage valuation. There are some private employers staff schemes and local authority mortgages where the borrower will be lent 100 per cent of the purchase price. Some feel that 100 per cent mortgages should be the rule rather than the exception, but such a practice would lead to an enormous increase in the price of houses because there are not enough houses to meet this kind of demand.

Now for some general points:

(1) There are expenses to be incurred for house purchase. Surveyor's fees, solicitor's fees and incidentals including stamp duty. Excluding stamp duty these will cost 2 per cent of the purchase price. Stamp duty is on a sliding scale as follows: up to £5,500, nil; exceeding £5,500 but not exceeding £7,000, for every £50 or part of £50 in excess of £5,500, 25p per each £50; exceeding £7,000 for every £50 or part of £50 in excess of £7,000, 50p per £50. Stamp duty on the mortgage was abolished in August 1971, previously it was 10p per cent.

(2) There is an earnings test which decides the amount of the mortgage, which varies with lenders. Here are some examples of what building societies will lend: (a) not exceeding three times the borrower's annual gross income; or (b) his net weekly income to be at least as much as the monthly mortgage outgoings. Normally the wife's earnings are ignored although the earnings of a wife such as a nurse or school teacher and the like will be a favourable factor in assessing the amount of the mortgage.

(3) The term of a house purchase mortgage will usually be for fifteen to thirty years.

Now turn to the table which assumes the following; (a) a mortgage of £5,000; (b) a repayment period of twenty-five years; (c) interest at 8 per cent; (d) a man aged 31 next birthday; (e) six differing methods of repayment as set out; (f) borrower paying income tax at 38·75p in the £ on an amount sufficient to cover his mortgage interest; (g) a continuance of the present rates of life assurance premium relief and loan interest relief for tax purposes.

Commenting on the figures in the table separately:

(1) Is, of course, a straightforward building society mortgage without life cover, repayable by fixed instalments of principal and interest which would cost first year £348, last year £459, average over twenty-five years £388, with a total cost of £9,700. With fixed annual instalments of capital and interest the actual cost increases each year because the interest portion subject to tax relief gets less each year and the instalment of capital increases.

(2) Is a similar mortgage but with the reducing outstanding amount of the mortgage covered for life assurance in the event of death. First year cost £356·83, last year cost £467·83, average annual cost, £396·83. Total cost £9,921.

(3) Is similar to (2) plus in addition a payment under the life policy of £1,000 at the end of twenty-five years. First year cost £377·19, last year £488·19, average annual cost £417·19. Total cost £9,430.

You will note that this method is cheaper than method (1) Thus the life cover in effect costs nothing. The annual cost is, however, higher.

(4) This method includes a with-profits policy for £1,000 otherwise it is similar to (3). Total estimated cost £8,600. The cost is lower still but the annual payment of interest and life premium is higher. First year £393, last year £504, average annual cost £433.

(5) Here the mortgage is repayable by a twenty-five year non-profit endowment policy. Fixed total annual interest and life premium payment £394·13. Total cost £9,853. This is exciting in that the annual cost differs little from method (1) and is less than any other method quoted, involving life assurances, and life assurance for £5,000 continues throughout the twenty-five years.

(6) This is a with-profit endowment policy to repay a mortgage of £5,000. The annual cost is increased to £466·38 and on a modest bonus scale assumption (special bonuses declared in the past are omitted) the cost is reduced to £5,536, clearly the best proposition if you can afford the annual cost.

The comparative costs of the six methods is as follows: (1) £9,700, (2) £9,921, (3) £9,430, (4) £8,600, (5) £9,853, (6) £5,536.

As clearly stated, the figures quoted above are for a man 31 next birthday, namely, age 30, and for a mortgage period of twenty-five years. If the man was 40 and the term of the loan twenty years the figures would be respectively (1) £8,623, (2) £8,938, (3) £8,479, (4) £7,924, (5) £8,798, (6) £5,863. The cost is less mainly because the loan period is five years less and less interest is payable. In fact the gross interest for (1) to (4) amounts to £5,200 and for (5) and (6) £8,000, whereas with the twenty-five-year loan period gross interest is (1) to (4) £6,725 and for (5) and (6) £10,000.

To sum up and accepting the view that life assurance cover is essential and that cost must be kept down, the cheapest annual cost is (5), the non-profit endowment assurance, but the two with-profit policies (4) and (6), particularly the latter, give the best net cost position.

The figures will, of course, be different at different ages as life assurance premiums go up as ages go up, but the increase for the younger ages is small.

I have quoted premiums for males, the premiums for females are those for males aged four to five years younger. This is due to the fact that the mortality tables of the life offices show that women live on the average about four to five years longer than men. Incidentally, it is not quite so easy for women to get mortgages. If you are a woman and you require a mortgage do not give up after your first or even second disappointment, there are building societies which will meet your requirements.

Some twenty insurance companies transact house purchase business and of these the Sun Life, Norwich Union, Standard Life, Provident Life, Friends Provident and Century, and Scottish Provident are probably the most active.

Further, many building societies have arrangements with insurance companies so that a borrower may use an endowment policy to repay a loan, although building societies prefer the straight repayment method of principal and interest because this means that money is coming in all the time and the potential for lending so much greater.

Those lenders who accept a conventional with-profits endowment policy in repayment of a mortgage will not accept it at its assumed maturity value but rather at its sum assured.

The equity-linked endowment has not caught on to any extent as a method of repaying a loan. But its time will come. The annual cost will probably be greater than either of the conventional endowment policies, but the rewards could be greater.

•

Amount of loan: £5,000.   Male, aged 31 next birthday,   rate of interest: ... per cent per annum ...
Term of loan: Twenty-five years.

Method	Annual outlay net after deducting tax from interest £		Average annual net cost £	Total outlay £	Total net cost £
(1) Fixed instalments of capital and interest gross of £469 for term of mortgage (without life cover)	First year	348·00	388·00	9,700	9,700
	Last year	459·00			
(2) Fixed instalments of capital and interest gross of £469 for term of mortgage (with life cover for outstanding amount of mortgage only)	First year	356·83	396·83	9,921	9,921
	Last year	467·88			
(3) Fixed instalments of capital and interest gross of £469 for term of mortgage (with non-profits life policy for outstanding amount plus £1,000 payable at end of term of loan)	First year	377·19	417·19	10,430 / 1,000[1] / 9,430	9,430
	Last year	488·19			
(4) Fixed instalments of capital and interest gross of £469 for term of mortgage (as (3) but with a with-profits policy for outstanding amount plus £1,000 (and bonus) payable at end of term of loan)	First year	393·00	433·00	10,825 / 2,225[1] / 8,600	8,600
	Last year	504·00			
(5) Fixed loan – repayable by twenty-five year non-profit endowment assurance for £5,000		394·13 per annum throughout	394·13	9,853	9,853
(6) Fixed loan – repayable by twenty-five year with-profit endowment assurance for £5,000		466·38 per annum throughout	466·38	11,659 / 6,123[2] / 5,536	5,536

Total gross interest for twenty-five years for (1) to (4) is £6,725, and for (5) and (6) is £10,000.

[1] Deduct bonuses from policy.   [2] Deduct proceeds of policy.

Assumptions

Income tax relief on loan interest: 38·75 per cent in the £ on seven-ninths, i.e., after adjusting for loss of earned income relief.

"   "   premiums: 38·75   "   "   "   ",   two-fifths.

Bonuses at £3·25 per cent per annum compound throughout term. Special bonus has *not* been included.

Part VI

Overseas Investment

CHAPTER 21

Overseas investment

We have seen in the previous chapters that we can invest our money in cash deposits, in Stock Exchange securities, both fixed-interest and equities, in life assurance policies and annuities, and in land and buildings. There has been no mention of investment overseas. However, there are companies whose stocks and shares can be bought which have considerable interests overseas but care must be exercised in choosing the good companies, Unilever for one, Shell for another. You can acquire considerable interests overseas but you still have an investment which is a sterling investment and which is freely marketable in this country. You can secure a stake in overseas investment through investment trusts and some unit trusts.

In Part V, Land and Buildings, I have made no mention of investing in properties overseas. This is not that I would rule them out altogether. There are complications in investing overseas but this does not mean that overseas properties should be excluded by large funds. British companies which have assets overseas will almost certainly hold land and buildings in overseas countries. However, direct investment in overseas countries for individuals has its complications. It involves the purchase of currencies other than sterling and the investment in currencies other than sterling. It involves foreign laws with all their intricacies. It also involves proving death on the death of the owner and this can be a very expensive operation involving the appointment by the executors in England of administrators overseas. Further the non-resident investor is involved in the tax laws of that country and in the law being changed to the disadvantage of non-residents. However, what I am going to deal with in this chapter is just investment overseas by the purchase of stocks and shares, and I must once again stress that investing overseas does involve a currency risk. There are some countries in the world, particularly those in South America, where the currency is a very fragile thing and where devaluations are frequent. There are other currencies such as the dollar which are very stable, usually more stable than the £. There is the Deutschmark, the currency of defeated Germany, which because of its strength has twice been revalued as compared with Britain, one of the victors of the Second World War, whose currency has twice been devalued. Worth a thought? Whilst on the subject of devaluation there is a case for buying the currencies or the stocks and shares of a country which has either never been devalued or has been upvalued. The case could be even stronger for a British company such as an insurance company which has large assets overseas, particularly in the United States. There is a strong case for all large funds to have a hedge against inflation or the possible devaluation of sterling by investing overseas in a country with a strong currency.

Another reason for investing overseas is in selecting a country which has had a very good growth rate, say a growth rate superior to Britain. When one talks about growth rates one has got to have a time horizon and if we look at the past ten years, certainly France, Holland, Italy, Japan, Germany and the United States have had superior growth rates to Britain. Personally I have a prejudice against investing in Europe because of its history. Here I am most influenced by what happened immediately following the First and Second World Wars where countries disappeared or where there was revolution and where investments in those countries almost or entirely disappeared. Things are changing of course, and the Common Market has now established itself. Indeed Britain is likely to join. Nevertheless, the German, the French and the Italian stock-markets have been risky markets. Their shares have become over-priced and there have been bigger differences between the highs and lows than there have been in Britain. Japan has been another market where there has been enormous growth in share values and where prices have, at times, been pushed so high that they have boiled over with enormous falls. As an expert on the British market I am inclined to stick to the market I know. And if I were to start investing in Europe then I would want to be advised by experts, as I would for Japan also. However, I have an investment connection with Wall Street, although I would not claim to be an expert. I feel that no large fund should be without a stake in U.S. common stocks.

The investor who wants to invest in Europe without the worry of selecting investments should consider the following trusts: Société Nationale d'Investissement (France), Holland Fund (Holland), Concentra (Germany), Itac (Italy), Eurit (all Europe), and for Japan, Anglo Nippon. There is no withholding tax (see page 161) in all cases except Itac and Eurit, which are Swiss trusts where the withholding tax is 20 per cent, which is a disability.

As regards the United States there is every reason for investing in the common stocks of that wonderful country. Wonderful in the sense that it has all the primary products and metals. It has scope for further tremendous development. It is still a young country in numbers and wealth. It has the greatest potential for skills and inventiveness of any nation. Although the world has got smaller it is still a long way from Europe. Moreover, it is the greatest capitalist country in the world, a country where investing is not a dirty word and where dividend limitation has never been said in anger. Furthermore, through its Stock Exchange protection committee, companies requiring finance have to comply with severe regulations for the safety of investors. The Wall Street market, which includes the New York Stock Exchange, the American Stock Exchange, and what is termed over the counter bargains, is by far the biggest in the world. London firms and European firms of stockbrokers are tiny partnerships compared with their opposite numbers in the United States where a stockbroking firm will have as many as fifty branches spread all over the United States with a head office near Wall Street and with two branches in New York itself. At the head office there will be a top investment analyst for each section of the market who will be allowed to have his own clientele and will earn a salary equivalent to what the partners will draw from the business. Computerization is commonplace. The prices at which shares are dealt in Wall Street are immediately signalled to price boards all over the country. There is one in every branch of a stockbroking firm, in a room where clients can watch themselves getting richer or poorer. And do – I have seen some glum faces on occasions.

To invest in the United States a British investor has to buy dollars out of the investment dollar pool, which means paying the current premium for dollars, or to raise a dollar loan. The premium has been as high as 55, it is now running round about 25 per cent. That is not the whole story. On the sale of a dollar investment 25 per cent of the dollars have to be sold to the Bank of England at the official rate of exchange which means that 25 per cent of the dollar premium is lost on the whole transaction. Some investors immediately buy back the dollars but that involves paying the then current dollar premium. Some hold the view that the dollar premium is with us for good, others that it will disappear certainly if we enter the Common Market, but if it disappears the growth in American investments will soon take care of the loss.

Another objection is the withholding tax of 15 per cent (it could go up or down) which is deducted from dividends before payment. Gross funds, that is funds which are not subject to income tax, cannot claim back the withholding tax but the investor who pays tax gets it taken into account in assessing his tax liability.

In considering the yield on United States common stocks it is appropriate to look at the *Dow Jones Index* of thirty common stocks. This at 735·15, an index low over the last six years, gave a dividend yield of 4·31. The high of the index to date is 995·15 (February 9th, 1966). The comparative yield on the 425 shares of the *Standard and Poor's Index* is 3·50. Assuming a purchase of each *Index*, with a dollar premium of 25 per cent, these two yields become 3·45 and 2·80 respectively. And where the 15 per cent withholding tax cannot be recovered 2·93 and 2·38 respectively. These yields are calculated at six-year low indices, the yield norm is much lower. However, many investment managers, particularly those versed in the U.S. market, feel that it is right to pay a high price for the dynamic growth in the United States economy where the capitalist society thrives and workers are highly paid. The large fund can certainly afford to accept a lower return on the expectancy of greater growth. If it puts 10 or 15 per cent of its money in America it will have very little effect on the all-over yield of the fund.

It is possible for a fund to raise a dollar loan in New York and to buy American equities with it in which case no dollar premium arises and on a sale 25 per cent of the proceeds does not have to go into the dollar pool. The transaction is also outside the currency provisions. One has to be careful in putting this transaction through in that the security is to a large extent based upon the common stocks purchased and if there is a substantial fall in the market then the company might be forced to realize some at a loss in order to keep the loan within the agreed limits. Also current U.S. interest rates are high and capital growth must more than make the difference up if the transaction is to be viable. Which reminds me that the American market is subject to fairly heavy swings in prices; with waves of confidence it can sometimes be heavily over-bought in which case the price of shares reach what later turn out to be absurd levels, and with the swing of the pendulum the falls are equally drastic. However, a skilled operator can succeed in the sophisticated U.S. market by careful timing. This applies to most stock-markets, but particularly to Wall Street.

In any case there are always shares which are overvalued and the skilled investor times the sale of overvalued shares pretty accurately and buys the undervalued investment and gets his timing reasonably correct. British investors in the American market should buy U.S. stocks by means of American Depository Receipts (A.D.R.) as this method greatly facilitates transfer. For further information on this subject readers should apply to the London offices of the Morgan Guaranty Trust of New York or to the head office of any of the big banks.

There is an enormous public interest in investment in the United States. As I have mentioned, all American stockbrokers' offices have a room where clients can sit down and watch a reproduction of the tape of Wall Street share prices. This tape moves at the rate of 900 characters per minute. It is possible, indeed I have seen this happen, to give an order, have it completed and to see your order going along on the tape a minute or two later. The number of shares and the dealing price is shown. There are times, however, of extreme activity when the tape gets behind. As you watch your order ticking along on the tape on the Wall Street Stock Exchange it is being watched ticking along similar tapes by thousands all over the country. As I have mentioned, public interest is so great that at times the market is over-bought and this involves violent changes in prices from time to time. Timing of a share purchase or sale is always important; even more important in the United States. Indeed, there are times when one should keep out of the American market and times when one should buy, although on the long term it is right to buy American equities. When I originally wrote this chapter the *Dow Jones Index* was plummeting to below the 750 level, indeed, it was testing the 700 level. It reached a seven-year low of 631·16 on May 26th, 1970, only to recover to 950·82 in 1971. At page proof time the *Index* was 893·98. All this highlights the risks of equity investment. Four years ago investors were asking themselves whether the 1,000 level would be reached. In fact it reached 1,000 during dealings but only the opening and closing *Index* counts for the record.

Investment is certainly big business in the United States, and is backed by a vast army of analysts. Investment analysis goes far beyond anything produced in England. There are vast hoards of statistics. Chartism is avidly practised. However, I do not feel that American stockbrokers are any better at forecasting the future than their English cousins even though their research work is in much greater depth and even though analysts are welcomed by companies to roam freely through works and factories and to consult freely with the boards and staff as regards future prospects. American firms provide quarterly figures of profits and stockbrokers are able to estimate the next quarter's profits fairly accurately, but when it comes to a year or so their efforts often fall far short of reality and, if not falling short, they are not able to estimate what other causes will affect the course of the market. However, Wall Street is so scientific that one almost believes that in the United States investment has become a science. The American stockbroker is mechanized far beyond the dreams of the English stockbroker, although the English stockbroker is catching up. The American stockbroker will have on his desk an electronic machine about the size of a small adding machine. This on dialling and giving the appropriate code number will provide, for some four thousand stocks, yesterday's close, the last dealing price, the bid price, the asking price, the current yield, the total shares traded in on the day, the last four quarterly earnings, indicated yearly dividend rate, and the time of the last sale. The American stockbroker is backed by many first-class investment services. There is *Standard and Poor's* monthly stock guide, which is only one of its services. The guide gives the following information:

(1) A list of recommended stocks for potential price appreciation.

(2) A list of stocks recommended for safety and income.

(3) The daily indices for the month for its composite index comprising:
   (*a*) 425 industrials;
   (*b*) twenty rails and its industrial common stock index of 215 industrials;
   (*c*) fifty utilities.
   And the highs and lows for these indices for the last six years.

(4) The earnings trend of the one hundred most widely held companies.

(5) A list of some nine thousand common and preferred stocks in alphabetical order giving, *inter alia*
   (*a*) *Standard and Poor's* earnings and dividend ranking;
   (*b*) institutional holdings of the stocks;

(c) the stock characteristics, i.e., what the company manufactures or the services provided;

(d) highs and lows for current year, previous year, and over the previous thirty-year period. The latter almost leaves an English investment advisor breathless;

(e) sales of the stocks in previous month;

(f) dividend yield;

(g) details of dividends, latest pay date, amount to date, previous year;

(h) annual earnings over five years;

(i) details of the financial position of the company, etc.

(6) Changes in ranking of any stocks.

(7) Any new exchange listings and listings pending.

(8) A classification of the stocks listed under (5) by industry.

(9) *Standard and Poor's* stock rankings (they rank shares as the A.A. ranks hotels).

(10) The various commission rates for buying and selling stocks.

(11) Finally, a 1,000-word explanation of the stock guide.

Indeed, apart from *Standard and Poor*, I seem to have come across scores of specialist research firms in the United States, including a monthly chart service for over nine hundred stocks by Trendlines which renders enormous help to the advanced service provided by the large research departments of the American broker.

In the United States the theory and practice of charts is very advanced. Charts are one of the stockbrokers' normal tools. Similar charts are not possible for British shares as the London Stock Exchange does not disclose full trading figures in each share.

Some idea of the performance of the equity market is illustrated by the graph on Table I, see page 168. The long-term growth of the American market is fully illustrated. It almost forms a straight rising line from 1949 whether the lows or highs are taken. But many still remember the Wall Street crash of 1929, when in a matter of weeks the *Index* dropped from 381 to a low of 40. This was at a time when there was a world depression and economists now hold the view that they know enough about the economy to prevent a repetition of this. It was also before the setting up of the Securities Control Commission which keeps a close control on the market and acts as an efficient watchdog.

While writing the first draft of this chapter Wall Street was going through a time of trouble. Interest rates have been very high. The United States balance of payments have been adverse. The military commitments in Vietnam and Cambodia have been unpopular. As a consequence the *Dow Jones* had pierced one support base after another, to breach the 700 line, making a seven-year low of 684·79. Table II shows the traumatic fall in the *Index* from a near 1,000 high at the end of 1968. I have great faith in the economy of the United States and think that the market will recover. It was back at 893·98 when I was checking the proofs.

As I have mentioned, two main indices for equities in the United States are the *Dow Jones* and the *Standard and Poor*. The *Dow Jones Index* is world famous and it consists, like the *Financial Times Industrial Share Index*, of thirty common stocks. The *Dow Jones Index* also provides indices for home bonds, rails, and utilities. *Standard and Poor*, which should be the better index, has as we have seen, the common stock industrial index of 215 equities and the composite index which consists of 425 common stocks, 50 utilities, and 25 rails.

Mentioning utilities reminds me that, unlike the case in England, an ordinary investor can still buy the shares of electricity supply companies, gas companies, natural gas, water, railways, but legislation is beginning to make it difficult for utility companies to increase their prices. A few years back I would have started any new portfolio of American stocks with utilities because they gave fair yields and had reasonable growth. Today I would hesitate as there is at the present time a question mark as to whether the current yield on utilities is high enough to take into account the lower growth rate which can be expected over the next ten years. Somewhat influenced by the view of an American stockbroking friend, I still have a sneaking feeling that utilities in the United States, where the growth of population potential is enormous, will still prove to be very attractive investments and in the meantime the yield secured will be much higher than can be obtained on a batch of selected growth common stocks. Elsewhere in this book I give you some current yields for half a dozen British equities. I now do the same for half a dozen American equities. I sometimes call them equities rather than common stocks, so that the reader gets familiar with the terms. Here they are and I have included two utilities in the list. I give two yields, (*a*) the quoted yield, and (*b*), the yield after taking into account withholding tax and a dollar premium of 25 per cent.

	July 20th, 1971 Price	P/E	Dividend Yield (a)	(b)
General Electric	57	21	1·9	1·6
General Motors	78	26	3·4	2·9
Minnesota Mining	119	35	1·2	1·0
Standard Oil of New Jersey	78	13	3·6	3·0
American Electric Power	29	12	4·7	4·0
American Telephone and Telegraph ..	45	11	4·6	3·9

Yield (a) allows for a dollar premium of 25 per cent;
    (b) for both the dollar premium; and
the 15 per cent withholding tax on dividends.

For those who feel their funds are too small for a direct participation in America there are the British investment trusts, some of which have nearly 50 per cent of their funds in America. This aspect is dealt with under investment trusts. There are also American unit trusts, termed mutual funds, to name two, the Boston Fund and the Tri-Continental, which are actually closer to our own investment trusts in their operation. A number of our own unit trusts specialize in American investments.

In reading books about American investment one must bear in mind that terms used in the United States are somewhat different and are sometimes confusing to the Englishman. The American calls the 'Underground' the 'Subway' and he has some fine descriptive terms, family formation for natural growth in the population. A two for one split for him is a one for one bonus issue for us.

Each day in the *Financial Times* details are given of the *Dow Jones* averages (Indices), the industrial dividend yield, the issues traded in, the *Standard and Poor's* indices, the industrial dividend yield, price earnings ratio, also the yield on long-term Government bonds. There is a list too of the most active stocks traded in. As I wrote these words they were Chrysler, Control Data, C. & A. Financial, Texaco, Telex, American Airlines, Itex, Middle South Utilities, Unilever, Computing, and Teledyne. There were 335,100 shares traded in Chrysler, and the others in descending order, the lowest being Teledyne with 130,700 shares. Every day there is a list of share prices. It is a very limited list but includes 200 common stocks covering railroads, industrials, public utilities and banks. No yields are given. There are other overseas markets quoted but only to a limited extent. These are the various European markets, Germany, Amsterdam, Oslo, Paris, Brussels, Switzerland, Vienna,

Milan, Stockholm, Copenhagen. There are twenty shares quoted on the Tokyo Stock Exchange shown. There are quotations also for Canadian shares quoted on the Toronto and Montreal Stock Exchanges and shares quoted in Australia and Johannesburg.

There is a strong political element with South Africa but there are some fine companies operating there, particularly the mining companies. However, this market is vulnerable to bad political news and at the time of Sharpeville the market was very depressed.

Both the Canadian and the Australian share markets become overheated at times and when everybody is telling you you ought to have shares in Australia or Canada that is the time to be very careful. I remember the Canadian share market being run up to very dizzy heights some ten years or so ago.

The Canadian economy is tied very closely to that of their near neighbours the United States.

Apart from the United States I feel that my favourite country for investing outside Britain is Australia. This vast Continent must grow and grow, in the numbers of its population, in the exploitation of its natural wealth, in the development of its industries. There is no dollar premium to pay when investing in Australia. Australia is a most loyal friend of Britain. Providing the investor does not buy at the top of a boom he cannot go wrong if he invests in the larger industrial and mining companies of Australia. Here is a list of stocks which can be recommended, with their dividend yield and price earnings ratio. But the purchase must be nicely timed.

	Price	Dividend yield per cent	P.E. ratio
Mining			
Broken Hill Proprietary	635	1·8	35·5
Breweries			
Carlton & United Breweries ..	177	3·5	18·7
Transport			
Thomas Nationwide Transport ..	76	4·4	12·7
Banks			
Bank of New South Wales	312	3·0	—
Stores			
G. J. Coles	42	7·0	9·2
Myer Emporium	120	4·4	9·8

I reiterate that when dealing with the investments of overseas companies, it is essential to have the help of an expert in the field, a merchant bank, a specialist stockbroker, or a first-class stockbroker in the country concerned.

INVESTMENT FOR ALL

DOW JONES INDEX OF INDUSTRIAL COMMON STOCKS
1945 – 1965

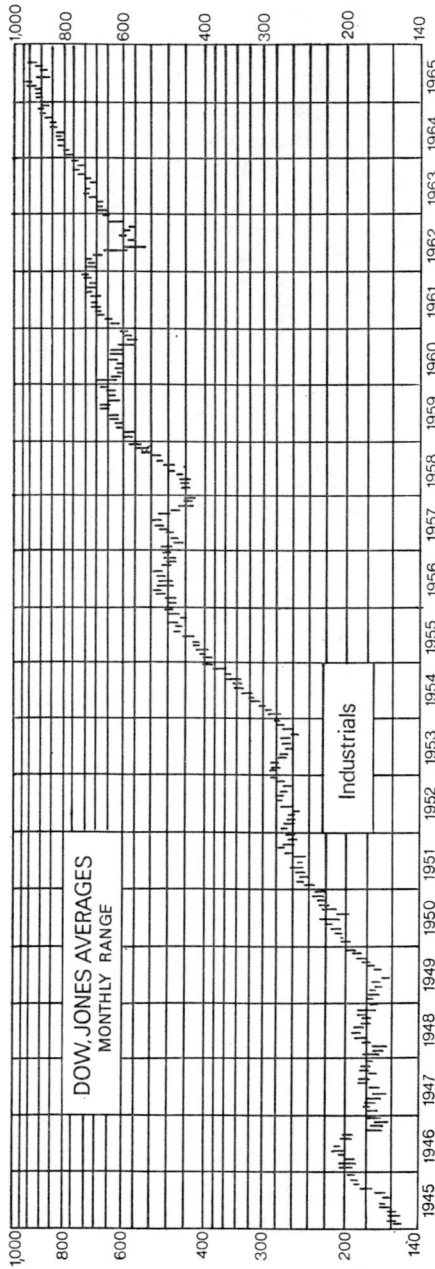

DOW JONES AVERAGES
MONTHLY RANGE

Industrials

TABLE I

DOW JONES INDEX OF INDUSTRIAL COMMON STOCKS
1965 – 1971 to date

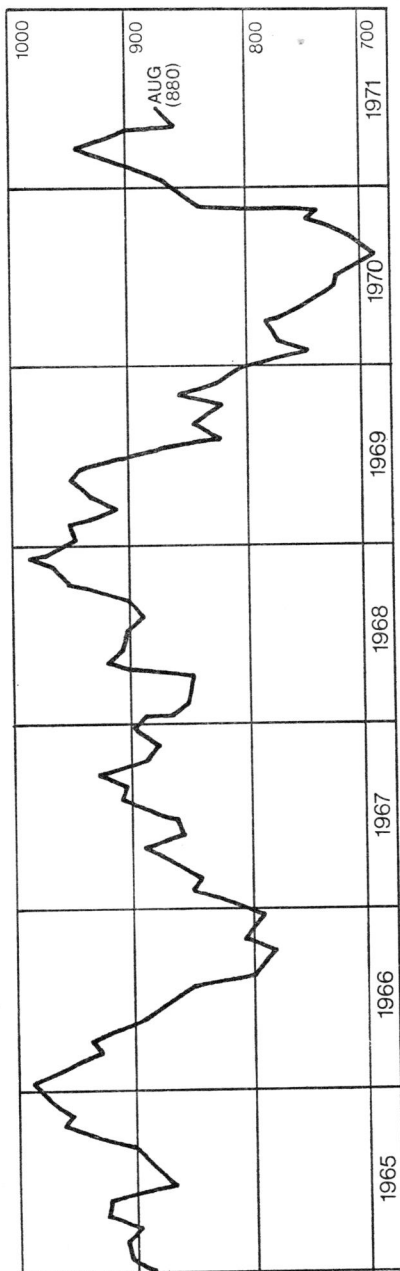

TABLE II

Part VII

General Investment Considerations

CHAPTER 22

The money game, investment factors for consideration
Buying investments can hardly be classed as a hobby, although it
can for some individuals become an obsession every bit as much
as collecting postage stamps, coins and the like. But taken to
excess it is far more dangerous. I know of some people who collect
share certificates and handle them as lovingly as rare postage
stamps or coins. Such a person has been hooked on the 'Money
game' and in no time he can become the modern Silas Marner.
He becomes a collector of money via growth equities and he
savours the periodic valuation of his growing portfolio with a
miserly relish.

The Money Game by Adam Smith, published by Michael
Joseph, is a satire full of investment truths and warnings amount-
ing to do not get hooked on the money game. I quote one example
of hooking which impressed me and reinforced my own experience
as a trustee manager responsible for many years for the administration of wills and trusts and the investment of trust funds:

'Once upon a time there was a very astute gentleman we will call Mr
Smith. Mr Smith was so astute that many, many years ago he invested in a
company called International Tabulator, which was a predecessor of IBM.
Mr Smith had great faith in the company, which in due course became
IBM, waxed fat, and prospered. Mr Smith and Mrs Smith had issue, and
the children grew up to be nice children. Mr Smith said to them, "Our
family owns IBM which is the greatest growth company in the world. I
invested $20,000 in IBM and that $20,000 has made me a millionaire. If
something happens to me, whatever you do, don't sell the IBM." Mr Smith
himself never sold a share of IBM. Its dividends were meagre, naturally,
and so Mr Smith had to work hard at his own business to provide for his
growing family. But he did create a marvellous estate. Eventually, he
became a grandfather, and he made gifts of the stock dividends* of IBM
to his grandchildren, and at family Thanksgivings, he counselled: "If
anything happens to me, whatever you do, don't sell IBM."

'Mr Smith died; the IBM was divided among his children. The estate
sold only enough IBM to pay the estate taxes. Otherwise the children – now
grown, with children of their own – followed their father's dictum, and never
sold a share of IBM. The IBM grew again, made up for what had been
amputated to pay estate taxes, and each of the children grew as rich as Mr
Smith had been because the IBM kept growing and growing. They had to
work quite hard at their own businesses, because their families were
growing and their only money was in IBM. Only one of them even borrowed
on his IBM, to get the down payment for a heavily mortgaged house. And

172

the faithful children were rewarded by seeing IBM multiply and grow. Mr Smith's original $20,000 has become millions and millions.

'The Smiths are now in their third generation of IBM ownership, and this generation is telling the next, "Whatever you do, don't sell IBM." And when someone dies, only enough IBM is sold to pay the estate taxes.

'In short, for three generations the Smiths have worked as hard as their friends who had no money at all, and *they have lived just as if they had no money at all*, even though the various branches of the Smith family all put together are very wealthy indeed. And the IBM is there, nursed and watered and fed, the Genii of the House, growing away in the early hours of the morning when everyone is asleep. IBM has been so good to them that even after divisions among children and rounds of estate taxes they are all millionaires or nearly so.

'Presumably the Smiths will go on working hard, paying off their mortgages, and watching their IBM grow with joy, always blossom, never fruit. It is a parable of pure capitalism, never jam today and a case of jam tomorrow; but as any of the Smiths will tell you, anyone who has ever sold IBM has regretted it.'

N.B. – A stock dividend is an American term for a bonus issue of shares.

Obviously there is every good reason for an individual building a nest egg against the uncertainties of the future or as a supplement to his pension and in this inflation rears an ugly head. Think for a moment. A man who retires from an executive position now would, because of the uplift in executive salaries owing to inflation, receive a pension of twice that of the man he succeeded who retired ten years earlier. The danger is that once a man starts on the road to building a nest egg, he can build himself a prison – he gets the portfolio building bug.

There are, of course, very sound reasons for investment and on the whole investment skills are directed to good ends. Speculation, particularly of the get-rich-quickly variety, when money is not really available for permanent investment or borrowed money is used, is bad and anti-social. It gives the Stock Exchange a bad name. Further you can be assured that if it is possible to make money quickly it is even easier to lose money quickly. Skilled speculators, to take profits, need some mugs to take the losses. Share prices are in my experience, moved more by mysterious and unpredictable factors than by known factors.

Investment skills are applied to improve the returns on pension funds, to reduce the premium rates on life assurance, to keep general insurance premiums as low as possible, and to aid charities in their good works. Even the Church of England parson has to thank the investment managers of the Church Commissioners that his stipend is not a lot lower.

Investment skills are, however, not confined to selecting good shares. They involve selecting the right stock or share or property, or other investment best suited to the individual or fund. This brings into consideration such factors as the time horizon – is it short- or long-term, and the latter can extend for ever. Another factor is the taxation position of the individual or fund, from no tax to 88·75 per cent going out as tax. And circumscribing all factors are the investment powers of the fund which can vary from statutory powers of investment, as set out in the Trustee Investments Act 1961 (see Chapter 26), to unlimited powers, with many a midway stage between.

Just as it is appropriate for the punishment to fit the crime, so an investment must as near as possible fit all the circumstances.

So in the following pages I will devote chapters to 'Time horizon', 'Taxation considerations', 'Investment powers', including the powers of the Trustee Investments Act 1961, and finally, the costs of buying and selling shares.

Time horizon, the period which investment activity is likely to cover, is discussed in the following chapter.

The taxation position of the investor is almost a paramount consideration and this is dealt with in Chapter 24, and is followed by Chapter 25 which shows the yields from various investments at various tax positions.

The powers of investment (see Chapters 26 and 27) available to the investor are of prime importance when the investor is acting for third parties. The individual himself can, of course, do what he likes – he may utterly regret it afterwards – with his own money.

In Chapter 28 I include what is relevant to purchases and sales of investments through the Stock Exchange, namely, what it costs to acquire investments.

The factors for consideration in dealing with investments vary with differing circumstances and with the funds involved. This is dealt with in Chapters 29 to 33. Some of the points made would already have been dealt with but it seems appropriate to me to stress them again in these chapters.

CHAPTER 23

Time horizon

With individuals it is obviously relevant whether the investor or the beneficiary of the fund is an infant, young, middle-aged, or old. With a pension fund the investment managers have to have regard to getting a high return on their funds to provide immediate pensions as cheaply as possible. This may involve buying high yielding fixed-interest securities or alternatively equities to ensure that the return on the fund will grow so as to keep pace with inflation; and what is more inflationary than basing future pensions on final salary or the average salary of the last, say, five years?

A general insurance company, in order to meet claims for fire, motor, marine and other risks will, to the extent that current premiums are inadequate for working capital, have to keep large funds in short-dated or readily realizable stocks. The life assurance company will have, on a time scale, to match its investments to its ascertainable money commitments, although again current premiums will be a great help in financing liabilities. The charity which has no time horizon because it is virtually a permanency and which, as is often the case, cannot spend capital without the consent of the Charity Commissioners is mainly interested in the right mix of fixed-interest stocks and equities to give maximum income. And do not forget it, a charity in carrying out its objects is as vulnerable to inflation, indeed more so, than an individual. It catches it both ways in overheads and in the rising cost of carrying out its benevolence.

The individual trustees and in particular the trust corporation who will be trustee for hundreds of trusts, will have to examine the time horizon and taxation position of every trust. Indeed, the facing sheet of trust particulars might well have notes on the time horizon, the ages of the life tenant (the person entitled to the income), and the ages of the reversioners, those entitled to the capital on the death of the life-tenant. There should also be some brief notes on the taxation position of the life-tenant, including a brief note of the extent of the life-tenant's other income. If the life-tenant is elderly then an appropriate part of the fund must be sufficiently liquid to provide roughly what are anticipated will be the death duties on the life-tenant's death. This can be a great worry. I recall one very large fund which was invested in first-class equities, subject to death duties of 80 per cent, where in the time between death and securing probate the equities fell below the amount required for estate duty. This is a special case, but it is most unsatisfying to have to realize funds for death duty and to know that the funds are worth a good deal less than their value at the date of death.

There was a time, and that was a mere few years ago, when the income of a child's trust which was accumulated was the child's income for tax purposes. From April 6th, 1969, it was taxed as part of the parent's income. Before the change it was obvious that an infant's trust fund should be invested to provide maximum income as the child was separately assessed for tax and was entitled to the usual tax allowances, but if after the change the parent paid surtax there was a lot to be said for a child's fund being invested in low-yielding growth equities. Now with the Finance Act 1971, and from April 6th, 1972, a child's income other than income received from his parent whilst under age 18, is his for tax purposes.

For an individual who is providing for his own retirement or setting up a fund to augment his own pension his time horizon will vary with his age, and his taxation position will come into his time horizon. Indeed, it is difficult to separate the two. Whilst his family is growing up he will probably need maximum income, then later with the growth of his income and his family responsibilities becoming less he will probably want to change his investments to low yielding growth equities keeping a certain amount liquid against the unexpected happening. On retirement then another change in investment policy becomes desirable for once again he needs maximum income. It might indeed be part of his investment plan to buy an annuity, in which case well before his retirement date he should provide for this by investing the necessary cash in short-dated low coupon Government stocks, so that he can realize investments without capital loss when the time to buy the annuity comes. Low coupon stocks have low current yields which suits the high taxpayer and are usually standing at a substantial discount and, if the stock has been held for a year, like all British Government stocks, no capital gains tax is payable on the difference between the price paid and the maturity value, which is usually par, namely, £100 per cent.

CHAPTER 24

Taxation
In earlier pages I have had at times to refer to how the incidence
of taxation affects investments and it seems appropriate to have a
chapter on taxation, even if it means repeating some of the factors.
I am, of course, only drawing attention to important factors and,
of course, I can only skim the taxation surface in a book on
investment. Most individuals of substance and all institutional
investors will have their own professional accountants to advise
them.

We have seen that some funds, pension funds and charities,
pay no tax, not even capital gains tax. As regards pension funds,
some schemes give members the right to commute up to one-
quarter of their pension for cash. This is a very useful option
because the cash will buy an annuity which, with the non-taxable
capital proportion, will give a substantially higher spendable
income than the pension given up. Pension schemes which include
this option have to pay tax on the proportion of the fund which
can be commuted. If it is a quarter, then the fund pays one-
quarter of the standard rate of income tax and one-quarter of
capital gains tax on the profits less losses of the whole fund.
Alternatively, the pension scheme trustees can set up two funds,
the three-quarters non-taxable and the one-quarter fully taxable.
However, in arriving at the tax, expenses of management and
pensions paid can be allowed for (see page 182).

The general insurance companies pay corporation tax on the
interest from their invested funds and other income plus or minus
profits or losses on underwriting their fire, motor, marine, accident and other insurance business, less of course, the expenses of
running the company. Profits and losses on investments are taken
into account in assessing profits subject to tax. The general
insurance companies' holdings of British equities and preference
shares are of especial value because they are franked for corporation tax and can be offset against the companies' liability to
corporation tax. The income from funds representing overseas
insurance is treated as trade income and thus qualifies for double
taxation relief. This is, as I have stated earlier, a concession
extracted from the Government at the inception of corporation

tax which many commentators overlook. It is of considerable help to the insurance companies.

The taxation of life offices varies within the company itself. Income from funds in respect of fully approved pension schemes under section 208, Income and Corporation Taxes Act 1970 (formerly section 379 of the Income Tax Act 1952) is fully relieved from all tax by that section. Ordinary life assurance business is assessed on interest, less an allowance for expenses of management. Profits less losses on investments are taxable. The annuity fund is taxed on profits. Both the life and annuity fund are taxed at the concession rate of corporation tax of $37\frac{1}{2}$ per cent. This is equivalent to the concession rate of income tax of 37·5p in the £, while profits, after deducting losses on the sale or realization of investments, are taxed at not more than 30 per cent.

Industrial and commercial companies pay corporation tax on the profits, including net capital gains.

Where corporation tax is payable, investment income received which has borne corporation tax has, as in the case of insurance companies, a premium value. Such investments would be equities and preference shares but not the debentures or unsecured loan stocks of industrial companies and obviously not the fixed-interest stocks of British Government or other fixed-interest investments. The point is that the gross dividend received from an investment in preference shares or equities is not further taxed in the hands of the company paying corporation tax. It is franked, as it is described, for corporation tax. It has the added advantage, and this applies to all investment income which has had income tax deducted at source, that the tax can be used as a set-off against the income tax the company has to deduct in paying its own dividend. So in effect the gross dividend of an equity or preference share held by a company subject to corporation tax is truly gross, whereas an investment in a fixed-interest stock has to pay corporation tax rate, currently 40 per cent, so a 10 per cent unsecured loan stock is worth 6 per cent only.

As is often the case, an individual's circumstances are the most complicated of all. He may not be subject to tax, and the ceiling above which a man or woman pays tax varies with the tax allowances to which he is entitled. This is not a book on income tax but clearly the ceiling will vary due to tax allowances, as to whether the taxpayer is married, has children or dependent relatives or is elderly, as there is old age relief. Another important allowance is earned income relief which is now two-ninths on the first £4,005, and 15 per cent thereafter.

However, for practical purposes the taxation split between individual investors when considering their investment needs are (*a*) non-taxable, (*b*) taxed at standard rate, (*c*) surtax payers.

Clearly an investor not subject to income tax should not invest in a building society because all he gets is the current rate and no more. For the same reason savings certificates are not suitable. However, from the point of security and the ability to get his money out quickly both are excellent. Three and a half per cent War loan has, in one way, a great attraction for the investor not liable to tax. Interest is paid gross, but capitalwise it has proved a most dangerous investment. It was as high as 107 in 1950 and has since been well under 40. The non-taxpayer is, of course, entitled to reclaim from the Revenue any tax deducted at source on any stocks or shares held by him. Perhaps the best investment for someone not liable to tax is a short-dated local authority mortgage, but even then he needs some money on current account such as the Post Office. Provided he retains £50 on Post Office ordinary account which earns $2\frac{1}{2}$ per cent interest per annum – $3\frac{1}{2}$ per cent from January 1st, 1972, but see page 15 – plus, of course, many facilities, he can have the rest of his money on investment account with a current rate of $7\frac{1}{2}$ per cent – his deposits being repayable on one month's notice.

An investor liable to tax at the full standard rate has a straight-forward investment problem. Apart from free-of-tax investments, building society deposits, national savings certificates, and the SAYE scheme, which are excellent for him, all investment income suffers tax at the standard rate. Apart from life assurance schemes he has thus a clear choice between tax-free investments and fixed-interest stocks and equities, between the higher current yields on fixed-interest stocks and the lower but growing yields of equities.

The investor with a problem is, of course, the surtax payer, and by quoting the current rates the problem is immediately highlighted.

Earned income fares reasonably well for surtax. It effectively starts at £5,550 for a married man with two children, but un-fortunately for surtax the husband's and wife's income was aggregated until 1972–73, but thereafter husbands and wives can be separately assessed.

On income of	On the last	Rate in the £	Total surtax payable on	
£	£	p	£	£
2,001– 2,500	500	10·0	2,500	50·50
2,501– 3,000	500	12·5	3,500	112·50
3,001– 4,000	1,000	17·5	4,000	287·50
4,001– 5,000	1,000	22·5	5,000	512·50
5,001– 6,000	1,000	27·5	6,000	787·50
6,001– 8,000	2,000	32·5	8,000	1,437·50
8,001–10,000	2,000	37·5	10,000	2,187·50
10,001–12,000	2,000	42·5	12,000	3,037·50
12,001–15,000	3,000	47·5	15,000	4,462·50
15,001–upwards	—	50·0	—	—

With unearned income surtax starts at £2,501, which is the excess of unearned income above £2,500.

Apart from small incomes the following allowances are applicable:

(1) Child allowance – £155 each child, rising to £180 and £205.

(2) Housekeeper allowance – £75.

(3) Additional personal allowance – £100.

(4) Daughter's services relief – £40.

(5) Dependent relative relief – up to a maximum of £75 or £110 each relative.

(6) Personal allowance – single: £325; married: £465.

(7) Wife's earned income relief – seven-ninths, limited to £325.

Obviously the man who pays 38·75p income tax and 50p surtax – the rates may come down, but for him they will always be penal – has a big investment problem. Building society interest has to be grossed up at the standard rate of tax – with 38·75p in the £. £5 per cent becomes £8·16 gross and is subject to surtax. Even the first £21 of Post Office and Trustee Savings Bank interest which is free of income tax has to be grossed up at standard rate for surtax purposes. This I confess I did not know until a reader of one of my 'Observer' articles pointed it out. He knew, for he had suffered himself. Surtax is payable on £34·29 (namely, £21 grossed up at 38·75p). I can see the argument but it is logic gone mad in my view.

The surtax payer is also hemmed in by capital gains tax, although long-term capital gains tax on investments held for more than a year is for him a mere 30 per cent. A safe haven is British Government securities on which you only pay capital gains tax if sold within twelve months of purchase.

However, a stock like 3 per cent Savings Bonds 1965–75 at a current price of 89, with a running yield of 3·38 is attractive to a surtax payer as the stock will be repaid at £100 on August 1975 and the appreciation of 11 is not subject to tax or capital gains tax. Clearly a surtax payer, particularly if subject to penal rates, should invest in low coupon British Government stocks, first-class properties, or low yielding growth equities. But he should always have his quota (and his wife's and children's also) of free of all taxes national savings certificates and, if he can bear the trouble, the maximum in SAYE, see page 17.

Annual premium bonds running for ten years or more, which are dealt with on page 127, are particularly attractive to surtax payers.

CHAPTER 25

Comparative yields after various taxation rates

We have already seen that the purchase of an investment on the London Stock Exchange will certainly involve a payment of commission and is likely to involve the payment of stamp duty. Further, there are two prices, the higher the purchase price and the lower the selling price. But the yield shown on the back pages of the *Financial Times* can only be used as a guide as it does not take into account commission or stamp duty and the price taken is the middle market price, the mean between buying and selling prices.

We have also seen that the difference between the buying and selling price varies from stock to stock and that the commission is higher for some investments. But these differences pale to insignificance when one considers the differences which are involved in true yields due to the varying taxation positions of the fund or the investor. To recapitulate – the charity for example pays no tax. The pension fund where there is no right to commute part of the pension for cash pays no tax. At present the pension fund which permits pensioners to commute up to one-quarter of their pensions, which is the maximum permitted, will pay tax at one-quarter of the various rates – one-quarter of income tax, one-quarter of capital gains tax. But pension schemes are in a transitional phase and by 1980 all approved funds will be exempt from tax and members will have commutation rights up to $1\frac{1}{2}$ times final salary. Life assurance companies are taxed in a special way (see page 178) and end up by paying less than other industrial companies.

All industrial companies, including general insurance companies, pay corporation tax, for which the current rate is 40 per cent.

Turning to individuals, some will not pay tax, others will pay tax at the standard rate, and some in addition will pay surtax, and surtax at the top level is 50p in the £. So for an individual we can have a span of no tax up to tax at 88·75p in the £ on the top slice of the investor's income.

Apart from all these complications there is the complication of franked income (see page 178) whereby a company does not pay corporation tax on income which has already suffered corporation tax. Further any income tax deducted from its investments can be set-off against the income tax it has to pay over to the Revenue in paying its own dividend.

Then there is the further problem that some interest is received free of tax, SAYE, national savings certificates, while building society interest, for example, is free of income tax but not free of surtax.

All these matters are dealt with in broad terms under taxation – see page 177.

Bearing all this in mind I have prepared the following table to show the percentage return after tax on various types of investment at various rates of income tax and surtax. I have included as a footnote a return to a company which is paying corporation tax at the full rate. This table highlights at once that someone who is not paying income tax should not put his money with a building society but should aim to get the highest possible rate of interest compatible with security. His choice might fall on a British Government stock which he can buy through the savings bank but he must remember this, that whereas his money with a building society cannot fall in money terms, if he invests in a British Government stock its value will vary with market conditions. He has, however, the alternative of putting his money with a local authority, but unfortunately the local authority will deduct income tax at source and the person not subject to tax will have to reclaim it back from his Inspector of Taxes. It is all very complicated and it is not surprising, therefore, that many investors do not buy the right stock to match their circumstances.

I have ignored capital gains tax, another complication, in my yield. The difference between cost price and sale proceeds or redemption value is subject to 30 per cent, except in the case of British Government stock held for more than one year.

Since I checked the galley proofs there have been changes in some of the rates quoted following the reduction in Bank-rate to 5 per cent. I have not altered my figures as the comparisons fully illustrate the point I am making.

TABLE I

RETURN ON £100 FOR VARIOUS TAX POSITIONS – INDIVIDUALS

Nature of deposit or investment	Return before tax	(i) No tax payable	(ii) After income tax at 38·75p	(iii) After surtax at 12·5p	(iv) After surtax at 50p
	£	£	£	£	£
1. Post Office and Trustee Savings Bank deposits:					
First £21 of deposit	3·50	3·50	3·50	2·8	0·64
Thereafter	3·50	3·50	2·14	1·71	0·39
2. Trustee Savings Bank investment account	7·50	7·50	4·59	3·66	0·84
3. National Savings Certificates	5·70	5·70	5·70	5·70	5·70
4. British savings bonds (7 per cent)*	7·88	7·88	4·83	3·84	0·89
5. Tax Reserve Certificates	3·50	3·50	3·50	3·50	3·50
6. Building societies					
Deposit account	8·16	8·16	5·00	3·98	0·92
Share account	8·57	8·57	5·25	4·18	0·96
7. Deposit with joint stock bank	4·00	4·00	2·45	1·19	0·45
8. Local authority					
365 days' deposit	7·10	7·10	4·35	3·46	0·80
Seven-year mortgage	8·50	8·50	5·21	4·14	0·96

TABLE II

RETURN ON £100 FOR VARIOUS TAX POSITIONS – INDIVIDUALS

Nature of deposit or investment	Price	Return before tax £	(i) No tax payable £	(ii) After income tax at 38·75p £	(iii) After surtax at 12·5p £	(iv) After surtax at 50p £
9. 3½ per cent War loan	39½	9·05	9·05	5·54	4·41	1·02
10. 3 per cent Savings, 1965–75	90⅛	5·83	5·83	4·56	4·16	2·95
11. 5½ per cent Funding, 1982–84	84¾	7·46	7·46	5·06	4·29	1·97
12. 6 per cent British Petroleum debenture, 1976–80	81¾	9·00	9·00	5·80	4·92	2·29
13. 8 per cent British Petroleum cumulative £1 preference shares, irredeemable	80xd	10·00	10·00	6·12	4·87	1·12
14. Shell 7 per cent second cumulative preference shares	72	9·72	9·72	5·95	4·74	1·09

N.B. – The yields on the dated stocks 10, 11 and 12 are redemption yields.

TABLE III

RETURN ON £100 FOR VARIOUS TAX POSITIONS – INDIVIDUALS

Nature of deposit or investment	Price	Return before tax	(i) No tax payable	(ii) After income tax at 38·75p	(iii) After surtax at 12·5p	(iv) After surtax at 50p
		£	£	£	£	£
15. Alliance Trust Ltd 25p stock units	207½	2·7	2·7	1·65	1·32	0·30
16. British Petroleum £1 stock units	617	3·5	3·5	2·14	1·71	0·39
17. British Motor 25p shares ..	38¾	2·5	2·5	1·53	1·22	0·28
18. Boots 25p shares	198	2·4	2·4	1·47	1·17	0·27
19. M. & G. General Trust units	11·4xd	3·79	3·79	2·32	1·85	0·43
20. Annuity – male aged 65 .. .. (Non-taxable capital proportion £7·05)	100	13·97	13·97	11·29	10·42	7·83

COMPANIES – subject to corporation tax at 40 per cent

	Price	Return before tax	Return after tax
21. Deposit with joint stock bank	—	4·00	1·47
22. 3½ per cent War loan	39½	8·95	3·30
23. Allied Breweries 7¼ per cent Debenture, 1988–93	77½	9·35	3·40
24. British Petroleum £1 stock units	623	3·4	1·25*
25. Tax Reserve Certificates	—	3·5	3·5

* But income is franked for corporation tax so the true return is 3·4 per cent.

CHAPTER 26

Investment powers

The law does not restrict the investment powers of an individual. The law may, however, stipulate that he cannot invest in a foreign currency or that he cannot send money out of the country but when it comes to investment in Britain the law, having set up all the necessary legislation which up to that date is felt suitable for the protection of the investor, permits him to invest how he likes. He thus can be beguiled by advertisements offering get-rich-quickly opportunities and he may have no personal protection experience to help him in his choice. If the individual is a conservatively minded man who does not like speculation he is pretty safe but if he is a man who loves a speculation and easily believes rosy stories then he is certainly at risk.

Although there is no protection for the individual as an individual, there is protection for an individual or an institution when acting in the capacity of trustees. The powers of investment, where a trust deed or a will sets up a trust, should be set out in the document. If it stipulates for statutory powers of investment or makes no reference to investment powers at all, the investment powers of the Trustee Investments Act 1961 apply. This is dealt with in the next chapter.

Prior to the passing of the Trustee Investments Act the statutory powers of trustees were governed by the Trustee Act 1925. In the expectation of giving trustees absolute protection this Act limited trustees' investment powers to British Government and local government securities and some prescribed fixed-interest securities, many of which have since disappeared owing to changes – nationalization, end of colonial status, etc. Things did not turn out in the manner the legislators expected because the value of gilt-edged stocks went down and down under the pressure of inflation and the value of equity stocks which were tabooed, despite periods of depression, went up and up. Things got so bad that pressure was brought on the Government and this led to the 1961 Act which enabled trust funds under certain conditions, including a once-and-for-all 50–50 division of the fund, dealt with in the next chapter, to invest up to 50 per cent of the fund in equities.

Any person, whether he be a trustee or in any way responsible for the investment of funds must, before he does anything at all, consult the document which created the trust or the rules and regulations governing the organization or the documents setting up the charity, the pension fund, the trade union or whatever, so as to ascertain what restrictions there are, if any, on the powers of investment. If the document is silent then, as we have seen, the investor is restricted to the investment powers of the Trustee Investments Act 1961. A trustee who purchases unauthorized investments becomes liable for any loss which occurs as a result and is not allowed to set-off the profit made on other unauthorized investments.

I have found some of the investment clauses very long and tortuous and even, although used to the kind of phraseology, very obscure. However, a trustee or someone responsible for the investment of the funds whatever the trust deed prescribes is entitled to at least the powers of the Trustee Investments Act 1961.

CHAPTER 27

Trustee Investments Act 1961

As stated earlier, if the document setting up a trust or charity or association or whatever makes no provision for investment, the powers of investment are limited to those laid down in the Trustee Investments Act 1961. Broadly, the trustees or those responsible for investment who are subject to the investment powers of the Act may put up to 50 per cent of a trust fund in equities and preference shares and 50 per cent or more in fixed-interest stocks other than preference shares. The Act defines the fixed-interest stocks authorized as the narrower-range investments and the equity and preference shares authorized as the wider-range investments; there are other conditions.

Although ten years after the passing of the Act it seems unlikely that there are many funds limited to statutory powers of investment (i.e., the powers of this Act) which have not yet been split in accordance with the terms of the Act, it must be made clear that before advantage can be taken of the investment powers of the Trustee Investments Act 1961 a valuation must be made of the fund and the fund then split into two halves, one called the narrower-range fund, and the other the wider-range fund. This is a once-and-for-all division and thereafter the two funds must be kept separate. Narrower-range investments (see page 190) can form part of either fund, but wider-range investments (see page 192) must be kept exclusively on the wider-range fund. Any temporary investment of the wider-range fund in narrower-range investments can be realized at any time and invested in equities. In fact on the wider-range fund there can be interplay between fixed-interest stocks and equities, but not on the narrower-range fund.

It will be appreciated that once the 50–50 split has been made it is extremely unlikely that a valuation of the fund will ever again produce a 50–50 division. In the long-term the expectancy is that the wider-range fund will be worth appreciably more than the narrower-range fund. I know of a number of funds where the ratio now is 75 per cent equities, 25 per cent fixed-interest stocks.

All additions to the fund must be divided between the two funds on a 50–50 basis, whatever the actual split on the valuation reveals.

The Act provides that every trustee of a fund to which the Act applies, other than a recognized investment expert, must seek the advice of an investment expert on all purchases and sales of investments except the purchase of defence bonds, national savings certificates and Ulster savings certificates, deposits in the Post Office Savings Bank, ordinary deposits in a Trustee Savings Bank. Even Post Office and Trustee Savings Bank investment accounts need expert sanction (see page 192, Part II).

An investment expert is defined in the Act as 'a person who is reasonably believed by the Trustees to be qualified by his ability and practical experience of financial matters'. The definition is an odd one. What, for example, constitutes reasonable belief? It will be years before beneficiaries become aware of the results of investment decisions and longer still before the claims of a particular investment expert are tested in the Court. I expect a crop of cases before we settle down to a realistic definition.

Further, the Act prescribes that an investment expert must be consulted:

(*a*) as to the need for the diversification of the investments of the fund in so far as it is appropriate to the circumstances;

(*b*) as to the suitability to the trust of the investments.

Further, so long as any investments made in exercise of the powers given by the Act are retained, the trustee must obtain advice on the lines of (*a*) and (*b*) above at such intervals as the investment advisor regards as appropriate.

Here now are the investments authorized by the Act:

NARROWER-RANGE INVESTMENTS

'PART I (not requiring advice)

'1. Defence bonds, national savings certificates, and Ulster savings certificates.

'2. Deposits in the Post Office Savings Bank, ordinary deposits in a Trustee Savings Bank and deposits in a bank or department thereof certified under subsection (3) of section 9 of the Finance Act 1956.

'PART II (requiring advice)

'1. Securities issued by Her Majesty's Government in the United Kingdom, the Government of Northern Ireland or the Government of the Isle of Man, not being securities falling within Part I of this Schedule and being fixed-interest securities registered in the United Kingdom or the Isle of Man, Treasury bills or tax reserve certificates.

'2. Securities the payment of interest on which is guaranteed by Her Majesty's Government in the United Kingdom or the Government of Northern Ireland.

'3. Fixed-interest securities issued in the United Kingdom by any public authority or nationalized industry or undertaking in the United Kingdom.

'4. Fixed-interest securities issued in the United Kingdom by the Government of any overseas territory within the Commonwealth or by any public or local authority within such a territory, being securities registered in the United Kingdom.

'References in this paragraph to an overseas territory or to the Government of such a territory shall be construed as if they occurred in the Overseas Service Act 1958.

'5. Fixed-interest securities issued in the United Kingdom by the International Bank for Reconstruction and Development, being securities registered in the United Kingdom.

'N.B. – Fixed-interest securities are defined in the Act as securities which under the terms of issue bear a fixed rate of interest.

'6. Debentures issued in the United Kingdom by a company incorporated in the United Kingdom, being debentures registered in the United Kingdom.

'7. Stock of the Bank of Ireland.

'8. Debentures issued by the Agricultural Mortgage Corporation Ltd or the Scottish Agricultural Securities Corporation Ltd.

'9. Loans to any authority to which this paragraph applies charged on all or any of the revenues of the authority or on a fund into which all or any of those revenues are payable, in any fixed-interest securities issued in the United Kingdom by any such authority for the purpose of borrowing money so charged, and in deposits with any such authority by way of temporary loan made on the giving of a receipt for the loan by the treasurer or other similar officer of the authority and on the giving of an undertaking by the authority that, if requested to charge the loan as aforesaid, it will either comply with the request or repay the loan.

'This paragraph applies to the following authorities:

(*a*) any local authority in the United Kingdom;

(*b*) any authority all the members of which are appointed or elected by one or more local authorities in the United Kingdom;

(*c*) any authority the majority of the members of which are appointed or elected by one or more local authorities in the United Kingdom, being an authority which by virtue of any enactment has power to issue a precept to a local authority in England and Wales, or a requisition to a local authority in Scotland, or to the expenses of which, by virtue of any enactment, a local authority in the United Kingdom is or can be required to contribute;

(*d*) the Receiver for the Metropolitan Police District or a combined police authority (within the meaning of the Police Act 1946);

(*e*) the Belfast City and District Water Commissioners.

'10. Debentures or guaranteed or preference stock of any incorporated company, being statutory water undertakers within the meaning of the Water Act 1945, or any corresponding enactment in force in Northern Ireland, and having during each of the ten years immediately preceding the calendar year in which the investment was made paid a dividend of not less than 5 per cent on its ordinary shares.

'11. Deposits by way of special investment in a Trustee Savings Bank or in a department (not being a department certified under subsection (3) of section 9 of the Finance Act 1956) of a bank or any other department of which is so certified.

'12. Deposits in a building society designated under section 1 of the House Purchase and Housing Act 1959.

'13. Mortgages of freehold property in England and Wales or Northern Ireland and of leasehold property in those countries of which the unexpired term at the time of investment is not less than sixty years, and in loans on heritable security in Scotland.

'14. Perpetual rent-charges charged on land in England and Wales or Northern Ireland and free-farm rents (not being rent-charges) issuing out of such land, and in feu-duties or ground annuals in Scotland.

WIDER-RANGE INVESTMENTS

'1. Any securities issued in the United Kingdom by a company incorporated in the United Kingdom, being securities registered in the United Kingdom which satisfy the conditions mentioned below.

'2. Shares in any building society designated under section 1 of the House Purchase and Housing Act 1959.

'3. Any units, or other shares of the investments subject to the trusts, of a unit trust scheme in the case of which there is in force at the time of investment an order of the Board of Trade under section 17 of the Prevention of Fraud (Investments) Act 1958, or of the Ministry of Commerce for Northern Ireland under section 16 of the Prevention of Fraud (Investments) Act (Northern Ireland) 1940.

'The powers of investment set out above can be extended by Order in Council (section 12).'

Further conditions. – The following further conditions must be noted:

(1) Investments must be quoted on a Stock Exchange in the United Kingdom or the Belfast Stock Exchange.
But see 'Part IV Supplemental', paragraph 2 of the Act.

(2) Repayment of an investment must be in sterling.

(3) As regards shares and debentures these must:
  (a) be fully paid-up within nine months of issue; and
  (b) have been issued by a company incorporated in the United Kingdom which has:
    (i) a total issued and paid-up capital of not less than £1 million;
    (ii) paid a dividend on all its shares in each of the five years prior to the calendar year in which the investment is made.

Generally

(1) Local authorities are permitted to pool funds for investment in the form of unit trusts.

(2) The Court still has jurisdiction on application to increase a trust's powers of investment beyond the powers granted by the new Act.

(3) The Act applies to trustees in England, Scotland, Wales and through Northern Ireland legislation to Northern Ireland.

It will be noted that the purchase of freehold or leasehold property is not authorized.

Both unsecured loan stocks and convertible debentures or unsecured loan stocks are narrower-range stocks, but if a convertible stock is converted into equities they cannot be retained on the narrower-range fund, the wider-range fund must buy them. This could be simple if fixed-interest stocks were held temporarily on the wider-range fund, otherwise other equities would have to be sold to pay for the 'converted' equities.

As mentioned earlier when an old fund has powers which are less than those of the Trustee Investments Act, the new powers are available to such a fund also.

The provisions of the Act, which for the first time give trustees restricted to statutory powers of investment the right to buy equities, are most complicated. The Act will prove in practice very difficult to administer, and a holy terror for the small investor and others. I would strongly advise trustees to examine from time to time the trust deed or document setting up the fund and if they have not the power to invest in any type of investment including overseas investments to get busy extending the trust's powers of investment. Those responsible must remind themselves all the time that breach of the powers of investment contained in the document setting up the fund or, failing prescribed investment powers, any breach of the powers of the Trustee Investments Act 1961 will rebound on their shoulders, as under English law, if the one responsible were, say, to buy twelve unauthorized investments, eleven of which showed handsome profits but the other one a loss he would be personally liable to make good the loss without taking into account a penny of the profit made on the other eleven.

It will be noted that the new statutory powers omit overseas investments which means that no direct devaluation hedge is possible where trustees are limited to statutory powers, but an indirect participation can be secured through investment trusts or unit trusts.

Trustees and others responsible for the investment of funds which are set up by documents which limit investment either by prescription or default to the investment powers of the Trustee Investments Act 1961 can apply to the Courts under the provisions of the Variation of Trusts Act 1958, for an extension of the statutory powers of investment; or, indeed, for their own powers to be extended if their own rules and powers preclude any simple procedure for extending their existing powers.

The Act gives power to the Treasury to increase the wider range proportion up to 75 per cent by order in Council.

CHAPTER 28

Purchases and sales costs
Jobber's turn
There is first of all a difference between the selling price and the buying price, the buying price always being higher than the selling price. The difference is often referred to as the jobber's turn. As I have pointed out, the differential in the case of British Government stock is very small; for very big deals it can be as low as one sixty-fourth. With corporation and county stocks, public boards and the big Commonwealth issues, the margin is also very keen but not as keen as the British Government market. The large issues of debentures and unsecured loan stocks of the major companies can also be dealt in on reasonable margins. The same applies to the ordinary shares of large companies where there is a big turnover of shares. I have, however, known there to be a difference of five points, eighty-five for sales, and ninety for purchases, for the debentures of a fairly unimportant company.

Stamp duty, which is at 1 per cent, has a bearing on the cost of the purchase of an investment. It was 2 per cent on August 1st, 1947, until August 1st, 1963, when it reverted to 1 per cent. British Government stocks are not subject to stamp duty, neither are certain corporation stocks, public board stocks and Commonwealth stocks. Indeed, it pays before buying a stock to make sure whether stamp duty is payable or not. Debentures are subject to stamp duty, also unsecured loan stock, convertible loan stocks, preference and ordinary shares (equities), in fact one might put it the other way that stamp duty of 1 per cent on the consideration money is payable on all purchases other than British Government stock and certain corporation and public board and Commonwealth stocks. Purchases of partly-paid stocks and shares normally liable to stamp duty are not subject to stamp duty whilst partly paid.

Commission
Here again British Government stocks are favoured and equities pay the top rate of $1\frac{1}{4}$ per cent. It would take up much too much space to set out all the Stock Exchange rules for commission, but the following rough figures will give you some idea:

COMMISSION

British Government stocks
Corporation stocks
Public boards
} with less than five years to final redemption } At discretion

British Government stocks
Corporation stocks
Public boards
} with five to ten years to final redemption

0·5 per cent on first £2,000 consideration
0·1 per cent on the next £2,000 consideration
0·05 per cent on the next £46,000 consideration
0·07 per cent up to £4 million consideration
0·035 per cent in excess of £4 million

British Government stocks
Corporation stocks
Public boards
} with more than ten years to final redemption

0·5 per cent on first £2,000 consideration
0·2 per cent on the next £12,000 consideration
0·1 per cent on the next £36,000 consideration
0·14 per cent up to £4 million consideration
0·07 per cent in excess of £4 million

Debentures and unsecured loan stocks

¾ per cent on consideration up to £5,000
⅜ per cent on consideration exceeding £5,000 up to £475,000
with a maximum of £93·75 for consideration of £25,000

Preference shares and ordinary shares

1¼ per cent on consideration up to £5,000
⅝ per cent on consideration exceeding £5,000 up to £75,000
with a maximum of £156·25 for consideration of £25,000

Note. – For debentures and unsecured loan stocks, reduced rates apply to consideration in excess of £475,000 and for preference and ordinary in excess of £75,000.

Part VIII

Varying Rules for Differing Circumstances and Funds

CHAPTER 29

Varying rules for differing circumstances and funds
In general and for individuals

You have not finished your education in the art and practice of investment when you have acquired a comprehensive knowledge of fixed-interest stocks and equities. How this knowledge is adapted to the circumstances and need of the investor or fund is in the end as important as being able to assess the merits of individual investments. The investment needs will, as we have seen, vary greatly according to the time horizon and taxation position. Investment powers may be limited. The effect of capital gains tax must be carefully considered.

Clearly the reader will realize as soon as I point it out that the investment requirements of the funds of individuals, personal trust funds, pension funds, charities, insurance companies, both general and life, investment trusts, unit trusts, building societies, not to give an exhaustive list, will vary in each case. It is my intention in this chapter to contrast the investment needs and requirements of some of these quite distinct investors.

Before an investment consultant can advise an individual he must have full information about him. His age, whether married, and if so his wife's age and the ages of all their children. Details must be furnished of all his assets and, if he or his wife are gainfully employed, information concerning their earnings. This kind of information establishes both the time horizon and taxation position.

My first rule for individuals and you must be familiar with it now, is that they should not buy equities or even medium, long-dated, or undated fixed-interest stocks until they have established a safe investment position which matches the needs of their dependants.

First there is everything to be said for buying a family home by mortgage; second there must be adequate life assurance; and thirdly a nest egg in ready money investments against the unexpected. After that an individual can buy risk investments such as medium, long-dated, or undated fixed-interest stocks or equities, choosing those which give him maximum income

198

or maximum capital growth, or a mixture of both. His choice will depend on whether he wants to maximize his income or whether, because of his high taxation rate, he wants low current income and as much capital growth as he can assuredly get with fixed-interest stocks. Such an investor could hardly do better than buy a British Government stock, paying a low interest rate because the stock will be valued much under par and on maturity it will provide a large capital profit, which in the case of British Government stocks will pay no tax after one year, whereas other fixed-interest stocks pay capital gains tax at 30 per cent. If the investor prefers the more uncertain but greater potential growth of equities, he will normally select an investment trust with a high United States content in its portfolio of investments or some of the well-known and established growth equities with plenty of cover for their dividends and with a record of persistent and substantial profit growth. The reason for the choice is obvious. Current income for an investor paying the maximum rate of surtax would be taxed at 88·75p in the £ (the total may be different by the time you read this but the principle will remain unchanged) whereas capital growth only pays capital gains tax at 30p in the £ when it is realized and then not on British Government stocks held for more than one year.

The investor with a substantial fund in excess of what is needed to provide for any known and unexpected contingency will obviously get together as diversified a portfolio of investments as suits his circumstances or he may just buy investment trusts and in this way leave the responsibility for changes in his investments to the skilled investment managers of the investment trusts. To put it another way, his own portfolio of investment trusts remains relatively static but the portfolios of the individual investment trusts will be changing all the time according to what their investment managers feel circumstances require. Such an investor, that is one who does not himself want to build up a diversified portfolio of individual shares or pay an investment consultant to do it for him, could buy the units of one of the unit trusts which sets out to provide the kind of portfolio which meets the needs of such an investor.

I have been writing about a married man, but the investment requirements of an unmarried man or woman differ only in that the married man or woman usually has greater family commitments.

With the individual investor the time horizon is of paramount importance. It is no good buying growth equities in a bear (falling) market of unpredictable length if you are elderly. For the investor who is gainfully employed retirement age is of investment significance. On retirement it might make sense to invest some of his funds in an annuity or to reorganize his investments so that they provide maximum income. Indeed, if the purchase of an annuity is a likely possibility, then well before the purchase date his investments, or some of them, should be got into short-term Government stocks which will well maintain their value. The danger is that his retirement date could coincide with one of those plunging equity bear markets.

The incidence of estate duty is something which must be seriously considered by an investor. If, for instance, he makes a will giving his wife a life interest, estate duty is payable on his death but not on his estate on his wife's death. An investor should certainly consider making some disposition of his estate bearing in mind the incidence of death duty. Since the Finance Act 1969, estate duty is levied, like surtax, on a sliding scale. The rates are as follows: Estates not exceeding £12,500 =nil.

Exceeding	But not over	Rate
£	£	Per cent
12,500	17,500	25
17,500	30,000	30
30,000	40,000	45
40,000	80,000	60
80,000	150,000	65
150,000	300,000	70
300,000	500,000	75
500,000	750,000	80
750,000	—	85

The all-over rate will not exceed 80 per cent.

It will be noted that any reduction in the value of an estate by giving part away or by setting up suitable trusts saves estate duty at the appropriate top rate.

With regards gifts to individuals or to trusts, other than charitable trusts, full relief of estate duty is not available until the expiry of seven years from the date of the gift, and no relief at all where death takes place within four years of the gift. There is a sliding scale of relief between four and seven years as follows:

Death in the fifth year 85 per cent of duty payable
```
   ,,      ,,     sixth   ,, 70    ,,    ,,    ,,    ,,
   ,,      ,,     seventh ,, 40    ,,    ,,    ,,    ,,
```

This waiting period was toughened up in a recent budget, the four years had been two years and the seven years, five. I would not be surprised if a subsequent Government changed back to the previous formula or something similar.

Gifts to charities are free from estate duty after the expiry of one year from the date of the gift.

This is a brief but essential reference to estate duty. But it is a subject in itself. I merely draw attention to the subject and its essentials – further advice must be sought from a solicitor or accountant or a trust corporation or an insurance broker if any action is contemplated.

CHAPTER 30

Trust funds for individuals

Taxation, time horizon, estate duty, capital gains tax will apply every bit as much to trust funds for individuals as to individuals. Much the same investment consideration will apply but with reservations. A trust fund can be primarily for an infant. A trust interposes a trustee between the settlor who made the trust and the beneficiary or beneficiaries of the trust. The trustee's ideas of investment may differ both from the settlor and the beneficiaries. Further, a trust fund more often than not makes investment two dimensional. There is the life-tenant who is entitled to receive the income for life and the reversioner who receives the capital on his death. Indeed, there can be a series of life-tenants provided the laws of perpetuities and accumulation are not broken which is that a trust can last for lives in being and twenty-one years thereafter, and such income cannot be accumulated for more than twenty-one years. A trust can continue for the life of a man's wife and after her death for their children for life with the capital passing to grandchildren. Discretionary trusts can provide a greater number of life interests. A discretionary trust is where beneficiaries are not named but discretion is given to the trustees to appoint a beneficiary or a number of beneficiaries out of a number of distinct classes named in the trust deed. A recent Finance Act has somewhat tightened the loopholes here.

It will be seen at once that there could be a conflict of interests between life-tenants and reversioners. The former might want maximum income even to the point of risking capital whereas the reversioner could be concerned only to acquire in due course maximum capital. In a nut-shell the life-tenant might like the 10 per cent plus which can be secured on a first-class unsecured loan stock and the reversioner the capital uplift which goes with, say, 3 per cent Transport stock 1978–88 at $53\frac{1}{4}$ which gives a current yield of about £5·63 but provides a certain tax-free capital profit of $46\frac{3}{4}$ by 1988. It is up to the trustee to hold the investment scales evenly between the life-tenants and reversioners.

From April 5th, 1969, the trust income of a child under 18 was aggregated with his parents' income and the parents bore the tax. From 1972–73, the income reverts back to the child for tax purposes. Once again most parents will want their child's trust to have the maximum income so that their child has the maximum benefit of his tax allowances. For the three years to 1972–73 parents were more concerned that the children's trust should be invested in low coupon (such as 3 per cent Savings bonds 1965–75) stocks with a tax-free run up to redemption or growth equities with low yields – another example of how taxation affects investment policy. (But see page 176.)

Clearly with trusts the circumstances which have to be considered will vary greatly. There will be trusts as we have indicated in favour of infant children, for young married children and for individuals of all ages. There will be trusts with a long period of life before them and trusts which are about to terminate or to take on a new aspect with the imminent death of a beneficiary – both cases involve death duty problems.

There will be trusts for a variety of classes of beneficiaries – for wife; for children; for grandchildren; for nephews and nieces; for mistresses; for charities and other good works; for alimony, for grandchildren to go to a public school, perhaps based on life policies; all posing distinct investment considerations and varying time horizons and taxation and other considerations.

With a trust too the powers of investment of a trustee have to be carefully borne in mind all the time. The powers of investment should be prescribed in the document which sets up the trust. If the document does not set out the investment powers of the trustee then the trustee's powers of investment are those set out in the Trustee Investments Act 1961, which is fully dealt with in Chapter 28. They are complicated and woe betide the trustee who does not keep to them.

Some of the powers laid down in trust deeds are long, tortuous and complicated – more so in that they are couched in an archaic language and include investments which have disappeared with our Colonial Empire.

Investing for trusts is probably more difficult than any other type of investment, what with restrictive powers of investment, differing beneficiaries, differing time horizons, conflicting interests, estate duty, etc. Apart from trusts invested by trust corporations as trustee and some golden exceptions, trust funds have probably been badly invested in past years and in some cases appallingly invested.

If any funds need expert management, trust funds do. Indeed

as will be seen from Chapter 28, the Trustee Investments Act 1961 prescribes that a trustee who is not an investment expert must secure regular investment advice from an expert as to the suitability of the investments and as to the diversification of the investments of the fund.

Some investment powers prescribed in trust deeds in effect give trustees the same full powers as if they were investing their own funds. These are clearly unlimited powers. But there is a lot of difference between investing your own money and investing trust funds. A trustee has a much greater measure of responsibility for he is acting for others and is answerable to others. If he is irresponsible or incompetent investing his own money and makes losses that is hard luck, but if he acts similarly with trust funds and incurs losses then he could have a law suit on his hands.

A trustee who is an investment expert, let us say a stockbroker or trust corporation, will have to be very careful because investment is not, as we have seen, a science and if losses are incurred which would not have been incurred if due care had been exercised such a trustee might be in trouble.

Some trusts are further complicated by the fact that there are up to four individual trustees all of whom have to agree on investment policy.

One of the big problems for trustees is how to split the fund between fixed-interest stocks and equities. The proportions should vary with market conditions and with the type of trust. The Trustee Investments Act limits in the beginning the equity proportion to 50 per cent, but see Chapter 27. Provision for estate duty is a difficult problem. To provide estate duty when an equity bear market is near the bottom could be an embarrassment, especially if it has taken a lot of time, perhaps twelve months, to assess the duty and in the meantime there has been a dramatic fall in share prices. In the case of a fund subject to estate duty it is sound investment to have a part of the fund in readily realizable securities. It is a problem because to get at the rate of duty on the trust fund the beneficiary's free assets and any other property passing on his death have to be aggregated together to get at the rate of duty and the appropriate rate applied to that amount of the trust fund passing on his death. The appropriate duty is then paid by the trustees out of the trust fund.

CHAPTER 31

Pension and superannuation funds

In contrast to the investments of the trust funds of individuals the investment of the pension fund is relatively simple. Most trust funds are static funds, new capital is seldom added to them. With pension funds they are growing all the time. New money, often at the rate of 10 per cent of the current fund, is coming in for investment annually.

Further, although technically a pension fund has a limited life, as it, like other trusts, is circumscribed in theory by the law against perpetuities, namely, lives in being and twenty-one years thereafter, in practice new trusts are made continuing the expiring ones. And to get as much length as possible some trusts define their horizons as – I quote one I have seen – 'the pension fund is to be wound up on the death of the last surviving issue of His Majesty King George V living on the date this trust deed was executed'. However, since the passing of the Perpetuities Act 1964, a trust can be made for eighty years although this type of formula could push the period up to one hundred years. To all intents and purposes, when investing a pension fund you are dealing with a permanent fund and certainly estate duty cannot be involved.

Neither is a properly constituted pension fund subject to income tax or capital gains tax. If, however, under the terms of the scheme a part of a pension allotment can be commuted for cash, the Revenue allows up to one-quarter to be converted in this way, that part of the fund which can be converted has to bear income tax at the standard rate and capital gains tax, but in assessing the tax, pensions and expenses of management will be taken into account.

With pension funds the major problem for the trustees is, with expert advice, to get right the proportions of the fund in fixed-interest stocks and equities including properties.

This affects the next important prerequisite of pension fund investment which is to get a high return on the fund's investments. Remember the fund is likely to pay little income tax, if any, so the higher the income the more there is to accumulate, the more there is to invest. The magic of compound interest works very effectively for pension funds.

I have mentioned that pension funds are almost perpetuities

so the trustees are going to have to invest through periods of high and low interest rates, through periods of equity bull markets and equity bear markets, through times of recession and times of boom, through times of inflation and times of deflation, although at the present time it hardly seems feasible that we shall ever get deflation again. I predict that we will nevertheless.

Clearly because of inflation and, whatever periods of deflation we get, we will certainly have inflation over the long term, a pension fund must not year after year invest exclusively in fixed-interest stocks just because they give the higher running yield or put a large amount of the fund in high coupon fixed-interest stocks standing at a substantial premium. Such a premium, in effect, converts capital into income. If such a policy were followed the fund would be most vulnerable to inflation and would also chalk up considerable depreciation of book values over market values when current interest rates were above the average rate at which the fund made its purchases of fixed-interest stocks. On the other hand if it consistently invested in equities including at the top of equity booms – I admit the fund would get the benefit of averaging – the return on the fund certainly currently might not meet the actuary's assumed rate of interest, on which all benefits under the fund are based. Incidentally, in my view it is essential for the trustees of all self-administered pension funds, as distinct from insured funds, to employ an actuary to ensure that the fund is viable and remains so, although unlike a life assurance company a pension fund does not have to pass a solvency test. However, the great investment advantage which pension funds have is in the regular supply of new money, because the new money can be invested in that section of the stock-market as is at present attractive. With skilled investment, fixed-interest stocks can be purchased when they appear cheap and equities when they appear attractive. The successful utilization of this advantage of new money will over the years serve the fund exceedingly well. Looking back only ten years there have been times when all new money could go into equities and other times when it seemed right to put the lot into fixed-interest stocks. Sometimes no particular signal seemed to favour either, in which case a 50–50 split between the two seems a satisfactory solution and this I know in my experience has been done.

As with other trusts the trustees' powers of investment should be set out in the documents setting up the pension fund and in the absence of any prescribed investment powers, the trustee will have to rely on our old friend the Trustee Investments Act 1961.

There are some very large pension funds with assets in excesss of £100 million. These and smaller funds should invest a proportion of their funds in property and overseas investments, in particular in Australia and the United States. Although a pension fund's commitments are in sterling there seems no reason not to have a devaluation hedge and in any case both Australia and the United States have had and are likely to have a greater growth rate than Britain.

Clearly what I have written elsewhere in this book on investments must be borne in mind in selecting investments, of fixed-interest stocks, equities and property of the mixed fund, in testing performance, and reviewing investments and generally.

Switching British Government securities is a useful source of income to pension funds. The differentials between differing issues do get out of line – the yield curve gets distorted – switches are thrown up. Pension funds, because of their size and their large holdings of British Government stock, can take full advantage of any such differences. They should not overlook the possibility of equity switches as some equities become over-valued and others under-valued.

In a book covering in simple terms the whole spectrum of investment there is no room to go into details but I have written a book entitled *The Principles of Pension Fund Investment* which is still selling and which those who want to delve further into the subject of pension fund investment will find, I am sure, of particular interest.

Those funds who desire to invest their own funds without outside help could consider the specialist unit trusts which the unit trust movement provides for the purpose, to name two, the M. and G. Pension Fund, and the Tyndall Exempt Fund.

The smaller local authority's superannuation funds have their own unit trust called Local Authorities Mutual Investment Trust known among its members as Lamit.

Pension fund investment is big business. I estimate current funds at approximately £7,500 million, excluding insured pension schemes and the growth rate is 8 to 10 per cent per annum.

CHAPTER 32

Charities

If pension funds are near perpetuities, charities *are* perpetuities.

The rules and conditions for securing charitable status are very strict but it is not appropriate here to go into the legal position, I will just stress that it is much harder to secure charitable status today than in the past and many charities which have existed for years would not today be granted charitable status.

The great advantage which follows charitable status is that a fully fledged charity is not subject to tax. But there are many charities which do not get this tax concession.

A charity is, of course, a trust and its functions are normally set out in the documents establishing it. Any change in the charitable objects has to be approved by the Charity Commissioners with whom all charities have to be registered.

The trust documents should give the investment powers of the charity. But many charities go back into obscurity. Indeed, some have ceased to have any purpose, the object of their beneficence having ceased many years ago. In such cases the Charity Commissioners set up new trusts under the *cy près* ruling, namely, objects as near as possible to the stated objects of the charity.

Where no investment powers are stated, and this applies to many hundreds of charities, the investment powers are those set out in the Trustee Investments Act 1961. Prior to that Act, the Trustee Act 1925, and previous Acts, virtually limited trustees to British Government securities, Colonial and Commonwealth countries and some British Railways debentures and preference shares. Any one of which, both from the angle of increasing interest rates and inflation has proved disastrous for charities. Consider the fact that British Government securities have at times been on running yields of $2\frac{1}{2}$ to $3\frac{1}{2}$ per cent for long periods – a $2\frac{1}{2}$ per cent stock £100 nominal would only be worth about £28 today compared with £100 at the time, and on top of that the purchasing power of the £28 would only be £14 compared with twenty years ago.

Most charities are static funds. In other words they get little in the way of new money. True they have their money-raising efforts but they are on the whole to meet revenue expenditure. Legacies unders wills are frequent additions to the resources of charities but once again these are often spent by the hard-up charity as income. So the old static invested fund limited to trustee securities has suffered greatly from the poor investment performance of fixed-interest stocks. Those trustees who bravely split up their funds into narrower- and wider-range securities under the terms of the Trustee Investments Act 1961, see page 189, have benefited greatly and the 50–50 of 1961 is now probably 25–75, the 75 being the wider-range equities fund. But it did need courage because on August 4th, 1961, when the Act became operative the yield on $2\frac{1}{2}$ per cent Consols was 6·85 per cent and on the *Financial Times Industrial Equity Index* 4·80 per cent. An immediate drop in income was inevitable. It was eased by buying some higher yield equities and some debentures on the narrower-range.

So in investing the fund of a charity we have to remember:

(1) that they are perpetual funds and thus vulnerable to inflation;

(2) they are not subject to income tax or capital gains tax;

(3) their powers of investment may be limited to those of the Trustee Investments Act 1961;

(4) they will need as much current income as possible because the office and organization expenses are going up all the time. Also in many cases the demands upon them are growing all the time too. A benevolent fund which helped an old-aged pensioner in 1950 with a cheque for £5 at Christmas would have to give £10 today to provide similar help;

(5) the funds, like all other trusts, are the responsibility of the trustees. These trustees will usually be busy laymen with little investment knowledge;

(6) their organization will often be very casual due to lack of adequate staff;

(7) but in most cases they will be performing most useful functions.

A skilled investor can work wonders with the funds of a charity. An active investment policy can provide capital profits and these profits are not subject to tax. To achieve the benefit of skilled investment the individuals responsible must have full powers to act promptly. Investment by a committee which at most will meet once a month and more likely half-yearly, or quarterly, will not give good investment results. Indeed, investment by committees rarely works. Experts tend to differ. Laymen will also differ because investment is a skill which most committee men seem to think they have. They can always quote something they have read that morning on the financial page of their newspaper.

A charity, like a pension fund, or indeed any trust or organization which has funds to invest, needs a one-man expert who makes decisions.

I would venture the statement that on the whole charitable funds are appallingly badly invested. There are, of course, some with vast funds which are outstandingly well invested. The Church Commissioners' income from Stock Exchange investments is about £12 million per annum which must indicate Stock Exchange funds of about £210 million. Income on property is over £8 million and total income £24 million.

Those charities subject to statutory powers of investment will have virtually two funds, the narrower-range fund restricted to fixed-interest stocks and the wider-range fund which can be invested in either wider-range investments, that is equities, or narrower-range investments (see Chapter 27). As I have pointed out, immediately the once-and-for-all split of the fund is made the two parts will differ in proportions at each valuation. If the past ten years is of any indication the time could well come when the narrower-range fund was 5 per cent of the fund and the wider-range fund 95 per cent.

But clearly the narrower-range fund *is* limited to fixed-interest stocks and all the investment manager can do is to invest the funds as skilfully as possible shortening the maturity dates in anticipation of a rise in yield and lengthening maturity dates when yields seem about to go down. And at other times getting a balanced fund of maturity dates so that the fund is not vulnerable to unexpected changes one way or the other.

With the wider-range fund there is more scope for skill. One charity, which I advise, for example, sold out all its equities on the wider-range fund at a considerable profit when the *Financial Times Industrial Share Index* was in the 500 area and invested in British Government stocks at yields of 9 per cent, only later to sell out into equities when the *Financial Times Industrial Share Index* had fallen to 360.

In making these changes it is important not to sell stocks or shares which are full of dividend or near their dividend dates or to buy stocks or shares which are just ex-dividend otherwise the trust's income is going to drop badly.

Not all British equities are available for investment under the terms of the Trustee Investments Act – see Chapter 27, and overseas investments and property investment are excluded.

For the large charity the switching of British Government securities as individual stocks depart from the normal yield curve can be very profitable and it is almost risk proof. Here I am thinking of stocks redeemable about the same time. Cheap and dear stocks will be indicated by their respective redemption yields. But there is a more or less fixed pattern of yields between all dated stocks including the longest dated stock and undated stock. Differences thrown up by changes in the yield curve draw attention to exchanges between short,- medium- and long-dated or even undated stocks. There are dangers with this type of switching because an unexpected rise or fall in Bank-rate could put the switch wrong.

The smaller trust cannot afford to employ experts to invest its funds but it might be lucky enough to secure an expert, who was sufficiently interested in the charity's objective to give his services freely.

If the charity is not so lucky the intelligent layman secretary of the fund limited to the powers of the Trustee Investments Act, could with the help of a stockbroker, have no special difficulty in investing the narrower-range fund but (see Chapter 27) he has anyway to be advised by an expert. The wider-range does, however, present difficulties because the equities must be diversified. This can be achieved by the purchase of investment trusts or unit trusts. There are a number of unit trusts who claim that their portfolios are particularly designed for charities. The Municipal and General Unit Trust has its Charifund. Ebor has its Charities and Pension Fund. Barclays Unicorn has its Trustee Fund. Unit trusts, of course, are authorized investments only for the wider-range fund.

Perhaps the best course of all for the trustees of a smallish charity is to put all their funds in C.O.I.F., Charities Official Investment Fund, because this fund is not limited in the percentage it may keep of equities. It can have 100 per cent in equities, if it likes.

C.O.I.F. can, of course, invest overseas as well.

By buying C.O.I.F. units the narrower-range investments can be converted partly into equities. A new fund limited to the Trustee Investments Act would have to have 50 per cent in fixed-interest stock. If it put all its money into C.O.I.F. the money would be split roughly as 20 per cent fixed-interest, 80 per cent equities, including properties, by market values which is the latest disclosed split of C.O.I.F. funds.

Indeed, it might not be too late for harassed trustees of old charitable funds to pass on their funds to C.O.I.F. for investment. There would need to be a full appraisal of the situation first.

The current yield on C.O.I.F. units is about 6 per cent.

CHAPTER 33

Unit trusts, investment trusts, insurance companies and others
With a general heading covering the varying rules for differing
circumstances and for funds, the omission of a reference to unit
trusts, investment trusts and insurance companies would call for
an explanation.

I have, however, dealt with these important fields of investment
in some detail in Chapters 12 to 14 inclusive, under the main
heading of 'Equities'. They are also referred to in other parts of
the book – under 'Taxation' for example.

What therefore appears in this chapter need only be brief.
What stands out at once is the marked difference between the
three. They illustrate the need for varying rules to meet differing
circumstances.

In essence a unit trust is a portfolio of investments held in trust
for a large group of investors. The portfolios, as we have seen,
may be many and various. They can be matched to meet the varying needs of investors but the investor can more or less choose the
type of portfolio which most seems to fit his circumstances. He
can choose it just as he might choose a hat. It must fit him. He
must like it. The managers try to suit him with the right kind of
portfolio but they are in business for profit and for the whole
thing to work what they get out of it must be worth their while;
and this against a ceiling of fees fixed by the Board of Trade.

My chapter on 'Investment trusts' is fairly comprehensive.
They are immediately distinguishable from unit trusts in that an
investment trust is a distinct company governed by the Companies
Acts. The unit holder's stake in a unit trust is easily identifiable –
it is his proportionate part of the portfolio of shares. The assets
of an investment trust are the exploitation, on conservative lines
of course, of money put up by the company's bankers, by its
fixed-interest stockholders, whether debentures, loan stock, or
preference shares, by its equity shareholders (who own the company) and all the surplus profits on investment and of surplus
income ploughed back into the company. All markedly different
from a unit trust, giving the director of the investment trust full
discretion to the end that the total assets of the company are most
advantageously employed. Re-read the chapters on investment

214 INVESTMENT FOR ALL

trusts and unit trusts and the variance in the investment circumstances of each becomes at once apparent and how. What could be more different than the fact that investment trusts are taxed as companies, whereas the dividend distribution comes to the unit holder like any other dividend, the only difference being that the unit trust dividend is a precise share in many dividends.

Insurance companies are also dealt with quite fully under 'Equities', Chapter 14. Clearly they are in a class by themselves, with the mode of taxation differing markedly between life and general insurance business. Insurance companies have large investment departments, indeed, investment income is their lifeblood and with the general insurance companies who have for years lost money in underwriting insurance business, investment income alone makes the companies viable. Success in the investment departments has in recent years been the only road for the maintenance or advancement of dividends to their shareholders.

With the life companies, the flow of premiums, including an annual substantial growth in premiums, makes for self-financing, so apart from investing short-term on stock-market considerations, long-term investment is the rule. With the general insurance companies it is almost the exception. Their losses cannot be calculated as with the life companies with mathematical accuracy with the aid of mortality tables. The general insurance companies, on the contrary, have to face unexpected losses and of unprecedented magnitude almost at the drop of a hat. Reference has been made to hurricane 'Betsy'. It would be a poor lookout for shareholders if when losses had to be met on a scale never experienced before in any previous insurance catastrophe, the bulk of the insurance companies' assets were in equities and long-dated British Government securities at a time when both were at low levels. It is indeed essential for the general insurance companies to have a fairly high proportion of their assets in investments which can be readily turned into cash without loss.

Building societies have their own investment problems too. They have to keep $7\frac{1}{2}$ per cent of their funds liquid, which means they are restricted to investments with lives of up to five years. Does not sound long does it? But there are times when it pays handsomely not to be invested longer than six months. Incidentally many building societies do quite well for their depositors and shareholders in switching their gilt-edged funds.

The thought I want to leave with the reader is that when it comes down to investing the funds of an individual, or a company or an association of any kind, or a charity, you name it, the rules will be different in almost every case.

Part IX

Investment Management

CHAPTER 34

The mixed fund of fixed-interest stocks and equities
The nature and various classes of fixed-interest stocks are described in Chapter 4 and in Part III equities are dealt with at
length. Equity investment includes, of course, property (see
Part V) and overseas equities (see Chapter 21).

What do we mean by a mixed fund? Why a mixed fund? And
in what proportions?

The reader by now should have got the message that fixed-
interest stocks are inflation prone and that equities can protect an
investor against inflation but are subject to the wide fluctuations
of bull and bear markets.

Further, he should have discovered that at present the current
yields on fixed interest stocks are decidedly greater than those on
equities.

The yields on the following selected indices clearly demonstrate
this:

	October 8th, 1971	Yields
2½ per cent Consols	29¼	8·55
Financial Times/Actuaries twenty-year Govern-		
ment stocks	86·13	7·46*
Financial Times/Actuaries twenty-year deben-		
tures and loans¹	78·61	9·34*
Financial Times Industrial Share Index ..	420·8	3·68
Financial Times/Actuaries 500 Share Index ..	186·3	3·55
Financial Times/Actuaries All-Share (621) Index	184·1	3·35

* Redemption yields.

It will be seen that the 2½ per cent Consols and the Government
indices give yields of around 4 to 5 per cent more than the two
Financial Times/Actuaries equity indices and debentures about
6 per cent more to redemption. These differences are, of course,
historic and vary with the attitude of investors to the two classes
of investment, fixed-interest stocks and equities.

This is a considerable difference even allowing for the fact that
due to increasing dividends the yield on the equities should go up
year by year. Indeed, I am informed that dividends on the average
would have to improve by 4½ per cent per annum in perpetuity
to match in mathematical terms the yield on the British Govern-

218

ment stocks and by 6¼ per cent per annum to match the yield on debentures.

This difference between the current yields of fixed-interest stocks and equities was not always so. Quite the contrary, for up to 1959 investors expected, in their investment psychology at the time to get a higher yield on equities by about 2 per cent to allow for the greater risk of investing in equities. This was termed the yield gap. In the second edition of another of my books *The Art and Practice of Investment* I wrote 'The yield difference between 2½ per cent Consols and the yield on the *Financial Times Industrial Share Index* (or the *Financial Times/Actuaries All-Share Index* which I prefer) is one of the indications as to the attractiveness of fixed-interest stocks or equities. When the yields draw together it could be a signal for buying equities and when 2½ per cent Consols give a yield of 2 per cent or more than the yield on the *Financial Times Industrial Share Index* it might be a signal for buying gilts.' That was 1967. Inflation has been so rife in the meantime, interest rates have been so high, devaluation of the £ has taken place, that now we have a difference of 5 to 6 per cent between the two. Surely a sign to buy fixed-interest stocks. But in these last years faith has almost completely been lost in British Government stocks. Indeed, on January 31st, 1969, the difference was 5·4 per cent. As I write this we have been getting good trade figures and there has been a modest recovery in British Government stocks. It may well go on. It is certainly overdue. But until inflation can be cured or controlled I feel we need about 4 per cent per annum more yield on fixed-interest stocks compared with equities whose profits and dividends grow with inflation.

Obviously if the present pattern of yields is to persist many investors will want to take advantage of the higher yields offered by fixed-interest stocks. Taxation as you will have seen, page 177, is a factor. The individual or fund not liable to tax should not neglect the advantage of the fruity jam today yields on fixed-interest stocks for the jam tomorrow yields on equities. Charities and pension funds will come in this category but these, because they are near perpetuities compared with the individual investor, are even more threatened by inflation than he is. Many charities have, as I have already stated, suffered in the past by having too much of their funds in gilts and fixed-interest stocks. But yields were much lower in those days and many could not invest in equities at all until the passing of the Trustee Investments Act 1961.

Fixed-interest stocks, as we have seen in the chapters dealing with these stocks, have the great advantage – well, in the large majority of cases – of having fixed dates for maturing, usually at 100 per cent, par as it is called, but occasionally at other percentages, 105 per cent is sometimes prescribed. With equities, although we can be sure their trend is ever upwards in value, they have their troughs as well as their peaks. Lines drawn joining their peaks and their troughs will clearly show upward trends, but if an investor has commitments at fixed times or at any unpredictable date in the future he will be unfortunate if a necessary part realization of his 100 per cent equity portfolio corresponds with a bear market in equities as instanced by the following indices figures:

	January 15th, 1969	July 28th, 1969
Financial Times Industrial Share Index ..	520·1	357·4
	January 31st, 1969	July 29th, 1969
Financial Times/Actuaries All-Share Index ..	180·97	129·58

All in six months.

You can take it from me bull markets end with a surprising abruptness and the end of a bear market cannot be predicted with any certainty. Seek the views on the course of the stock-market from any dozen investment managers, you will find no unanimity. And at times when they have been unanimous they have been wrong. You must accept the fact that there are no scientific means of forecasting accurately when a market is about to change violently one way or the other.

Because of this no investor can afford to neglect the fixed-interest market unless he has a substantial fixed-interest income from salary or pension and needs inflation protection from equity investment.

Charities must have adequate current income otherwise they would have to cease their good work or cut it back. Pension funds must have an adequate income otherwise the roll up of income would be inadequate to meet present and future pension commitments. It is no good pointing out that growth in capital through the growth in value of dynamic low yielding super growth equities will do the trick, for these are equally vulnerable to the slings and arrows of international and national trade cycles and the top growth shares also fall, often to a greater extent, in value with bear markets. Profits on the appreciation of equities have either to be realized or show substantial appreciation before the actuaries to pension funds become very interested. They know that unrealized capital appreciation can disappear.

I have known the equities of a large pension fund to be slightly under cost at one annual valuation date and to be £8 million in excess at the next valuation only to be £1½ million in excess at the following valuation date. The changes would be even worse by comparison if the whole fund had been invested in equities. However badly fixed-interest perform, it is equities which have their glorious high peaks and terrifying chasm depths.

All this points to charities (they must if they are subject to statutory powers of investment), and pension funds, insurance companies and other investors having a part of their fund in fixed-interest investments. For tax reasons unit trusts will not. Even with investment trusts the incidence of corporation tax and the need for franked income (see page 178) limits their participation in fixed-interest stocks.

Growing funds like insurance companies and pension funds can adjust the proportion of their funds in fixed-interest and equities by merely directing new money for investment one way or the other. Static funds can only do this by selling and a redeployment of the proceeds.

Obviously, if a fund had sold 20 per cent of its equities in January 1969 on the basis that equity prices were high, the proceeds could have been invested in fixed-interest stocks on very satisfactory terms. The yield on the *Financial Times/Actuaries All-Share Index* then was 3·16 per cent, and the *Financial Times/Actuaries British Government Index* then stood at 80·6 to yield 8·08 per cent. Since January 1969 the lows of both indices have been as follows:

Financial Times/Actuaries All-Share Index – 114·27 on May 25th, 1970, and it is now 184·13 to yield 3·35 per cent.

Financial Times/Actuaries British Government Index was 68·43 on June 15th, 1970, and it is now 86·13 to yield 7·46 per cent.

I stress that having with the right instinct sold equities into fixed-interest in January the investment manager who made this move would have been in a position to reverse it very satisfactorily on many occasions subsequently.

Now I hold the view strongly that with current yields on fixed-interest stocks of nearly 10 per cent and on equities of under 4 per cent this is the point of time when 50 per cent of a combined fund by market values should be invested in fixed-interest stocks. And, as I see the position, this state of affairs would have been arrived at by selling equities from about October 1969 onwards until the equity market really broke.

In other words the percentage of the fund in fixed-interest stocks and equities (which includes properties) should be a varying one, changing either by the disposition of new money or by selling out of one into the other.

Put another way, pension funds, for example, will have two yields. The one is yield on the money which has been transferred to the fund since its inception which truly evaluates what the fund is earning. Supposing a pension fund, say, twenty years ago, which is before the advent of the cult of the equity, invested the major part of its money in equities, the yield on the money transferred to the fund would now be an extremely attractive one. The other yield is, of course, the current yield on the market value of the fund. This immediately highlights whether the fund could be invested to produce a higher income.

Those funds which went into equities in the early days would have done well. With hindsight it was a clever course of action but at the time it seemed speculative. Today I would expect to get 6 per cent on setting up a new fund and, to get this yield on the indices I have quoted, 45 per cent of the fund would have to go into fixed-interest and 55 per cent into equities.

I would remind my reader that although the current yield on the fixed-interest portfolio is $8\frac{1}{2}$ per cent the yield to redemption is $9\frac{1}{2}$ per cent. So there is another 1 per cent there. The yield on the *Financial Times/Actuaries 621 Share Index* is only 3·35 per cent so the mere fact of investing in equities at these levels assumes that the dividends will grow at over 5 per cent per annum for certainly twenty years. This rough statement implies growth in the market price of equities to keep abreast of the dividend increases. It would take eight and a half years with dividends growing at the rate of 10 per cent per annum before the same amount of money was received on equities as on fixed interest stocks.

In the course of time I would vary the proportion between the two funds on market considerations and with maximum yield and capital appreciation in mind. All said and done it is the surplus income in the kitty that shouts loudest when pensions are under review. The market surplus on investments, unless it is realized, can disappear.

In my view, getting the month-by-month proportions right of a fund in fixed-interest stocks and equities respectively, is one of the major factors in successful investment. Certainly yields of 10 per cent current and redemption on fixed-interest stocks and about 4 per cent on a mixed bag of diversified equities do point to an extraordinary fund for these days of inflation, namely, 100 per cent in fixed interest. But no investment manager would have the pluck to go as far as that. He might never, in the case of a very large fund, get back his beloved and cherished equity portfolio. There are times when first-class equities are in very short supply.

Getting the proportions right cannot be achieved by any scientific method. How are we to know when one sector is cheap and the other dear? I recall that when gilt-edged yields went up to 5 per cent most investment managers and commentators felt gilts were outstandingly cheap. The high of gilt yields was in July 1969 when the Government issued 9 per cent Treasury 1994, the Government thus committing itself to pay 9 per cent for twenty-five years. It proceeded to fall to 92 giving a running yield of 9¾ per cent. Ten-year corporation stocks in the early part of 1970 were issued at 97½ with interest of 9¾ per cent, giving running yields of 10 per cent and redemption yields in excess, and unsecured loan stocks were issued at current yields of 10½ per cent. Perhaps now there has been some recovery in fixed-interest stocks we can, with conviction, cry out fixed-interest stocks are cheap, but at the time these issues were made interest rates in money terms were subject to searing inflation and were being talked up higher.

The sophisticated investor has yet to discover a trigger mechanism to tell him when to sell equities and buy fixed-interest stocks and vice versa. A number of stockbrokers have tried out some formulae but the imponderables are so many and so important that I feel it will continue to be a question of shrewd judgement as to what the proportions should be at any point of time and the shrewd investor can hope only to get his sums right more often than he gets them wrong.

CHAPTER 35

The need for expert management and how to achieve it

I expect that I have written enough to convince the reader that investing is no simple matter. It is not a complete and exact science which any individual with application can learn. There is some theory but political decisions, changes in fashion, indeed many things can make a mockery of theory.

I confess here and now that I have been directly concerned with investment for well over thirty years, and I am at present directly concerned in investing the funds of private individuals, trusts of many varieties, including pension schemes and charities. To make a point I have seen the effects of my investing, have known when it has been good and when not so good. And there is no investment manager, even the top of the professionals, who with hindsight could not have improved on his performance, for the scales of uncertainty are loaded against him. But a first-class investment manager knows of the limitations imposed on him, learns from his experience and does not make extravagant claims for his skills. Truly he knows that investment is an art and not a science.

It is a salutary experience reading through the circulars, some in very glossy covers, of stockbrokers, the hundreds of thousands of words of financial journalists, the erudite predictions of investment analysts, called security analysts in the United States. On the same morning I have received circulars from two stockbrokers, both studies in depth, both including learned predictions in the future, but one advocating a sale, the other a purchase.

Elsewhere (page 51/8) I have considered investment analyses and charts, and the general tools of the trade available to the investment manager. I welcome all efforts to record the past performance of companies and their shares and the greater the depth the better. I welcome too, all efforts to probe the future and assess future trends. But as I have stated under investment analysis the chances of predictions being correct are little different from evens. I quote Dr J. T. Ross Jackson:

> 'Many theories, facile and sophisticated have been put forward to aid predictions of the price of stocks and shares. They crumble when statistical analysis reveals that price variations conform very closely to something as simple as the flick of a coin.'

This is the climate in which the investment experts labour, pity the layman.

I feel that the layman is often misled, not deliberately, of course, by unit trust advertisements and the financial journalists into thinking that successful investment is simple. Of course, if you buy the right shares when they are low and sell them when they are high you will make money subject to the payment of capital gains tax on your profits. With hindsight you will see the highs and lows and know all too well what could have been.

Let us examine what has happened to a top equity share. The General Accident Fire and Life Assurance Corporation. Here are the highs and lows and the average of the highs and lows for 1961 onwards:

				High	Low	Average ten-year high and low
1961	..	..	..	214	124	
1962	..	..	..	281	171	
1963	..	..	..	193	159	High – 177·9
1964	..	..	..	173	116	Low – 118·5
1965	..	..	..	125	100	
1966	..	..	..	137	100	
1967	..	..	..	153	120	
1968	..	..	..	195	137	
1969	..	..	..	187	84	
1970	..	..	..	121	73¾	
1971 to date (3.10.71)	..			197	115	

As regards share tipping by financial journalists I will quote from one of my books, *The Principles of Pension Fund Investment*:

'It must be said at once that these are, as a group, able, honest and conscientious exponents of the art of investment. Very willing to learn, they have the entrée to the parlours of most chairmen, particularly if they take a photographer with them. Having extolled their abilities and their virtue it should be stated at once that whilst the investment journalist is experienced in the field of comment, seldom has he had practical experience in the more humdrum work of buying and selling investments. Unlike the investment manager, he almost certainly has never had to put his recommendations to the test or have had to stand up to the criticisms which inevitably follow if a buy or sell recommendation turns out to be ill-advised. In the case of a bad one the odd letter of reproach will go to the editor, but the mud soon settles. The mistakes of the investment manager leer at him each time he opens the portfolio and exposes himself to the barbs of the comments of his trustees and especially so when he decides to cut a loss. An investment manager naturally tries to avoid getting into such situations.

'Investment managers realize, however, that investment journalists have

226 INVESTMENT FOR ALL

a profound effect on the market in the short term. A tip to a million readers, and I have no qualms in associating the investment recommendations with the Turf, must have an effect on the price out of all proportion. I can imagine the jobbers sitting up in bed on a Sunday morning sipping their morning cups of tea with a stack of Sunday papers before them, reading the City columns one by one and jotting down the names of the shares tipped in the newspapers. It is usually a tip to buy and like the stockbrokers' very seldom a tip to sell. Is this because a tip to sell if it is wrong looks so very wrong, whereas a tip to buy can be equated in terms of hope deferred, wrong timing, temporary unfavourable market conditions, etc.?

'In my imagination, I can see Edmund Durlacher in a brilliant dressing-gown marking up a list of shares tipped in the Sunday papers in readiness for Monday's dealings. From this it will be seen that very rarely is one able to buy a share at the price given in the newspapers and the first orders which come in will tend to put up the price of this share further. I am assured that readers demand these tips just as they appear to demand football match forecasts to help them to complete their football coupons. Many of the tips will be worth consideration, others are supplied out of the sheer necessity of having to produce them. However, the best plan is to take a note of any recommendation which convinces and wait until the market has settled down. For the layman, the dangerous recommendation is a share which is infrequently dealt in and of which there is a short supply. Buying orders in even small quantities will soon drive up the price of the share to quite unrealistic levels and as soon as interest wanes the share price will drop back to its original level and the investor may be locked in, with an indifferent performer.

'Anything which appears in print in a newspaper or journal seems to carry with it something of the Delphic oracle. If the reader were to know how quickly some of the comment is assessed he would treat all news with much greater caution. I remember being in the office of a City editor at a time when some important trade figures were coming through on the Telex, and as these figures came through he was writing his piece for the next edition of his newspaper coming out in an hour or so, and as he composed each sentence he was arguing with his deputy as to whether this figure or that figure was good, bad or indifferent. His piece appeared in the newspaper. It may have been right, I believe the comment was, but no man is capable of being brilliant all the time or able to churn out accurate comment minute by minute as the news comes through.

'One reads from time to time that "the institutions are back in the market". Such a statement should be treated with caution. I recall that a pension fund in which I was interested had on a particular day following its periodic meeting put £750,000 in some fifty different equities. The date of the meeting was pure chance and the money went into equities simply on the operation of a formula plan which inevitably put the fund into equities when they were particularly depressed. I understand that our fund was practically the only big buyer of equities on that day but a newspaper reported nevertheless that the institutions were back in the market.'

However, more recently William Davis who wields a delightful pen, formerly City Editor to the *Sunday Express*, the *Evening*

Standard, and *The Guardian*, and now editor of *Punch*, has reflected on financial journalists in an article in *Punch*, dated November 19th, 1969:

'The ugly truth, dear reader, is that share tipping isn't nearly as easy as City editors make out. There is a considerable element of hit and miss about it, and even experts frequently get caught. . . .

'There are, of course, various ways of helping one's tip along. The most obvious is to pick a share in which there is a "thin" market. Newcomers offer a fairly wide range of choice. . . .

'Even a small amount of buying can, in these circumstances, produce quite a sharp rise.

'The snag with this kind of thing is that a lot of newcomers don't retain their popularity. . . .

'The share tipster rarely tells his readers when to sell. It's such an unpopular thing to do. Whenever I tried it, in the *Sunday Express* and *Evening Standard*, I was swamped with abusive letters. . . .

'Much the best way of establishing one's reputation as a tipster is to use what one might call the "grapeshot" method. You tip thirty shares at the start of the year, on the principle that there's safety in numbers. . . . At the end of the year, you simply mention the few which have done well. Well, mention is perhaps too mild a word. You shout – or better still, you get your paper to shout for you. In the tipping business, modesty is a deadly sin.'

Personally, I have a prejudice against City Page fictitious portfolios, where a financial journalist sets up a fund with, say, £20,000, and buys shares and sells them from time to time – in theory of course. Every portfolio seems to make good profits. I would be impressed if the newspaper owners gave the particular financial journalist a sum of money and he actually bought the shares. There is all the difference in the world between an actual purchase and a decision to buy. If the owners of a newspaper are not prepared to risk their own money – but only to encourage their readers to risk their money – then I feel that the whole operation should be examined by a qualified accountant and his certificate appended to the effect that what is claimed has been done, could in fact have been done and the claims stand up to investigation.

I have referred elsewhere to Lesney Products, I could list many sound fashionable shares which blazoned the investment scene but have not maintained their brilliance. It is disastrous for the small investor to buy these near their highs. Indeed some fashionable shares permanently lose their glamour and never in afteryears attain their highs of fashionable days. The small investor can certainly suffer terribly from paying too much for a first-class blue chip. Look at the five-year highs and lows of British Petroleum and Marley (Tile).

British Petroleum				High	Low
1967	..	..	..	355p	294p
1968	..	..	..	718	305
1969	..	..	..	800	500
1970	..	..	..	575	340
1971 (to date) ..	..	..		628	403
Marley (Tile)					
1967	..	..	..	115	86
1968	..	..	..	151	91
1969	..	..	..	127	56
1970 (to date) ..	..	..		73	37
1971 (to date) ..	..	..		134	37

Surely I have convinced the lay reader that he is at risk as an individual investor. He is up against the same slings and arrows of outrageous investment fortune as the expert but without the expert's experience and knowledge. There's scope for profit too.

How shall he then limit the risks of investing, because there are risks even with British Government securities – even with those so-called gilt-edged stocks? War loan was £109 in 1947 and was as low as 35 in 1970.

He should, as I have frequently stressed, limit in the first place his investing to cash deposits, Post Office and Trustee Savings Bank investment account deposits, building society deposits and the like, national savings certificates, and life assurance savings schemes plus adequate life assurance cover, at least he will get the magic of compound interest. Then, and only then, should he consider equity investment and only then in unit trusts or investment trusts. These are dealt with earlier on pages 97 and 85 respectively. I freely admit that the best investment result can be achieved in selecting the best share for long-term growth. The right choice can be very thrilling but it takes many years of highs and lows to prove that the one selected is right. You learn the answer retrospectively – by hindsight. But in looking for the most brilliant performer you might pay a lot too much for what with hindsight turns out to be a disastrous performer.

I repeat small investors should stick to unit trusts and investment trusts. Buy them when the equity market is in the dumps.

As regards the trustees of a trust fund, the trustees of a charity or of a pension fund, these should employ outside experts as investment managers unless the fund is in excess of £5 million, in which case it could set up its own investment department.

Where are these experts to be found? The merchant banks, and the joint stock banks and the insurance companies have investment and trustee departments. It would be among their managers and staff that a fund would recruit its staff in setting up an investment department. There are also many firms of investment consultants and the number is growing all the time but you must choose very carefully and make sure you get a satisfactory reference.

Investment managers and consultants sometimes require the investments which they are managing to be registered in their names so that speedy action on a sale can be taken – no difficulty in executing transfers, etc. This is all very well with a large merchant bank or a joint stock bank but there is a security risk with a small concern. The bosses may appear to be as safe as houses but there have been the odd black sheep in the past – also there is the risk of one of their staff members who has access to documents and the seal, going wrong; speculating himself or betting on horses.

Most of the smaller investment firms have insurance cover against defalcation but the premiums might go into default or the cover become inadequate. My advice when employing a small company is either to have all shares registered in your own name or in the name of a bank nominee and let your advisers deal direct with them. This will eliminate any security risks.

With my few clients, which because of my many activities I have to limit, the investments are either in the name of the client or his nominee. I make this a condition.

Some of the smaller firms offer splendid investment management and advice and good expert advice is in short supply. It certainly is likely to be if you accept my idealistic definition in another of my books, *Purposeful Investment*, published by Hutchinsons, where in answer to the question 'What do we ask of an investment expert?' I quote:

'Apart from his investment experience ideally he must be something of an actuary or an accountant, an economist, a stockbroker, a man of affairs with a facile pen for his ten thousand word reports. Above all he must have the ability to make up his mind quickly on the merits and demerits of an investment, then to act quickly.'

I am of the firm view that the investment function cannot be satisfactorily performed by a committee even if that committee

is composed of first-class business men because the skill we are
looking for is expertise in investment. One of the ironies of investment is that many people will talk as if they were skilled in investment, even if it is only to repeat what they have read in the
Financial Times. My advice for funds above £5 million is to
appoint an investment manager who can clearly claim to have the
necessary skill and leave the investment initiative to him. The
committee or the trustees can lay down policy and the investment
manager should, as routine, report regularly what he has done.
Another reason for leaving the investment decisions to the investment manager is that to secure the best result decisions must be
made promptly. The stockbroker with a line of stock for sale
knows where he can soonest get a decision and not unnaturally
that is where he offers the stock.

Even worse than investment by committee is leaving investment
to an executive who has many other duties as well, someone who
is likely to be promoted in due course and who will be judged not
on his investment success but on his other work. Inevitably, he
will skimp investment work and cover up the deficiencies as much
as possible when the meeting of trustees takes place.

In cases where a fund has an investment department or has set
up one with a promising young investment manager but not fully
fledged with experience, it is a good plan to employ a consultant
to whom he can turn for advice and help when he feels in some
doubt or where he feels he needs support.

The smaller funds may not be able to afford any professional
advice which requires to be remunerated. In the case of charities
they can, as I have already suggested, make use of the Charities
Official Investment Fund (C.O.I.F.) in which case the trustees
purchase units of C.O.I.F. The current price is 111·34p and the
yield is 6·07 per cent. The price was 100 in 1963, when the units
were first issued. There are no restrictions as to the investment
powers of C.O.I.F. so a charity limited to the powers of the
Trustee Investments Act might, through C.O.I.F., secure a much
larger percentage in equities than if directly invested which would
mean a 50–50 fixed-interest/equity fund by book values at the
date of splitting the fund in accordance with the Act (see page
189). Unit trusts also provide investment facilities for charities
with specialist trusts for charities but only the wider-range equity
fund can be invested in unit trusts. The M. & G. has its Charifund,
Ebor its Charities and Pension Fund.

For the smaller pension funds, the unit trust movement offers a number of funds designed specially for pension funds. These include M. & G. Pension Fund and the Tyndall Exempt Fund. There is also a fund referred to as Lamit – the Local Authorities Mutual Investment Trust – designed for the pension funds of the smaller local authorities.

Above I have only named a few unit trusts. Many are quoted daily in the *Financial Times*. The point is that the trusts mentioned claim that they are specialist trusts for charities and pension funds. Two trusts are particularly suitable for trustees, these are the M. & G. Trustee Fund and the Barclays Unicorn Trust Fund. But when it comes to the investment of funds which, unlike pension funds and charities, are subject to tax, there are scores of unit trusts to select from. The tax deducted at source can be reclaimed from the Revenue by the unit holder not liable to tax. But for non-tax-paying funds there are distinct advantages of investing in a fund which does not pay tax.

Individuals and trustees who want to do their own investing might consider splitting their funds, say, 60 per cent in equities and 40 per cent in British Government securities, looking to the latter to push up the all-over yield on the fund. The 60 per cent in equities could be provided by a selection of investment trusts making sure that the funds of the investment trusts have adequate holdings of U.S. common stocks.

Now a few words about stockbrokers who have already been mentioned under 'Aids for investment'. No investor, whether he be layman or specialist, can afford to ignore the skills, the knowledge, the market sense, or the research departments of stockbrokers. The layman will largely rely upon their opinions and seek the help of their research. Perhaps the layman will be more concerned with history and figures than with future projections which are estimates. But even the expert might feel a lot happier if he found a first-class stockbroker's prediction coming to the same conclusions as himself. The expert usually knows what he wants and if the information is not on the *Moodies* and *Exchange Telegraph* cards or has not emerged during his vast reading of the financial papers and journals and investment opinion generally, he will soon be ringing up a favourite stockbroker.

The stockbroker who funnels orders to the firm's dealer in the house, and remember there will be different sections for gilts, other fixed interest and equities and a split up of equities into sections such as property, insurance and investment trusts, etc., acquires a wonderful market touch. His knowledge of the market is also of great value. He may be able to tell you that there are big buying orders for the shares you have to sell – 'wait for a bit' or that buyers are scarce – 'push it out in small lots and gradually'.

Yes, indeed, a first-class stockbroker is a most worthy exponent of the art of investment. Rents and salaries are high in the City so he cannot afford to spend much time on the small investor even though some small investors grow to very big ones – here he must use his judgement to spot the up and coming.

When it comes to selling, stockbrokers, like investors generally and financial journalists in particular, are slow to recommend sales unless it is to finance a purchase they are recommending. And like all investment advisers they not unnaturally don't like telling a client to take a big loss on a share they have recommended. We are all guilty of this especially if the company is a good one and is going through a bad patch and after a year or two things could be all right again. There is sometimes also a little bit of self-deception in this. Even selling to set up a capital gains loss does not disguise the fact that the original purchase was ill-timed, although it looks a lot better if having established the loss for capital gains the stock is bought back after the required interval at a lower price. All right if you require the share as a permanent investment but if you want to get out one day then you pay capital gains on the profit and you may be back to square one. As the saying goes 'You can't win'.

Finally, how do you recognize your expert. By his label – stockbroker, bank manager, investment manager. All of these could disappoint you. You need to know your man and time only will produce the proof. A recommendation from a satisfied customer is a help. If he is a chartered accountant, an actuary or a chartered secretary, that's proof that he has some background. He might be a member of the Society of Investment Analysts. They do not have examinations but they are tested for standing and experience before admission. The only Diploma of Investment I know of is the one open to those who have passed Part I of the examination of the Institute of Actuaries and the Faculty of Actuaries. The Corporation of Secretaries, now merged with the Chartered Institute of Secretaries, had a paper on investments in its final examination. The subject is included in one of the papers in the final examination of the Chartered Institute of Secretaries.

The latter's examination syllabus is now under review and I hope that this go-ahead Institute will give greater prominence to investment in the new syllabus. The Chartered Insurance Institute has questions on investment in its Fellowship examination.

CHAPTER 36

Reviewing and reporting on the fund

It is essential to review a portfolio of investments periodically and for this purpose a valuation of the investments must be made.

The valuation should be split into three main groups: properties, fixed interest, and equities. The fixed-interest stocks should be further split under their appropriate headings – see the chapter on 'Fixed-interest stock'. The equities themselves should also be split under the main groupings of the *Financial Times/Actuaries All-Share Index* (see page 238) or if the fund is a very large one, further split under the sub-group headings of the same *Index*.

For properties a schedule will be required giving the following information:

(*a*) details of the property and where situated;
(*b*) amount paid for the property;
(*c*) present book value – cost price, including cost of any additions to the property, capital repairs, improvements, etc.;
(*d*) amount of the latest valuation with date;
(*e*) details of any leases of the property with break clauses shown;
(*f*) expected net revenue for the year;
(*g*) yield on book value.

Note. – For leaseholds additional information would be:
(*a*) freeholder's name;
(*b*) ground rent;
(*c*) expiry date of lease.

The major job of reviewing properties is to get down to those properties where the rents come up for review.

In the case of fixed-interest stock, the following information is desirable:

(*a*) name of stock, nominal value, interest rate and redemption date;
(*b*) book value;
(*c*) current price;
(*d*) market value;
(*e*) running yield, alternatively called flat yield;
(*f*) redemption yield.

While, for equities, I like to have the following information:

(*a*) name of company;
(*b*) number of shares;
(*c*) book value;
(*d*) market price;
(*e*) market value;
(*f*) earnings and dividend yield per cent;
(*g*) highest and lowest price in respect of the twelve months under review;
(*h*) price earnings ratio.

Note. – (*b*) and (*g*) adjusted in respect of rights and bonus issues.

Book values

You will notice I have included book values. There are many investors who criticize the keeping of book values. I agree that book values should not influence an investment decision, but the capital gains tax position must be considered. However, I believe that book values perform a useful function in that they spotlight the investor's mistakes or lack of success – also any glorious successes. A fund invested in ten equities might in the course of years appreciate by 50 per cent – not an unsatisfactory performance – but an inspection of the book values might reveal the fact that four of the investments in the portfolio have performed very indifferently.

A large fund should be reviewed at least twice a year, but it would be sufficient to review a modest sized one annually.

A review of a portfolio of investments which has been chosen by a competent investor or his expert advisors would not normally spark off much action but the following factors would have to be considered:

(*a*) Whether there has been any change in the circumstances of the fund or its beneficiaries which makes it desirable to modify investment policy. Estate duty is always a problem with personal funds and it becomes urgent to deal with this impending liability when a life-tenant grows old. Such a fund needs to have an appropriate portion of its fund invested in cash deposits or in investments which can be readily realized at or around their cost such as short-dated British Government stocks, not a long-dated stock where the market value can vary greatly.

(*b*) Whether the proportions of the fund in fixed-interest stocks and equities are correct in all the circumstances including stock-market conditions and whether some variations between the two should be made.

(*c*) Also whether the distribution under the various groups is correct and if not, to make the necessary adjustments.

(*d*) The reduction by sales of those holdings which have shown remarkable growth and now represent too large a proportion of the fund and the investment of the proceeds in other shares, thereby achieving further diversification.

(*e*) Whether there has been any change in the standing of any investment or in its prospects.

(*f*) Selling any investment which is not showing the growth expected of it.

The object of a review is to probe whether the fund has any weaknesses and if so to deal with them. Changes for the sake of change must be resisted. Buying and selling securities is expensive; there are, as already mentioned, the jobber's turn both ways, commission both ways and stamp duty on all purchases, except British Government, corporation stocks, public boards and some Commonwealth investments.

CHAPTER 37

Investment indices

There are 5,269 fixed-interest stocks, 303 convertible stocks, and 3,452 equities quoted on the London Stock Exchange, a total of 9,024 investments. Three years ago the figure was 9,481 of which 3,874 were equities. The 422 drop in equities despite a considerable number of new quotations is due to elimination by mergers. Dealings in these appear in the *Stock Exchange Daily List* and in a supplementary list which is issued monthly. Some idea of the course of the market can be obtained by a comparison of the number of fixed-interest stocks which have gone up with the number which have gone down and similarly for equities. This, however, can only give a rough idea of what is happening. It is to the various investment indices to which the investment managers and others look to ascertain what the market is doing, and in the previous pages indices have been frequently mentioned.

An index is made up of a number of stocks which are valued daily and the comparisons of the performance of those stocks is represented by an index figure which is published daily. The most famous index of all is the *Financial Times Industrial Share Index* which has been going since 1935. It has always been represented by thirty stocks, although those thirty stocks have altered as mergers have taken place. Whenever one share has gone a very great effort has been made to substitute it with a stock of a similar type. The *Financial Times* has other indices. There is the Government Securities Index, the Fixed-Interest Index, and Index of Gold Mining Shares. Others to have indices are *The Times*, *The Economist*, *The Exchange Telegraph*, *Moodies Service*. The Institute of Actuaries have had an index going since 1930, but in 1962 the Actuaries and the *Financial Times* joined together to start the *Financial Times/Actuaries Index*. Of these, the most quoted is the *All-Share Index* which comprises 621 industrial shares. There is in addition the *500 Share Index* which excludes the financial group. There is also the *498 Index* which excludes oils and is regarded as the *Financial Times/Actuaries Industrial Share Index*. There are indices also for the commodity share groups, namely, rubbers, teas, coppers, mining finance and tins.

The *Financial Times/Actuaries Indices* include indices for fixed-interest stocks. They comprise (*a*) the twenty-year Government stocks, and (*b*) twenty-year redeemable debentures and loans, and (*c*) two preference stock indices, one for investment trusts and the other for commercial and industrial preference stocks; also the $2\frac{1}{2}$ per cent consols yield.

I think it is appropriate to list the groupings of the *Financial Times/Actuaries All-Share Index* because it covers the whole spectrum of industrial share investment.

EQUITY GROUPS

Groups and Sub-groups

1 CAPITAL GOODS GROUP (185)
2 Aircraft and components (3)
3 Building materials (29)
4 Contracting and construction (19)
5 Electricals (excluding electronics, radio and TV) (13)
6 Engineering (81)
7 Machine tools (15)
8 Miscellaneous (25)
9 CONSUMER GOODS (DURABLE) GROUP (56)
10 Electronics, radio and TV (14)
11 Household goods (15)
12 Motors and distributors (27)
13 CONSUMER GOODS (NON-DURABLE) GROUP (176)
14 Breweries (21)
15 Wines and spirits (7)
16 Entertainment and catering (15)
17 Food manufacturing (24)
18 Food retailing (17)
19 Newspapers and publishing (15)
20 Packaging and paper (17)
21 Stores (30)
22 Textiles (21)
23 Tobacco (3)

24 Toys and games (6)
    OTHER GROUPS
25 Chemicals (19)
26 Office equipment (10)
27 Shipping (10)
28 Miscellaneous (unclassified) (42)

---

29 INDUSTRIAL GROUP (498)

---

30 Oil (2)

---

31 500 SHARE INDEX

---

32 FINANCIAL GROUP (121)
33 Banks (6)
34 Discount houses (6)
35 Hire-purchase (6)
36 Insurance (life) (9)
37 Insurance (composite) (9)
38 Insurance (brokers) (10)
39 Investment trusts (20)
40 Merchant banks, issuing houses (15)
41 Property (31)
42 Miscellaneous (9)

---

43 All-share index (621 shares)

    COMMODITY SHARE GROUPS
    (not included in the 500 or All-share indices)
44 Rubbers (10)
45 Teas (10)
46 Coppers (4)
47 Mining finance (11)
48 Tins (8)

Figures in parentheses after sectional names show number of stocks.

Note. – Information for each group and sub-group is given as follows for each day:

(*a*) index;

(b) percentage change on the day;
(c) estimated earnings yield and estimated price earnings ratio based on corporation tax of 40 per cent;
(d) dividend yield;
(e) index for four previous days;
(f) index a year ago;
(g) highs and lows of the index:
   (i) current year;
   (ii) since compilation.

Here are some historical figures selected on the same day. *Financial Times/Actuaries All-Share Index* 184·13 yield 3·35.

Because the *All-Share Index* includes some financial groups it is not possible to give the estimated earnings yield or the estimated price earnings ratio. However, this is given for the *500 Share Index*. The *Index* as at the date selected was 186·34. The dividend yield was 3·55, the estimated earnings yield was 5·47, and the estimated price earnings ratio 18·28. A comparison of the dividend yield with the estimated earnings yield gives some idea of what cover there is for the dividend. The highs and lows of the *500 Share Index*, since its compilation are 193·73 (January 31st, 1969) and 84·86 (August 25th, 1962) and for the *621 Share Index*, 187·32 (September 8th, 1971) and 83·72 (August 25th, 1962). The wide differences constitute the tops of bull markets and the bottoms of bear markets. An inspection of the highs and lows of the various groups and sub-group indices is very revealing. Clearly the groups and sub-groups do not move with the *Index* highlighting the fact that great skill is required to time a purchase or sale effectively.

Just as in the case of the *Financial Times Industrial Share Index* the component parts of the *Index* are adjusted when mergers take place, every effort being made to keep the index comparable.

An index which is in such depth as the *Financial Times/Actuaries All-Share Index* will, by reference to the sub-group indices, tell an investment manager many things. It will show what parts of the market currently appear to be dear or cheap. It will draw attention to the reality or otherwise of the yields, and at a glance show whether the price earnings ratio is high or low. It will do a lot more than this. It will provide the means by which investors can check the performance of their own fund. Without doing elaborate tests the performance of the *Index* will give a rough guide. I will go more into performance testing later.

You will have noticed the highs and lows of the *Financial Times Actuaries Index*. It will be helpful to have a look at the highs and lows of the *Financial Times Industrial Ordinary Share Index*. Its all time low was 49·4 on May 28th, 1940, which is well into the war years, and its high 529·9 on September 19th, 1968. Indeed, during 1969 it had a high of 520·1 on January 15th, 1969, and a low of 357·4 on September 22nd, 1969. What clearer demonstration could you have of the vulnerability of share prices? The *Financial Times Government Securities Index* started in 1929, had a low of 64·21 on June 11th, 1969, and a high of 127·4 on January 9th, 1936. The *Fixed-interest Index* started in 1928, had a low of 67·12 on June 11th, 1969, and a high of 150·0 on November 28th, 1947. It is of significance that it is in the last year or so that British Government and fixed-interest stocks generally have reached their all-time low. I find a perusal of the course of the various indices and their yields most exciting and the performance of the various groupings and sub-groupings of the *Financial Times/Actuaries Index* over the short and the longer term most challenging and instructive.

One final word, the *Financial Times/Actuaries Equity Indices* are geometric indices and are weighted for the market capitalization of the share. The *Financial Times 30 Industrial Shares* is an arithmetical index and is not weighted – very inferior to the 621 shares not only because of lack of spread but because it is arithmetical and not weighted.

It is, of course, the *Financial Times Industrial Share Index* which is news. When I was checking the galley proofs the *Financial Times* on August 25th emphasized the fact that the *Financial Times Industrial Share Index* at 417·8 had reached its highest point for nineteen months with a headline 'Equities up 5·7 to a nineteen-month peak'. Whereas little in the way of head-lines appeared in the Press when the so much more sophisticated and so much more reliable *Financial Times/Actuaries 621 All-Share Index* reached an all-time peak on July 27th (1971), and this *Index* is the true measure of the equity market.

To put it another way the *Financial Times Industrial Index* was on August 25th (1971), still 20 per cent below its high of 521·9 (September 19th, 1968), suggesting that the equity market could still rise appreciably and yet the *Financial Times/Actuaries 621 All-Share Index Index* had already reached a new peak. One has to remember, however, that the *Financial Times Industrial Share Index* is indeed an *Industrial Share Index* whereas the *Financial Times/Actuaries 621 shares* covers the whole market including the Financial

Sector and some might well argue that you should compare the *Financial Times Industrial Share Index* of thirty shares with the *Financial Times/Actuaries 500 Share Index*. However on August 25th, the latter was only 4 per cent below its peak. On the other hand the Price Earnings Ratio of the *Financial Times/Actuaries 500 Share Index* was on the same day 18·05 whereas at its all-time high, January 3rd, 1969, it was 23·6. So currently the price earnings ratio is 23 per cent below its high and assuming the next equity boom goes to a similar Price Earnings Ratio the *Financial Times/Actuaries Industrial Share Index* does seem to justify the *Financial Times Industrial Share Index* assessment of industrial shares but not of the whole market. As for myself I shall continue to believe that the true measure of the equity market is the *Financial Times/Actuaries All-Share Index*.

When I checked the page proofs in early October, all the indices were higher. The up-to-date indices are set out on page 218.

CHAPTER 38

Testing the performance of the fund with the use of investment indices
Indices are essential to performance testing. To take a very simple
example, if you bought one share only you would soon know by
looking at any equity indices whether your share had done better
than the *Index*. It is almost as easy if you had fifty shares at the
beginning of the year and the same fifty at the end of the year,
again, it would be easy to check their performance against the
indices. You merely value the shares at the middle market price
at the beginning of the year and again at the year's end. The
percentage fall or rise in the value of your portfolio over the year
is then calculated and is compared with the percentage rise and fall
of the indices. You could for comparison use the *Financial Times
Industrial Share Index* or the *Financial Times/Actuaries All-Share
Index* or indeed any reliable index.

It is hardly any more difficult if you have been active over the
twelve months and no new money in the form of cash or shares
has been added during the year. You ignore the changes and value
your portfolio of shares at the beginning and the end. You do not
credit your fund with the expenses of buying and selling because
if an exchange is justified it must justify the expenses involved.
It might be salutary to test what would have happened if you had
kept the portfolio unchanged over the year. Would you have done
better or worse? Look at each sub-group separately. Take capital
gains tax on profits (less losses) into account.

Although the *Financial Times Industrial Index* and the *Financial
Times/Actuaries Index* are so differently composed and the former
is an arithmetical index and the latter a geometrical index they
perform surprisingly close to each other at times. But it is generally
found that it is easier to beat the *Financial Times Industrial Index*
than the *Financial Times/Actuaries All-Share Index*.

It is possible that you will not readily be able to isolate new
money and sales and purchases. In that case every transaction
which takes place has on your performance testing to be matched
by hypothetical purchases and sales of the *Index*. Where you can
isolate sales of existing holdings and their re-investment I do not
think you should, for the reasons already given, make an addition
for expenses in 'buying' or 'selling' your units of the *Index*.

I know this is a handicap and that what turns out to be an excellent sale and purchase takes time to fructify but it comes through in the end and your fund performance eventually gets the benefit.

But if we have a mixed fund of fixed-interest stocks and equities we ought also to test whether we have held them in the right proportions. Here we are getting on difficult ground because the permutations are many, it can be fixed-interest 0, equities 100, to 100 fixed-interest, 0 equities; 101 different proportions, and the same can apply to new money going into the fund. Getting the right proportions between fixed-interest stocks and equities is as important, if not more so, as selecting the right shares and stocks. If an effort is made to test the fund's proportions against the proportions which would have performed best it is essential to take income receipts into account.

To explain, supposing a fund was worth £200,000 and £100,000 was invested in fixed interest at a yield of 8 per cent and £100,000 in equities with a yield of 4 per cent, and these rates were what was actually earned on each portion of the fund during the year. Supposing the fixed-interest index did not change over the year but the equity index improved by 4 per cent, then clearly with a non-taxable fund such as a pension fund or charity both the fixed-interest and the equity fund have performed similarly. It is the same in theory for a company which pays corporation tax of 40 per cent on its income and capital profits although capital gains tax is not payable until the profit is realized. Likewise a 100 per cent fund in fixed-interest stocks would thus have performed as well as a 100 per cent fund in equities. But the surtax payer pays capital gains tax of 30 per cent on capital growth realized, whereas income bears both income tax and surtax, so for him the equity fund has done better.

I have yet to hear of a reliable method of testing what should be the correct proportions between fixed-interest stocks and equities, over the past let alone the future.

I believe the time will come when a computer will calculate what would have been the best performance from 100/nil in either way to a level 50–50 for a portfolio based on various indices. The number and frequency of the calculations involved are certainly beyond a man's time but one would have thought that a programme could be computerized which would show what was the best proportion as between fixed interest and gilts over a certain period. It would, of course, be an exercise in hindsight but it would presumably establish the basis of the most successful investment of the period. Such an exercise must also take income into account. Here is a difficulty because income can be taxed from nil to 88·75p in the £, namely, 88·75 per cent.

There are other factors which have a bearing on the skills of an investment manager. Should he for example be tested on the timing of his purchases? I think he should and to do this the hypothetical purchase of the units should be made on the day he *receives* the new money. But, should he be tested on going liquid? Here I do not think he should, except perhaps for British Government stocks where there is no stamp duty, stockbroker's commission rates are low and there is an excellent market. In the past it has frequently been evident that gilts are going down and it seems likely that part or all of a gilt-edged fund could be sold and the proceeds put on deposit pending an attractive buying time in the future.

Testing portfolio performance is a complicated process when the fund is growing rapidly and the fund is very active. I have gone into the subject fairly fully in one of my books, *The Principles of Pension Fund Investment*, published by Hutchinson, and question whether the time spent on performance testing in great depth could not be put to better use. However, performance testing is becoming a fashionable pastime and the results are acclaimed from the housetops when they are good. But how good are they? They ought to have an auditor's certificate as to their accuracy.

As I have frequently stressed in this book, the small investor who has money to put into equities will, if he is sensible, limit his purchases to investment trusts, for which, as you know, I have a preference, and unit trusts. He can easily check the performance of his investment trust or his unit trust with the indices. Indeed unit trusts do endeavour to check the performance of their funds with the indices. It is, however, a poor consolation to an investor if his unit trust or investment trust has beaten the *Index* but his investment is still worth considerably less than what he paid for it. One of the odd quirks of unit trust investment, and this I have already mentioned, is that investors are always prepared to buy unit trusts when the market is blazing ahead, and as we have seen the best sales of units in recent years were achieved when the *Financial Times Industrial Index* was around 500. It would certainly be a poor consolation to a unit holder to discover that if he had invested in the *Index* he would have lost 40 per cent of his money but instead by investing in the particular unit trust he has only lost 30 per cent of his money. I cannot reiterate sufficiently that the essence of an investment is timing. It is more than likely that when the market is blazing away to a high, although no one knows where that high is going to be, it would be much more sensible for an investor to keep his money in a building society or on deposit account and await the time when the index is at least a good deal lower than its last high and, although he may not select the low point of the index he has at least invested at a time when shares are considerably below their top if it is also as events turn out quite a bit above the next low.

I certainly regard the periodic reviewing of a fund as essential.

Performance testing can get very involved and in a book mainly addressed to the student, the individual investor, and the staff of an investment department, I must keep my remarks simple and resist the temptation to debate the matter with investment analysts.

Let us consider a closed equity fund, which never has any new money paid into it. This fund could be valued at the beginning of a period and valued at the end of the period and the percentage fall or rise calculated. Supposing this fund was worth £150,000 at the beginning of the period and the *Financial Times/Actuaries All-Share Index* was 150 we could hypothetically utilize our £150,000 in purchasing 1,000 units of the *Financial Times/Actuaries All-Share Index*. Supposing at the end of the period the *Financial Times/Actuaries Index* had gone up to 160, then the hypothetical value of the fund invested in the units of the *Financial Times/ Actuaries Index* would be worth £160,000. If the value of the fund, which was £150,000 at the beginning of the period, was worth more than £160,000 at the end of the period then it has beaten the *Index*.

You should calculate annually what income your fund has earned and whether this is more or less than that which would be provided by investing the fund in the *Financial Times/Actuaries Index*. Obviously, it is no good performance testing the capital of the fund without taking income into account. In a sentence you could buy a very low yielding ordinary share which could have a capital appreciation of 5 per cent in a year and a very high yielding ordinary share which could have a less appreciation but could have provided 3 per cent more of income. Obviously, with a charity or a pension fund which is not subject to income tax the difference in the income is worth more than it is to a fund or an individual which has to pay corporation tax or income tax or income tax plus surtax.

If you have not done as well as the *Index* you might excuse yourself by saying that in making purchases and sales during the period tested you have incurred expenses and the jobber's turn. But surely if you do make an exchange you ought at least to justify the expense of making that change. I would, however, allow you some latitude because the benefits of a successful exchange sometimes take some time to come through. Performance testing is indeed useful in the case of a very active fund which seems to exist merely to provide commission for a stockbroker. Therefore, I feel that one should be as tough as possible in testing the performance of a fund and that no allowance should be made for expenses of exchanges.

Performance testing is more complicated with a growing fund, one where new money is coming in all the time. Take, for example, a pension fund. This is usually growing at the rate of 10 per cent per annum. Now how can you check the performance of a pension fund which is growing all the time? The fund is valued at the beginning of the period and again at the end of the period and the growth calculated. With the value of the fund at the beginning of the period units of the *Financial Times/Actuaries All-Share Index* units are hypothetically bought (I am still testing an equity fund). On the same day as the new money comes in a similar amount is invested in units of the *Financial Times/Actuaries All-Share Index* taking into account stamp duty and the broker's commission. No allowance for expenses, however, must be made for sales of shares and the re-investment of the proceeds because these as I have already mentioned, should stand on their own feet without being subsidized. At the end of the period the stock of units is valued and you calculate how much the unit fund has gone up. I am assuming growth because of the new money which has gone into the fund but if the *Index* was 150 at the beginning and 100 at the end – not an impossible position – then despite the new money the value at the end can be less than the beginning but you can still calculate how your hypothetical fund has performed compared with your own fund.

There are many refinements of this, and with a large fund diversified through the whole spectrum of industrial and financial shares, you could compare the performance of the group and sub-groups of your fund with those of the *Index*. You might, for example, find that your composite insurance shares have performed better than the sub-group index. The sub-group index comprises nine composite insurance companies. If you had picked the three best then obviously you would have beaten the *Index*.

We have been considering how to test an equity fund. There are indices – see page 61 – which can be used to test a fixed-interest fund and an exclusively British Government fund.

Supposing you have a fixed-interest fund or part of your fund is invested in fixed-interest securities, it will probably consist of: (*a*) British Government stocks, (*b*) debentures and loan stocks, (*c*) some convertible stocks and perhaps (*d*) some preference shares.

The whole fund could be tested against the *Financial Times Fixed-interest Index* which covers six British Government, five corporation stocks, two public board stocks, and seven debentures and preference shares – quite a good spread or you could check the performance of your various fixed-interest groups against the *Financial Times/Actuaries Twenty-year British Government Index*, the *Financial Times/Actuaries Twenty-year Debenture and Loan Stock Index* and the *Financial Times/Actuaries Commercial and Industrial Preference Share Index*. In both cases you would have to keep out your convertibles. I know of no index to test a selection of convertible stocks.

Again income must be taken into account, but the exercise does not test what would have been the best spread between the various groups although the indices will show which group has performed best.

CHAPTER 39

Investment protection societies

The investor is obviously in need of protection. From time to time the Government pass Acts which help to protect the investor whether he be depositing cash or buying shares or taking some interest in an investment. There is the Prevention of Fraud Act. There are the provisions in the Trustee Investments Act for the investment of trust funds. There is the Companies Act, indeed, there are a number of statutes which exist to protect the investor. There are the activities of the Board of Trade. The London Stock Exchange with its regulations also helps to look after the investor starting from the date a share or stock issue is made, or when a company obtains an official quotation for its shares when stringent regulations have to be complied with.

All the statutory provisions and all the *ad hoc* regulations which are stipulated by a variety of organizations concerned with investment are efforts to keep things on straight and narrow paths. Not only to protect the investor from the fraudulent and vicious promoter but against the many things which can happen as a result of the actions of someone who has no intention of taking advantage of an innocent investor.

Here I am concerned with efforts which have to be made to preserve an investment in the course of its life or when it has gone wrong or is in danger of going wrong. There are a number of societies and associations to protect the investments of its member associations and companies. Obviously you would expect the large investor to ally himself with other investors and it is these which I will deal with first.

Perhaps the most influential of all is the Investment Protection Committee which is part of the British Insurance Association. The life and composite insurance companies are still the largest investors in fixed-interest stocks and equities. The I.P.C., as it is called, takes action or considers whether it is necessary to take action when one of its member companies draws to its attention a particular investment which has either gone wrong or is in danger of going wrong, or where some proposal affecting the interests of the shareholder or stockholder is proposed by the company.

Any change in a security may affect an investor unfavourably.

249

Every time any change is contemplated the company has to advise the investor; for example, if it wants to extend the term of a debenture or if it wishes to release some of its security, offering as an inducement an increased rate of interest. There may be a scheme of arrangement whereby the preference capital is paid off in exchange for debentures or loan stock. Often the terms of a suggested arrangement are fair, in which case the I.P.C. would not hear about it from a member. But where the terms are doubtful or where the investor feels that the terms could be improved by a body of strong investors taking a firm line, then this is a matter for the I.P.C. to consider and if felt fit to bring pressure to bear on the company.

So powerful is the I.P.C. that many companies will consult the I.P.C. before publishing a scheme of arrangement. It will be seen that although the I.P.C. is looking after its own members in doing this it is also helping all investors in the particular issue involved.

For many years the I.P.C. has worked in close collaboration with the Investment Committee of the Association of Investment Trusts. To give you some idea of the respective power of these two organizations the investments of the insurance companies by book values total £15,533 million (market values not available) and the investments of the investment trusts by market values total £4,469 million. It will be seen that these two organizations are very formidable. And that if a company wishes to bowl a fast ball then it is likely to be met by very solid defence from these two committees.

Another powerful investors' organization is the National Association of Pension Funds, of which I am an associate member. It has a membership of some 2,100, of which 1,027 are commercial and industrial and miscellaneous companies. As to the rest there are municipal pension funds, co-operative society pension funds, insurance companies, banks, shipping, breweries, in fact it is a cross-section of the whole of the financial/commercial life of the country. The invested funds of pension funds are catching up with insurance companies. Many pension funds are what are called insured schemes and the funds of these schemes appear in the funds of the insurance companies and I estimate them at £3,500 million against the £7,500 million of self-administered funds.

This association has an investment protection committee also and is in close touch with the other two investment committees. The Association of Pension Funds also provides a valuable platform for its members through the medium of its conferences. At these conferences, and there are more than one annually, the members can discuss with their opposite numbers the problems they have on their pension funds generally, including investment problems. You will hear the investment manager of a fund comment to another. 'I do not like the scheme which so and so is putting up. What do you think about it?'

I have no doubt that there is an equivalent committee of the Association of Unit Trusts because naturally they too are concerned to fight any proposal of a company which they do not consider to be reasonable and are ready to take action when clearly an investment is at any kind of risk.

Of the smaller protection societies, there is the Investors and Shareholders Association Ltd. This issues a monthly newsletter and woe betide any company who is trying to put a fast one over to the disadvantage of its cash depositors or its shareholders. This is a private concern to which individual shareholders can subscribe. The subscription is £2·50 per annum and it is open to all investors. It grew out of the Women's Shareholders Protection Committee which was started by Miss Freda Spurgeon. Because it represented women and was therefore something novel it got a considerable amount of publicity. It has now become an Association representing all investors with emphasis on the smaller investor. Apart from its excellent monthly newsletter it holds frequent meetings at which its members can attend. These meetings are addressed by prominent investment and financial people and at these meetings they discuss any particular problem going at the time. The Association is not only concerned with investments which have a quotation on the Stock Exchange but with many of the small investments which do not get that sort of status. It is also concerned with any scheme which is floated with the alleged purpose of making money for the investor. This Association is doing some fine work from very little money, all made possible because so many people associated with it give their services free, and on the committee there are two very colourful individuals, one Dame Pat Hornsby-Smith and the other Sir Gerald Nabarro. Also on the committee is Mr A. P. W. Simon, T.D., F.C.A., who is prominently concerned with unit trusts.

Unfortunately by the time I came to read through the page proofs of this chapter, Miss Freda Spurgeon was ill and the work of the Association in abeyance. I have however preserved the paragraph as a tribute to her great work for the small investor.

All this is great and the scope will continue to expand, but, as indicated in the earlier pages of this book, you don't only lose money by investing in companies that go wrong. You can lose money by buying the very best shares at a time when they are over-valued. I have already mentioned Lesney Products which is involved in the manufacture of toys and which had the reputation and deservedly so, of being an outstanding growth company. In the course of twelve months, well, less than twelve months, if you bought your shares at the top price which was 473p and sold them today you would have lost all but one-twelfth of your money. That is why I stress again and again that equities in no form whether by direct purchase, or through investment trusts or unit trusts are suitable for the individual who may want his investment converted into cash in any unknown foreseeable future. Equities can be magnificently successful investments on long-term and on the long-term it doesn't matter too much if you buy them in one of their top phases, because on the long term you will be all right. So before you embark on equity investment in any form make sure that you have sufficient cash to see you through any unforeseeable difficult financial problem.

CHAPTER 40

Capital gains tax
The subject is an intricate one and experience and practice are
still developing. Already there is quite a library of books dealing
with the tax, including the *Taxation of Capital Gains* by Percy F.
Hughes and K. R. Tingley, and many more will follow. The tax
applies not only to the type of investment dealt with in this book
but to practically everything that can be sold at a profit or a loss
or is disposed of at a price differing from the cost price. In a short
chapter dealing with the effect of capital gains tax on investment
and not a treatise on the capital gains tax it is possible only to deal
in generalities. In broad terms, the only exceptions are:

(1) gains on profits on British Government stocks sold after
    twelve months of purchase;

(2) owner-occupied property with land up to one acre is exempt
    on a sale of the house and land together;

(3) annual gains on sale proceeds not exceeding £500 – formerly
    annual relief was limited to gains not exceeding £50;

(4) national savings certificates, national development bonds,
    defence bonds and premium savings bonds, also private
    motor-cars;

(5) on the proceeds of life assurance policies and contracts with
    life assurance companies other than unit trusts linked to
    life assurance (see page 126).

The tax is levied not only on realized profits but on the transfer
of assets by way of gift. This does not apply to transactions
between a husband and wife.

Obviously I can within these pages only touch upon the tax in
broad outline and as it affects the type of investment dealt with
in the chapters of this book.

First a little history. The Tories having introduced a short-
term capital gains tax on capital profits arising within a six-
month period, the Labour Government extended the scope in
the Finance Act 1965. They laid down the rules then and they
instituted a long-term capital gains tax and extended the short-
term tax to twelve months.

The Tories ended the distinction between short-term and long-term capital gains as from April 5th, 1971, thus we are now left with capital gains tax at the original rate of 30 per cent for individuals and for companies at the corporation tax rate, in both cases subject to the exemptions set out in (1), (2), (3), (4), and (5) on the previous page.

Capital gains assessed on the death of an individual are now exempt from tax, formerly gains up to £5,000 only were exempt.

For annual gains of less than £5,000 the taxpayer can pay at half his top rate of tax on the gain.

Companies were made liable to pay capital gains on all profits less losses at the corporation tax rate as part of their profits. The rate can vary from year to year, currently it is 40 per cent.

Losses, as indicated, are allowed as a set-off against capital gains profits and losses not used up in one tax year can be carried forward to the next. Profits on the other hand cannot be carried forward to the next year and off-set against losses in that year.

There seems to be no time scale rules to cover the case where an investor wishes to sell stocks or shares and buy them back immediately. In such cases the general practice is to sell at the end of one Stock Exchange account and buy back at the beginning of the next provided, of course, the price favours such a repurchase.

It was a rule for short-term capital gains tax that having established a loss, the loss would be invalidated if the shares were repurchased within one month. This was a dreadful nuisance for short-term capital gains. I recall a first-class share which fell heavily with the market, indeed fell more than the market because the particular group was suffering from bad publicity. It was a share of such high standing that I would probably have been prepared to hold it indefinitely on any portfolio. The loss, however, was tempting so I took it and then waited for the month to go by. I certainly got out at the bottom but towards the end of the month the share started to leap forward. It certainly was a buy at the increased price and the same number of shares was repurchased. However, the capital gains loss, though substantial, was not enough to pay for the extra cost in replacing the shares. The one-month period had defeated my client and me.

I was delighted when short-term capital gains ended. It restricted market activity because the gain was treated as income for tax purposes thus liable to tax at the individual's top rate.

There is a concession for capital gains on holdings purchased before April 5th, 1965. The investor has the choice of selecting his original cost as a basis or the price at April 5th, 1965, whichever suits him best. With losses he does not get this choice and the basis becomes the lower of the two prices, his original cost and the April 6th, 1965, value. Thus he can have a small loss for capital gains tax and a big actual loss. If he sells to take the loss then he gives up what has come to be referred to as 'a run up'. Supposing he pays £5 for a first-class share and sells it for £2 and the share was £3 on April 5th, 1965, his capital gains loss is £1 a share. If he buys them back at £1·50 and they rise to £6 when he sells them for the second time, he has to pay capital gains tax on £4·50. If, however, he had retained the original holding and sold it at £6 his capital gains tax liability would only be £1 a share. By being active he has achieved a capital gains loss of £1 a share and a capital gains profit of £4·50 a share, giving a net capital gain of £3·50 that is £2·50 a share worse off than if he had retained the holding and sold at £6.

This sort of experience should be a warning to those who fall for the naïve argument that a true investor just makes his decisions on investment merits and ignores capital gains. I am personally responsible for many portfolios and I must confess that investment changes, which apart from the capital gains tax, would immediately be effected are often vitiated by events, but it was a lot worse when short-term capital gains were taxed in effect as income and not at 30 per cent. The ending of the distinction between short gains (within twelve months) and long (gains made after twelve months) was a great relief as was also the ending of capital gains on death.

The following example, prior to April 6th, 1971, illustrates the point. Supposing an investor bought Sun Life at £4 including expenses and sold them over a year later at £8·50 net of expenses and a few weeks later bought them back at £5 including expenses, a perfectly possible proposition. His gain is £4·50 a share, his capital gains tax £1·35 per share, net profit after capital gains tax £3·15 per share. Now assume that at the time of the investor's death the shares were 850p against the value of 500p for capital gains tax which at 30 per cent of 350p gives a capital gains liability of 105p.

The hypothetical capital profit and capital gains tax position is as follows:

					p
Net sale price per share	..	..	..	..	850
Original cost per share	..	..	..	..	400
Capital profit per share	..	..	..	..	450
Capital gains per share, 30 per cent of 450p =	..		135p		
Repurchase price per share	..	..	..		500
Value date of death per share	..	..	..		850
Taxable as profit on death*	..	..	..		350
Capital gains tax, 30 per cent of 350p	..	..	105		
Total capital gains tax	..	..	..	240	

*Prior to April 6th, 1971

The total number of shares remain intact. The deceased and his executors have together paid 240p a share in capital gains tax and against this the deceased made a cash profit of 450p a share.

The net position is a profit of 210p a share.

But if he had done nothing the capital gains tax at death would be 30 per cent of 450p (i.e., 850p — 400p) = 135p per share and no profit to set it against.

Better by 135p per share in both cases if the deceased's total capital gains did not exceed the £5,000 of capital gains which on death was up to April 6th, 1971, exempted from capital gains.

But supposing he had paid 850p a share including expenses for the shares and sold them for 400p net per share, taking the tempting loss for capital gains of 450p and hoping to buy them back at a low price later. He eventually buys the shares back at 500p including expenses. Supposing he dies when they are 850p. Here is the capital and capital gains position.

							p
Original cost per share	..	..	..	..	..	..	850
Net sale price per share	..	..	..	..	..	..	400
Loss per share	..	..	..	..	..	..	450
Value date of death	..	..	..	..	..	..	850
Repurchase price per share	..	..	..	..	..	500
Subject to capital gains tax on death*	..	..	..	..	350

*Prior to April 6th, 1971

Let us assume he was able to set off the 450p of capital gains loss against profits so the loss was worth 135p per share.

To summarize he has made a capital loss of 450p per share less capital gains tax relief of 135p per share which is 315p per share net.

On top of this unless his total capital gains are less than £5,000 his executors have a liability of 105p a share, namely, 30 per cent of 350p. Had he stayed with the shares there would have been no capital gains liability.

Let us assume an ideal situation. Assume he got the shares back after expenses at exactly the same cost for which he sold them. He is back where he started as to price and number of shares but he has established a capital gains loss of 450p which will qualify for relief at 30 per cent =135p. But if the shares are sold eventually for 850p or he dies when the shares are valued at 850p he or his estate has a capital gains profit of 450p and a 30 per cent liability of 135p and he or his estate is all square.

Note. – The share prices of Sun Life are historic and before the issue of fully paid bonus shares and share split.

I repeat all the examples above are hypothetical cases, but they do demonstrate what a blessing it is to an investment adviser that relief on capital gains at death no longer applies only to the first £5,000 of assessed gains but to the whole without limit.

Clearly in the new circumstances it will always pay to sell when shares are high (if you know when they are) and pay capital gains tax but you must get back into the shares when they are low and as you retain 70 per cent of the profit you should get a reasonable chance of getting back.

The main difficulty is the fact that when a sale is made the investor does not know whether he is making the sale at a top price. He may sell only to find that the share price subsequently advances substantially. Indeed, he may find he can never get back into what is one of his favourite shares at the price at which he sold them and he wishes he had stayed with the share.

Getting out and back into a favourite share is a dicey capital gains problem. It is much better so far as possible to sell and at the same time buy a different share in a similar class of business. But a precisely similar share is a near impossibility. Here are some suggestions for near shares – Sun Life into Equity and Law or Legal and General and vice versa, Royal into Commercial Union and vice versa, London Brick which I have sold recently on many portfolios to establish capital gains losses into Redland Holdings. On the assumption that these exchanges are spot on and the shares purchased rise in value you still have capital gains problems unless you or your client dies with them. But with sales and purchases effected on the same day you are not at risk for the required interval to get back to the same share. The expenses of the sale and purchase are commission $2\frac{1}{2}$ per cent, stamp duty 1 per cent, and you have paid for two jobber's turns – probably the all-in cost is 7 to 10 per cent, and these have got to be made up to break even.

Making losses is indeed a rare kettle of fish. As you will have seen you lose 70 per cent in real terms to gain 30 per cent and your share, if repurchased, stands at a lower cost for capital gains and even if you successfully repurchase the same number of shares with the sale proceeds you have a lower price for capital gains. Some investors comment 'I will die with the shares' and they do.

It is quite a different matter if you have made a bad purchase. Then it makes a lot of sense to cut your loss because at the minimum you recover 30 per cent of the loss as a set-off against capital gains profits.

To an investor or his adviser the irritating aspects of capital gains tax are: (1) the enormous amount of work it necessitates for the investor, his stockbroker, his bank, his accountant and for the Revenue. In my view the tax collected does not begin to compensate the country for all the non-productive time spent in maintaining and providing the necessary information and assessing the tax on changes in those investments; (2) the difficulty in coming to a ripe judgement as to whether the handicap of certain capital gains tax becoming payable justifies taking no action when, apart from this, action would have been taken; (3) the sluggish effect the tax has on the market by eliminating many a sale or purchase resulting in shares being held more firmly and creating a shortage which drives up prices against those rapidly growing funds – pension funds and the like – which must invest a portion of their funds in equities. The abolition of short-term gains tax was, however, a considerable liberalism.

The mention of pensions reminds me that charities and pension funds are not subject to taxation and thus escape capital gains tax. It is consequently a joy to administer their funds. There is, as I have already mentioned, some taxation payable on a pension fund where the pensioner has power to commute part of his pension – the maximum permitted is one-quarter. The trustees of some funds believe it is simpler to have a separate fully-taxable fund in respect of the commutable portion and a separate fund for the non-commutable portion, so that different investment consideration can be applied to both, and this concept is fully justified.

To summarize:

(1) The price for capital gains is the original cost or, if held prior to April 6th, 1965, the value on that date at the option of the investor. This is a useful concession. He can, however, take a once-and-for-all option to take April 6th, 1965, price for all shares held then. Obviously purchases since that date have to be taken at cost. Originally part sales were set against the most recent purchases; now the cost can be averaged. The Stock Exchange publishes a book, price 105p, which lists the April 6th, 1965, prices.

(2) For losses the purchase cost for investments held before April 6th, 1965, is the original cost or the April 6th, 1965, value, whichever is the lower – here the investor loses out. This was very unfair to holders of steel shares, which were compulsorily acquired by the Government, as most investors paid much more than the value at April 6th, 1965. So subsequent sales of the Treasury $6\frac{1}{2}$ per cent 1971 (the take-over stock) although resulting in heavy losses in most cases did not qualify to the full for losses for capital gains.

(3) Instead of paying 30 per cent on capital gains if less than £5,000 the investor can pay at half his highest rate of tax. Supposing a man pays income tax at the standard rate of 38·75p plus surtax at 12·50p, a total of 51·25p, it would pay him to elect to pay half the rate, 25·62$\frac{1}{2}$, but if he pays surtax of 22·5p a total of 61·25p he is better off with the 30 per cent which is 30p in the £.

(4) On death there is no capital gains assessment.

(5) Gains on proceeds of sales up to £500 in any one year are not subject to capital gains tax – a measly concession, particularly so for a husband and wife who are considered as one for the purpose, another example of the unfair treatment of married folk.

(6) Losses assessed on the proper basis can, as illustrated, be set-off against gains, and losses not so eliminated by gains in one year can be carried forward indefinitely against gains in future years.

(7) Gains tax has to be paid on net profits in the year they occur. They cannot be carried forward and set against losses incurred in subsequent years.

(8) All investments are subject to capital gains tax except:

    (*a*) gains on profits on British Government stocks sold after twelve months of purchase;

    (*b*) owner-occupied property with land up to an acre is exempt on a sale of the house and land together;

    (*c*) national savings certificates, national development bonds, defence bonds and premium savings bonds, also private motor-cars.

(9) No capital gains tax is payable on the profit from a conventional life assurance policy.

(10) There is no capital gains in connection with the replacement of a company's assets.

The capital gains tax position of insurance companies, investment trusts and unit trusts is dealt with under their respective chapters.

INDEX